# WE HAVE BEEN
## BELIEVERS

# WE HAVE BEEN BELIEVERS

*An African-American Systematic Theology*

James H. Evans, Jr.

Fortress Press                    Minneapolis

WE HAVE BEEN BELIEVERS
An African-American Systematic Theology

"We Have Been Believers" is from *This Is My Country: New and Collected Poems* by Margaret Walker (Athens: University of Georgia Press, 1989), copyright © 1989 Margaret Walker Alexander. Used by permission of the author.

"Conversion" is from *Cane* by Jean Toomer, copyright © 1923 by Boni & Liveright, renewed 1951 by Jean Toomer. Used by permission of Liveright Publishing Corporation.

Interior design: ediType
Cover design: Carol Evans-Smith
Cover art: "Jesus Loves Me," © Varnette P. Honeywood, 1983

**Library of Congress Cataloging-in-Publication Data**

Evans, James H., 1950–
    We have been believers : an African-American systematic theology /
James H. Evans, Jr.
        p.  cm.
    Includes bibliographical references and index.
    ISBN 0-8006-2672-9
    1. Black theology.  I. Title.
BT82.7.E84  1992
230′.089′96073—dc20                                    92-15333
                                                        CIP

The paper used in this publication meets the minimum requirements of American National Standard for Information Sciences—Permanence of Paper for Printed Library Materials, ANSI Z329.48-1984

Manufactured in the U.S.A.                              AF 1-2672
96                            4    5    6    7    8    9    10

To My Aunts and My Mother, Who Have Been Believers
To Janie, Azella, Annabelle, Amy, Annie Ruth
To Dettie Burke
And in Memory of Alice

# WE HAVE BEEN BELIEVERS
## By Margaret Walker

We have been believers believing in the black gods of an old land,
believing in the secrets of the seeress and the magic of the charmers
and the power of the devil's evil ones.

And in the white gods of a new land we have been believers, believing
in the mercy of our masters and the beauty of our brothers, believing
in the conjure of the humble and the faithful and the pure.

Neither the slavers' whip nor the lynchers' rope nor the bayonet could
kill our black belief. In our hunger we beheld the welcome table
and in our nakedness the glory of a long white robe. We have been
believers in the new Jerusalem.

We have been believers feeding greedy grinning gods, like a Moloch
demanding our sons and our daughters, our strength and our wills
and spirits of pain. We have been believers, silent and stolid and
stubborn and strong.

We have been believers yielding substance for the world. With our
hands we have fed a people and out of our strength have they wrung
the necessities of a nation. Our song has filled the twilight and our
hope has heralded the dawn.

Now we stand ready for the touch of one fiery iron, for the cleansing
breath of many molten truths, that the eyes of the blind may see
and the ears of the deaf may hear and the tongues of the people be
filled with living fire.

Where are our gods that they leave us asleep? Surely the priests and the
preachers and the powers will hear. Surely now that our hands are
empty and our hearts too full to pray they will understand. Surely
the sires of the people will send us a sign.

We have been believers believing in our burdens and our demigods too
long. Now the needy no longer weep and pray; the long-suffering
arise, and our fists bleed against the bars with a strange insistency.

# CONTENTS

# PREFACE

Since its emergence in the 1960s black theology in the United States has achieved a level of sophistication and complexity that is to be both expected and welcomed. However, black theologians must be on their guard against complacency. It is possible to fall asleep at the treasurehouse door if we no longer value its contents. We may awake and find that the gifts that have been entrusted to us no longer are ours to share. The strength and power of faith have been the bulwark of African-Americans against the principalities and powers of oppression. "We have been believers" as Margaret Walker reminds us. The faith of African-Americans has been tempered in the fire of oppression and galvanized by the quest for freedom. On the threshold of a new century the African-American community is threatened by a crisis of belief. This crisis is not simply a matter of intellectual acquiescence, but signals a deeper human loss. At this moment, looking out on the teeming avenues of a city in the throes of scarcity, I am reminded that material poverty is not always synonymous with the poverty of faith. While love is the bond of human community and hope fuels its engines, faith charts its direction. The question that has given rise to the chapters that follow is "what is the relation between faith and freedom?"

I want to thank my colleagues on the faculty of the Colgate Rochester Divinity School/Bexley Hall/Crozer Theological Seminary and St. Bernard's Institute for their commiseration and support. A special measure of gratitude goes to Ellen Wondra and Thomas Scott, who read parts of the manuscript, and to Linda Wickett who assisted in its production. I also want to acknowledge the contribution of the students in my black theology courses. Their probing questions nurtured many of the ideas in the pages that follow. Finally, I must express an inexpressible appreciation to my spouse, Estella, and my children, James III, Jamila, and Jumaane, for the quiet moments and the occasional insistence that I leave this project for rest and renewal.

The reader should understand that citations from other writers are usually presented in their original form. Therefore, in these instances, "humanity" is not substituted for "man," and "black" or "African-American" is not substituted for "Negro."

*Lima, Peru*
*August 1991*

# INTRODUCTION

Theological reflection is central to the ongoing life of the African-American Christian church. Theology is essentially the church's response to the autobiographical impulse, and it grows out of the need to proclaim with authority and commitment the identity and mission of the church in the world. That is, in theology, the church both asks and answers the questions, "Who are we, and where are we going?" It has unfortunately been the case that the work of black theologians and the work of African-American churches have often been construed as separate types of activities. It would not be an exaggeration to say that the leadership of many black congregations, large and small, and the ranks of professional black theologians have looked on one another with caution and, at times, suspicion. This has resulted in a chasm in the black religious community between the theology and practice of Christian faith, leaving the churches with a religion that appears to be no more than a cultural performance, and the theologians with a theology that seems to consist only of abstract concepts. The question, then, is "How can the dialogue between professional black theologians and other members of the African-American churches be strengthened so that it becomes clear that black theology is rooted in the faith of the church and that the faith of the church is given intellectual clarity and expression in black theology?"

This intellectual clarity is not a substitute for, but a complement to, genuine, personal, and communal expressions of faith. In other words, African-American church leaders should be reminded that leadership means more than habitually performing the liturgical functions necessary to the structural maintenance of the community. Genuine church leadership requires sound theological judgment. At the same time, professional black theologians need to be reminded that theology is more than the writing of scholarly articles and books. Genuine theological judgment requires a praxiological commitment to the community of faith. Theologians as theologians cannot tell other Christians what they should believe; rather their task is to help the community understand

1

more clearly what they do believe and to assess those beliefs in light of the major sources of Christian revelation.

Black theology differs from traditional theology in much the same way that African-American Christianity differs from the Christianity of Europe and the North Atlantic. Since the first Africans set foot on this soil, people of African descent have had a singularly unique experience in the New World. They brought with them an inherent philosophical heritage, including a distinctive religious sensibility; they encountered the most brutal form of slavery in human history; and they were introduced to North Atlantic Christianity. Because there was no precedent for the experience of people of African descent, they created distinctive ways of conceptualizing and speaking about their ultimate concerns. Black theology is a continuation of that discursive tradition. Therefore, African-American theological development can be best understood as the convergence of an African-derived worldview, the complexities of the experience of slavery, oppression, survival, rebellion, and adjustment in the New World, and their encounter with the biblical text. These realities shaped the African-American intellect and spirit.

Black theology reflects the passion, feeling, and expressiveness of African-American Christianity. It must be in touch with the "guts" of black religion. It must have, as Karl Barth once put it, "heavenly fire." Without this quality it would forfeit its claim to authenticity. On the other hand, theological reflection is not synonymous with the sermon, the litany, or the testimony, although they all participate in the same ethos of religious expression. Black theology is also a formal, self-conscious, systematic attempt to interpret the faith of the church. The form need not always be linear, nor the system based on Western philosophy. Black theologians may employ explanatory and formal devices such as story or biblical commentary. Black theology is passionate and incisive, reflecting what Paul Tillich called "ecstatic reason." The important factor, however, is that the theology that results must coherently interpret the experience of black people and the Gospel.

The contemporary African-American church needs theological acumen as much as it ever has. Not only must attacks on the integrity of black religion be resisted, but the continual evolution of religion in America and the often surprising turns that it takes require a constant "testing of the waters" by theologians of the black church. However, the need for theological reflection goes beyond the issues of the survival or integrity of the black church as an institution. In a world where black people, people of color, and poor people, are continually frustrated in their attempt "to have life, and have it more abundantly," black theologians must speak to those systems, persons, and conditions that impede the worship and adoration of the God of the Gospel and the living of a just life.

In light of these factors, there are several tasks that black theologians have before them today. *The first task is to clarify the contexts — histori-cal, sociopolitical, cultural, and intellectual — in which African-American Christian faith is affirmed.* The historical context of the faith of black Christians includes a shared legacy of slavery, the struggle to adapt to legal manumission, and the ongoing battle to be recognized as full human beings. The development of slave religion and its relation to the early freedom struggle among people of African descent is the his-torical source of contemporary black Christian faith. African slaves who embraced Christianity also modified and shaped it to meet their exis-tential needs and saw, even in the contorted presentations of the Gospel by some white people, a continuity between what they knew of God in Africa and the God of the Bible. Gayraud Wilmore describes the essential relationship between faith and freedom in the development of black religion:

> An exceedingly elastic but tenacious thread binds together the contribu-tive and developmental factors of black religion in the United States as one distinctive social phenomenon. It is the thread of what may be called, if properly defined, "black radicalism." Black religion has always concerned itself with the fascination of an incorrigibly religious people with the mystery of God, but it has been equally concerned with the yearning of a despised and subjugated people for freedom — freedom from the religious, economic, social, and political domination that whites have exercised over blacks since the beginning of the African slave trade.[1]

This thread can be traced through the public annals of professional historians, but is also present — perhaps in even more striking mani-festations — in the autobiographies, personal narratives, and journals of African-American women and men who felt compelled to give testimony to the work of God in their lives.

The sociopolitical context for the re-radicalization of African-American Christianity in the twentieth century is the civil rights/black power movement. Scholars differ on which aspect of the substantively crucial period in American history is most directly responsible for the religious and theological revival in the black community. Warner R. Traynham argues that the civil rights movement and its most visible leader, Martin Luther King, Jr., were most responsible for the reli-gious and theological reawakening.[2] Both James H. Cone and J. Deotis Roberts suggest that the radical critique of American racism inherent in the black power movement is the source of contemporary black the-ology and prophetic black Christianity.[3] Gayraud Wilmore argues that radical black Christianity and black theology in the twentieth century emerged after many of the leaders of the civil rights movement had been coopted by the white power structure and before the full measure of black power had been seized.[4]

It seems clear that while there are differences in interpretation, the civil rights movement and the black power movement are part of a continuous tradition of protest and struggle in African-American religious life. The civil rights movement was based on the notion that the equality of black people was a function of their legal status in American society. Equality had been denied by the Fugitive Slave Law of 1850, the Dred Scott decision (1857), and the Plessy vs. Ferguson decision of the Supreme Court (1896). These legal conscriptions were subsequently reversed or eliminated by the Brown vs. Board of Education of Topeka Supreme Court decision of 1954 and the voting rights laws passed in the 1960s. These advances were engineered by people and groups directly or indirectly related to the African-American church. They were visible evidence of the reawakening of the black church militant that had slumbered for decades.

Not since the end of slavery, however, had the attitudinal and psychological dimensions of racism come to the forefront of discussion. The black power movement was, in part, the result of the failures and limitations of the early civil rights movement; especially its dependence on enfranchisement as a tool for liberation. Black power advocates asserted that control of the institutions that regulated *intellectual commerce* and *social values*, not legal prescriptions, were the most effective means for achieving the liberation of black people. Racism was seen as an attitudinal, psychological, and structural aspect of American life. Therefore, it could not be eliminated simply through legislation because people tend to structure their behavior according to deep-seated values and not in strict accordance to extraneous norms. Thus civil rights laws were widely ignored. The psychological, attitudinal, and structural aspects of racism also meant that racism was supported by the pseudo-Christian values prevalent in American society.

The most profound contribution of the black power movement to the development of black theology was its challenge to black people to show how they could be black and Christian at the same time. This challenge was multidimensional. Black Muslims called Christianity a "white man's religion" that had nothing to do with the spiritual heritage of African-Americans. Black secular Marxists argued that Christianity was an unscientific, irrelevant, and counter-revolutionary illusion that only hindered the liberation of black people. Pan-Africanists eschewed Christianity to the extent that it obscured the reality that black people were part of the African Diaspora. Black nationalists rejected Christianity on the grounds that it prevented black people from seeing the necessity of separating themselves from white culture as a prerequisite for their liberation.[5]

Black theology was in part a response to these objections. Black theologians were not willing to concede Christianity to its white abusers and based their legitimacy on the fact that African-American Christianity was the result of the encounter of black people with the liberating essence of the Gospel. Black theologians viewed the history of black resistance to white oppression, and the fact that the leaders of that resistance were more often than not black Christians, as evidence that the black liberation struggle was rooted in black religion. Black theologians stressed that the connection with Africa was more evident in black religious life than anywhere else. Further, they pointed to the identification of black Christians with the biblical people of Israel as an example of an appropriate nationalist sentiment in the religious setting.

In addition to the historical and sociopolitical contexts, the cultural and intellectual contexts in which African-American faith is affirmed are part of the focus of this first task of theology. Black religion was shaped in the midst of a profound cultural conflict between the inherited cosmology, value systems, and philosophical constructs that African slaves brought with them to the New World, and the protean culture of the colonies that were struggling to define themselves over against the dominant European paradigm, and in light of the ironic position of the colonies as an imperialist presence. (The colonists presumably came to the New World to escape tyranny, but found themselves in the position of tyrants in relation to Amerindians and Africans.)

The cultural matrix of the African tended to affirm the infinite worth of the African as a human being in relation to other human beings and under the auspices of a benevolent creator God. The community (the no longer living, the living, and the yet to be born) was affirmed as the basic social unit and as the social framework in which the individual was defined. All creation, including nature, was seen as infused with the spiritual presence of God.

The formative culture of the colonies demeaned the African as a human being, by associating blackness, and thus black people, with evil; by denying the existence of an indigenous African culture and civilization; and by rejecting the notion that Africans had any idea of a Supreme Being, thereby condemning them to the state of God-forsakenness and justifying their continued enslavement and exploitation. The culture of the colonies devalued community and idolized the individual, making the protection of private property and individual rights the basis for social and political organization. Further, nature and those living beings thought to be most closely related to it became, in the minds of the colonists, the "wilderness" and the "savages," both of which were to be tamed, subdued, and domesticated.

This cultural conflict has not been resolved in contemporary American life. As African-Americans struggle with the pull of a secular, materialistic, hedonistic, narcissistic, and pessimistic culture, they also experience, to varying degrees, the magnetic hold of a spiritual, integrated, communal, and hopeful, counter-culture. African-American Christian faith is in part a response to this cultural conflict, attempting to navigate, with varying degrees of success, a course between the old and the new, the familiar and the strange.

The intellectual context of black faith reflects a similar struggle on the ideational and practical level. In the eighteenth century Gustavus Vassa, Phyllis Wheatley, and Jupiter Hammon attempted to reconcile the African intellectual tradition with their crisis-ridden status as slaves in the New World. In the nineteenth century, Henry Highland Garnet, T. Thomas Fortune, Martin R. Delaney, and Maria Stewart attempted to resolve the tension between the problematic presence of African-Americans with their relationship to Africa and the emerging national identity of the United States.[6] In the first two-thirds of the twentieth century Booker T. Washington, W. E. B. Du Bois, Marcus Garvey, Mary McCloud Bethune, Martin Luther King, Jr., and Malcolm X attempted to relate the plight of African-Americans to that of the insurgent liberation movements in Africa and the so-called Third World. The ideas generated in these historical moments owe much of their power and pertinence to the influence of African-American Christianity. These attempts to orient people of African descent in an alien environment were shaped by the fundamental encounter of a sternly held faith and the fierce desire for freedom. Moreover, black theology is the ideological progeny of these moments. Therefore, black theologians must take seriously these intellectual contexts and sources.

*The second task is to articulate, interpret, and assess the essential doctrinal affirmations of African-American faith for the contemporary African-American community of faith.* In spite of the unique history of the evolution of African-American faith, this faith cannot be reduced to its contexts. That is, sociological reductionism, cultural reductionism, or ideological reductionism does not reach the spiritual essence of black faith. Empathic intimacy with the heart of African-American faith requires that we move beyond the *contexts* to the *content* of that faith.

Briefly stated, the content of African-American faith is the story of God's dealings with God's people and the world. There are, in fact, two stories involved here. On one hand the Bible presents what I call "canonical stories." The canonical story is what we construe to be the message of the Bible and tradition. For African-Americans that story has always been, in some paradigmatic form, the story of the liberation of the Hebrew slaves and Jesus' liberating mission in his time. The elements in that story are linked by the providential will of God. That is, clearly God has been in control of events from the beginning and stands as the guarantor that, in the end, "everything will be all right." It is this guarantee that is the basis of faith. Yet there is a danger of distortion present here. It is also possible that this story can become a safe haven for those Christians who yearn to return to the pristine past or to create a religious subculture in which they might escape the demands of postmodern life.

On the other hand, African-Americans bring their own stories to bear on the Bible and tradition. They bring what I call "folk stories." Because we are historical creatures, we suffer under the tragic limitations of human finitude, and folk stories are our way of expressing the fears, frustrations, and struggle as well as the determination for freedom from existential anxiety, political oppression, and cultural exploitation that constitutes our experience. We live uncertain of whether our hopes will be vindicated or whether the struggle for freedom will end; therefore we can only infer that, given the faithfulness of God, one day "the wicked shall cease from troubling, and the weary shall be at rest." That is, African-American existence may be characterized by a rugged determination for freedom and not by any certainty that this freedom will be realized. There is a danger of distortion connected with this story as well. This existence may also portray a kind of pathos and despair in which anomie and disorientation in a mass culture and secular society have all but extinguished the fires of the will and determination.

The black theologian must relate the "canonical" story, in its prophetic mode, with the "folk" story of a people who hope against hope. To do this the theologian cannot be so immersed in the assurance, optimism, or myopia of the canonical story (the proclamation of the churches) that he or she is unable to see the challenge of the folk story. Conversely, the theologian cannot become so enchanted by the pathos of the folk story or so disillusioned by the tragic dimensions of African-American experience that the hope expressed in the canonical story is not seen. In sum, black theologians must tell a story that relates the hope of the biblical message with the realism of black experience. Through the arrangement and explication of the basic Christian doctrines, from creation to consummation, black theologians must fashion a story that brings together the twin commitment of African-American Christians to faith and freedom.

*The third task is to examine the moral implications of that faith for Christian witness in the world.* African-American Christian faith is shaped by a variety of *contexts*, has a distinctive and identifiable *content*, and matures only through the fulfillment of its *intent*. The intent, goal, or telos of African-American Christian faith is the moral ordering of personal and collective human existence through Christian witness in the world. Christian witness here is understood to involve three moral moments. First, Christians must engage in moral discernment. The challenge is to read the signs of the times, to look into the hearts of

people, institutions, and social systems, to find the sources of impedi-
ments to justice and truth. Therefore, Christians can and must employ
those modes of analytical discourse that can make plain the origins of
human misery. Depth psychology, literary criticism, and other forms of
analysis may be helpful in this regard. However, given the morphology
of human existence in postmodern society, it is imperative that moral
discernment today include a socio-economic and cultural analysis of
our world and its inner workings. Human suffering in our time cannot be fully explained by looking at the cruelty that one individual
inflicts upon another; it must also be seen as the result of conflicting
economic interests and conflicting social values.

Second, this moral discernment must be guided by moral norms.
That is, one must have a set of criteria by which one can determine
whether the present social order is just. These criteria must themselves
be drawn from the content of African-American Christian faith, rather
than from any extraneous philosophical norms of good and evil, right
and wrong. Therefore, one cannot introduce a notion of justice, for
example, as central to ethical behavior if the notion itself is not central to the theological affirmations of African-American faith. In other
words, one must be able to act and live in a way that is consistent
with one's beliefs.

Third, the moral norm must render judgment on society, and the
participation of African-American Christians in that society, in such
a way that one is forced to decide and is moved to action. It is not
enough to analyze society and to announce that injustice exists. The
full meaning of Christian witness in the world includes deciding for
the victims and acting in solidarity with them. It is interesting that
Jesus rarely talked about the issue of poverty, but constantly com-
muned with poor people. People are rarely moved to compassionate
acts by abstract issues, but are often moved by the encounter with
specific people. Christians must refuse to sacralize poverty or to abandon the poor. Christians must resist victimization and minister to
the victims. This requires a praxis that embraces moral acts as well
as moral existence. Christians must act morally, but moral acts are
grounded in a basic lifestyle and mindset that itself is moral. Christians must exist as moral people, but moral existence is buttressed by
moral acts.

In sum, authentic Christian witness is an engagement in moral discernment and making moral judgments, in light of moral norms, that
results in moral acts and lifestyles. Black theologians must contribute
in a substantive and comprehensive way to authentic Christian witness. As "organic intellectuals" (Antonio Gramsci) their work involves
social analysis, normative claims regarding the demands of the faith
in the postmodern world, and actual engagement in communities of

resistance. In this way, theology as a vocation can become a form of authentic Christian witness.

These, then, are the primary dimensions of African-American Christian faith. The contexts show how the external and internal forces that shaped and continue to influence black religious expression have brought faith and freedom into sharp relief. The doctrinal affirmations must form the story, or gestalt, of black Christianity around the twin elliptical centers of faith and freedom, the dialectic of which recasts and reinterprets the major sources of Christian revelation. The moral implications of this faith must guide and direct African-American Christian witness in the world in a way that manifests the twin commitments of faithfulness to God and the struggle for freedom.

The focus of this book is the second theological task as described above. Of course, the contexts of African-American Christian faith are always in the background and the moral implications of that faith must always be acknowledged to be in the foreground, but the concern here is specifically the content of African-American faith and its theological significance. The opening chapter on theological methodology will provide an examination of the distinctive problems and solutions that black theologians have had in analyzing and correlating black experience and divine revelation. It is followed by a chapter that examines the Bible as an imaginative text, the meaning of which is most clearly visible to those who experience marginalization and powerlessness. The next five chapters are devoted to a discussion of the doctrines of God, Christ, humanity, church, and eschatology in black theology.

In sum, this book is an explication and elaboration of the following theological affirmations:

- The content of God's *revelation* is *liberation*.

- The primary record of that revelation is the *Bible*, which has historically carried a special significance for those who are *outside* the corridors of power in society.

- It is *the ungiven God* of the oppressed who is revealed in the Bible.

- The zenith of God's self-revelation is *Jesus Christ*, who is affirmed as both *liberator* and *mediator*.

- Jesus Christ embodies *being black* in such a way that the result is the emergence of a distinctive *community of faith*.

- This community, vivified by *the spirit of freedom*, provisionally manifests and anticipates the justification of the present social and human order, a justification so radical and complete that those who are now counted as *last shall be first*.

Theology as introspection and as proclamation is crucial for the African-American church, and for all Christian churches, because the relationship between faith and freedom is, perhaps, the most pressing theological problem of our time. Faith seeks understanding; but in the present context that understanding must be a critical one. The point is not simply to understand the basis on which faith is affirmed, but to understand it in a way that makes the faithful a redeeming and transforming presence in the world. Faith seeks critical understanding. Likewise, freedom seeks expression; but the freedom of which we speak must be discernible in visible acts and modes of being in the world. Christian freedom, then, is never simply a spiritual reality, or only a spiritual possession, but is realized in and among those who, even in our midst, struggle for liberation. Freedom seeks public expression.

# 1

## REVELATION AND LIBERATION

The two stubborn facts of African-American Christian existence are that God has revealed Godself to the black community and that this revelation is inseparable from the historic struggle of black people for liberation. These facts are not merely the product of an experiential appropriation of the Gospel but are themselves reflected in the biblical witness. Both the call of Moses (Exod. 3:1–17) and the missiological declaration of Jesus (Luke 4:16–30), the scriptural touchstones of African-American Christianity, reflect the inherent connection between God's self-disclosure and the manifestation of God's liberating intentions in the context of a people who suffer under the yoke of oppression. The Hebrew term employed in the Old Testament to refer to God's liberating and illuminating word is *dabar*. Dabar, however, does not mean the disembodied utterance of a distant Deity, but rather refers to the active engagement of God in bringing about what God proclaims.

In the call of Moses God reveals no new knowledge, engenders no new mysticism, but situates God's appearance in the context of and as a response to the enslavement of Israel. What Moses learns in this encounter is that God has promised to fulfill the covenant relation established with Abraham, Sarah, Isaac, Rebecca, Jacob, and Rachel. The bondage of the people of Israel stands as an affront to the fulfilling of that covenant. Further, God informs Moses that the liberation of the slaves will bring the disfavor of their captors, but that even Pharaoh's army is no match for the power of God. Thus, in this encounter we have the backdrop of a prior, covenantal relationship between God and Israel, an immediate confrontation between Moses the chosen messenger and that God, and the pressing, existential situation of the enslavement of Israel.

In the annunciation of Jesus, he draws from the oral prophetic tradition of Israel and situates himself as the anointed one whose mission it is to bring the good news to the poor and oppressed. He tells his

11

listeners that even today the words of the prophet Isaiah are fulfilled. However, the reaction of the hometown folks of Nazareth turns from praise to condemnation when Jesus indicates that the poor and oppressed to whom he is referring are not the calloused, self-righteous, and complacent citizens of Israel, but are those marginalized people of Zarephath, Syria, and Sidon.[1] A similar pattern to that described above is evident here. We have the backdrop of the prophetic, justice-seeking, tradition of Israel, an immediate encounter between Jesus as the fulfillment of that tradition and the community of hearers, and the cries of oppressed peoples whose voices are not heard even in Israel.

There is within African-American Christianity a structural similarity to the instances cited above. That is, black Christianity developed against the backdrop of a religious sensibility born of African traditional religions, in direct response to the immediate encounter of African slaves with the Jesus of the Bible, and in the existential situation of oppression and unmerited suffering. The religious sensibility of African slaves prior to (and in spite of the conditions of) their introduction to European-American Christianity is evidence that Africans were not pagans or infidels. They were not forgotten by God. African theologians are quick to reply to suggestions that the European missionaries brought God to Africa. Their response is that "we already knew God before the missionaries arrived."

In spite of the ravages of their kidnapping and the disorientation that they endured, African slaves retained an outlook on their experience that continually reaffirmed their worth as individuals and as a people and affirmed God's unmistakable presence in the created order. The Jesus whom they encountered as they were exposed to the Bible was a caring and liberating friend who shared their sorrows and burdens. Further, this Jesus was able to bring real change in their personal condition and their collective estate. It was impossible, however, to speak of this Jesus without relating him to the condition of slavery and exploitation. There was no revelatory significance to the biblical account of Jesus if he could not speak to the real suffering of a voiceless and invisible people.

What this means, theologically speaking, is that to attempt to formulate an understanding of God's revelation apart from an analysis of the unjust structures of social existence does violence to both the significance of that revelation and to the integrity of the liberation struggles carried on by the victims of society. Such a separation would make God's revelation a quaint addition to our knowledge of an ancient religion with no salvific significance for the world in which we live. It would also distort the transcendent dimension of the universal human longing for freedom and justice.

The history of revelation and the history of liberation are the same history.[2] God's self-disclosure is not meant to increase humanity's storehouse of cognitive merchandise or to intensify one's inward feeling of piety, but to demonstrate that God's presence and power are limited by neither geographical boundaries nor political structures. What we learn in the revelatory moment is that God is invested in the struggle of the oppressed for freedom.

## The Meaning of Revelation

God's revelation is both dynamic and multidimensional. Its dynamism is evident in that it takes place in history. It is not an abstract, timeless event, but the manifestation of the will of a living God. The revelation of God is permanent, final, and ultimate in the sense that what we know of God is absolutely trustworthy. All of Christianity stands or falls with the promise of God to be faithful to God's word. Therefore, God's allegiance with the enslaved Israelites and Jesus' solidarity with the victims and outcasts of society are permanent in that they are axiomatic assumptions. From this perspective one can say that God has made Godself known to suffering humanity.

But God's revelation is also contingent, partial, and incomplete in the sense that human history is yet unfolding. Unanticipated, novel, and surprising moments await humankind. The open-endedness of our historical experiences and the limitations of our human condition suggest that this is a revelation that we do not possess, but that possesses us. This is the root of the dynamism of the revelatory moment. There are both novelty and continuity, confirmation and surprise in every encounter between God and humanity. Yet Moses' call and Jesus' annunciation are prototypes, or basic paradigms, through which all our subsequent revelations are judged. Therefore, revelation is dynamic in that while we may not know what God will do in the future, we do know that God's future acts will not contradict God's past acts. We may not know in what garb or visage Christ will appear among us in the future, but we do know that his future identity will not contradict his past identity. In the words of a hymn often sung in African-American churches, "We may not know what the future holds, but we do know who holds the future."

The dynamic character of God's revelation is important in understanding the shape of African-American Christianity because black Christians have lived face to face with the contingency of their own reality. From the sobering recognition of slave parents that their days with their children could be capriciously cut short by the auction block, to the dis-ease of black middle-class persons whose tenuous ties to a comfortable lifestyle may be suddenly cut by the market forces of an economy over which they have little control, the contingent nature of African-American reality is ever-present. Yet the truth of God's promise is not dependent on the human capacity to apprehend its totality, but is finally rooted in the unshakeable Word of God.

God's revelation is dynamic, and it is also multidimensional. Since the seventeenth century, theologians have responded to the Enlightenment claim that religion cannot share the same ontological ground with reason by attempting to demonstrate that revelation is a kind of knowledge. These theologians became so preoccupied with the problems of epistemology that they lost sight of the deeper meaning of God's self-disclosure. Much of this was based on René Descartes' notion that reason precedes existence (*cogito ergo sum* — I think therefore I am), and that knowing (*ordo cognoscendi*) precedes being (*ordo essendi*). What was lost is that God's self-disclosure was the disclosure of a self, not merely a disembodied rational mind, and that Jesus' revelatory declaration in the Gospel of Luke was not the disclosure of some new information but the uncovering of the God's preferential option for the poor and oppressed. Because of this detour in the history of theology, theologians limited their inquiry regarding revelation to two questions, "What is the content of God's revelation?" and "How is that revelation legitimated?"

From the perspective of the poor and people of color, God's revelation involves more than solving abstract epistemological problems. The emergence of the Enlightenment period accompanied the imperialistic expansion of Europe and the large-scale encounter between Europeans and aboriginal peoples. This encounter, and the exploitation of those peoples that followed, resulted in the demise of the classical homogeneous picture of humanity. In terms of the doctrine of revelation it was now necessary to address two further questions, "To whom is this revelation given?" and "Where does this revelation occur?"

The first question became necessary because of Western Christianity's confrontation with people designated as "the other," i.e., people of color and women. The confluence of Christianity and political confrontation meant that one could not speak of God's revelation without some consideration of the question "To whom is God revealed?" The ulterior motives of enslaving Africans, exterminating Jews, and rendering women invisible and aboriginal peoples extinct blinded theologians to the importance of this question, and in most cases they merely assumed that, of course, they (as members of so-called civilized European societies) alone were the recipients of God's revelation.

The second question became necessary because of Western Christianity's complicity in the territorial conquest of other (i.e., "foreign") lands. Christianity's relation to Constantinian expansion in the distant past and the colonial occupation of Africa and Asia in the recent past meant that one could not speak of God's revelation without considering the question of the locus of revelation. However, the incredible bounty extracted from these lands and their eventual enrichment of the European-American churches compromised the integrity of most theologians, and they merely assumed that the locus of God's revelation was wherever they (as bearers of so-called civilized culture) happened to be. The notions of some people designated as "other" and some places designated as "foreign" meant that those with military and political power in these contexts were tempted to deem themselves as the only chosen receptors of God's revelation and the ground on which they stood and lived as the only revelatory ground.

God's revelation is multidimensional for African-American Christians because they were the "other" to whom God's self-disclosure had been presumably denied. However, they knew differently. African-American Christians have always resisted ideas of revelation that confined it to pure abstract knowledge. To paraphrase Blaise Pascal, revelation has more to do with the reasons of the heart than with the reasons of the head. Further, African-American Christians have consistently resisted the tendency to divorce the fact of God's revelation from the identity and social location of those to whom it is given. This is why black religious testimonies are full of specific personal and topographical references when speaking of an encounter with God in Christ. African-American Christians will often cite the date, time, and place of their conversion/revelation experience as a sign of authenticity. In addition, many will affirm that God called them by name. God's revelation is multidimensional because it is essentially a personal encounter. That revelation concerns whole persons and whole communities in their particularity. It is the loving and gracious giving of Godself to the world.

## The Meaning of Liberation

Like the notion of revelation, the idea of liberation is also dynamic and multidimensional. Its dynamism lies in the fact that at any given time the desire for liberation is a response to the concrete historical and existential concerns of the oppressed. The term "liberation," unlike the word "liberty," is employed precisely because it points to the real, visceral character of the human struggle against the principles of evil in the world. The term "liberty" has become associated with laissez-faire economic theory, individualist political theory, normative ethical theory, and uncritical patriotism, to the extent that it has lost any symbolic power for those whose condition is more than theoretical. Liberation, to this point, has the advantage of being associated, for good or for ill, with concrete historical movements.

To speak of liberation as God's work and intention in the world means that one must understand liberation as a permanent, final, and ultimate feature of one's existence. That is, God's will is irresistible, and God's work cannot be thwarted. All Christian hope stands or falls with this conviction. God's liberation of the Israelites under the leadership of Moses and God's liberation of the oppressed through the death and resurrection of Jesus are the cornerstone of Christian hope. This liberation, however, is also partial, fragile, and incomplete, because the drama of the struggle is yet being played out on the stage of history. Although one might know the general theme of the story, and therefore be certain about the outcome, new plot twists and unexpected ironic reversals await humankind. This means that life must be lived, not only for the anticipated reward that awaits one at the end of the earthly journey, but because life itself is a gift from God.

To make liberation only a future reality leads to quietism and leaves the forces of dehumanization in the world unchallenged. More importantly, however, making liberation an eschatological carrot on the end of a stick cheapens life and robs each moment of the sense that it is an instance of the grace of God. The dynamic character of liberation is important for understanding the experience of African-Americans because they are a people who know what it means to wrest some small joy out of disappointment, to celebrate life's victories, to endure life's pains, and to sense a measure of triumph in the living of each day. This is why prayers commonly heard in African-American churches will offer thanks to God for "last night's lyin' down and this morning's gettin' up; for allowing our golden moments to roll on just a little while longer." This is the experience of a people who understand that liberation is fragile, but precious.

Liberation is also multidimensional. The most common distortion of the notion of liberation is that it unidimensional. While many people associate the term with movements for political independence or the overthrow of existing governmental structures, there are those who, seeking to coopt the term, speak of liberation as an inward reality, a kind of psychic or spiritual antinomianism. The fact is that liberation in the context of the revelation of God grasps humanity at every level of human existence. Liberation is multidimensional in that it includes the physical, spiritual, and cultural dimensions of human existence.

*Physical liberation* refers to the innate desire of all human beings to enjoy freedom of movement and association and the rights of self-determination. The prominence of the emphasis on physical liberation in African-American social thought is understandable in light of the fact that physical bondage was the distinguishing aspect of the existence of Africans in the New World for four hundred years and that complete freedom has not yet come to African-Americans as a whole. There are still neighborhoods where black people are not welcomed and where their homes are desecrated. There are still institutions in which limits are placed on their participation and influence. Because African-Americans are almost always viewed as "a social group" and almost never as human beings with the same needs and desires as any other human beings, their struggle for liberation appears to concern mainly their physical condition. While this certainly may be the case, there is more to the liberation struggle than one's physical condition.

The human spirit is meant to soar, lifting one to new vistas. Where there is no spirit, there is no life, even though one's biological functions may continue. To be created in the image of God or to be part of God's created order is to possess the spirit. *Spiritual empowerment* is that dimension of the liberation struggle in which African-Americans come to understand and reclaim their intrinsic worth as human beings.

Thus it is not accidental that with the political reawakening of African-Americans in the 1960s there was also a spiritual reawakening. Black Christians, along with Black Muslims, began to see the revolutionary potential in genuine faith. Old compensatory ideas of religion being "the opiate of the people" were challenged, and the prophetic strand of black Christianity reemerged. This Pentecostal liberation was never a naive assumption or an easy victory. African-American Christians understood themselves to be involved in spiritual warfare "against principalities and powers," both inside and outside the black community. However, the connection between the first two dimensions of liberation is evident in the physical language often used to express the spiritual triumph. "I looked at my hands and my hands looked new. I looked at my feet and they did too. . . . I have a new walk and a new talk." Spiritual liberation meant walking in the newness of life, no longer fettered by self-doubt and flagging confidence. It meant freedom from the sin of slavery as well as the slavery of sin.[3]

A third dimension of liberation in the African-American experience is cultural. *Cultural liberation* refers to freedom from negative self-images, symbols, and stereotypes. People of African descent have been historically victimized by a color symbolism that has consistently described the favorable qualities of goodness, purity, honesty, and cleanliness with the word "white," while describing the unfavorable qualities of evil, defilement, disreputability, and stain with the word "black." The association of blackness with sin in the Christian context has played a major role in the cultural oppression of people of color. However, the problem goes beyond the mere symbolic associations. Western culture, which has been built on this kind of symbolism, has led to a distorted view of life and themselves on the part of black people. Adjusting to this distortion often meant trying to see oneself as others see one and trying to escape the blackness that is intrinsic to one's being.

Part of the meaning of liberation is a reversal of the color symbolism that has afflicted African-Americans, an overturning of the historic association between blackness and sin, and a revalorization of one's identity. In the 1960s the slogan "black is beautiful" embodied the emerging liberation of black people from the cultural bondage that had for so long held them in its grip. In response to this the bondage, however, African-Americans have forged their own distinctive culture in spite of racial oppression and dehumanization. This culture was a product of the interaction between their African past and the demands of their present condition. The sustaining value of this culture is evident in the black "style of life" and "way of being" in the world. It safeguarded the essential conviction that the inherent sense of self-worth and indigenous values could not be destroyed by the experience of oppression.

These three dimensions of liberation must be seen as one piece. Where the liberation movements of black people have failed to realize their potential, that is, where the frailty and incompleteness of human liberation projects are most visible, an imbalance in these dimensions is evident. Where the political dimension dominates, one finds a utilitarian notion of human existence and spiritual poverty. Where the spiritual dimension dominates a kind of private docetism reigns as well as political asceticism. Where the cultural dimension dominates one often encounters a narrow spiritual parochialism as well as political insularity. While at various points in the history of African-Americans emphasis on one of these dimensions has been necessary, a full understanding of liberation requires that an appropriate balance among them be sought. In the contemporary world, the reality of racism, sexism, and classism both inside and outside the African-American community requires a multidimensional view of liberation. Liberation involves more than what humans alone can accomplish. It is a powerful symbol for the ultimate destiny of humankind.

## Two Aspects of African-American Religion

In African-American Christian faith there is a dynamic interrelation between God's revelation and human liberation. This interrelation is a product of the divinely inspired collective imaginative vision of black people and is most clearly visible in the concrete phenomenon of African-American religion. In classical Protestantism the relation between faith and religion has often been misconstrued because of the particular cultural, historical, and social circumstances of European-American Christianity. In the sixteenth century, Martin Luther was appalled by the corrupt religious practices of the established church and sought to define true faith over against mere religion. This was the import of his doctrine of *sola fide*. Likewise, the twentieth-century neo-orthodox theologian Karl Barth, dismayed at the shallow religious practices of bourgeois German society of his time, condemned all human religion as essentially idolatrous and sought to define the concept of a transcendent faith as the essence of Christianity.

When one examines the thought of African-American Christians it becomes readily apparent that one cannot (nor should one) radically separate religion and faith. The etymological root of the word "religion" is *ligare*, from which we get the word "ligament." It means "to hold together." Religion, then, is a way of holding together the various aspects of the human response to the divine encounter. Faith is embodied in religion. In religion, the faith and practice of the Christian community are united. Thus black religion has two major aspects, obedience to God's command and the pursuit of God's truth, the discovery of the verity of God's word and the structuring of one's reality in accordance with that word.

A watershed event in the development of contemporary African-American theology was the publication of Joseph Washington's controversial book, *Black Religion*.[4] In this work, Washington presented a thesis on the dysfunctional character of black religion and outlined a surprising proposal for the solution of that dysfunction. In the manner of classical Protestantism he argued that faith and religion are separate entities:

> Religion is always a partial expression of some faith.... Faith must always be a response to God. Religion may be a response to whatever the individual desires.... Religion for the Negro is inherited and changed by the contemporary mood without reference to the theological dimension of faith.... Though he is involved in a separated religion he cannot create a separate faith.[5]

Washington's major concern is that since black religion is so radically different from white religion in America it must necessarily be dysfunctional because it departs from the accepted norm. His conclusion is that black religion is not an expression of true Christianity, but a kind of "folk" religion with the physical condition of black people rather than matters of doctrine and orthodox liturgy as its primary concern:

> Born in slavery, weaned in segregation and reared in discrimination, the religion of the Negro folk was chosen to bear the roles of both protest and relief. Thus the uniqueness of black religion is the racial bond which seeks to risk its life for the elusive but ultimate goal of freedom and

equality by means of protest and action. It does so through the only
avenues to which its members have always been permitted a measure of
access, religious convocations in the fields or in houses of worship. . . .
[Black] religious institutions exist without any meaningful goals, with
the sole exception of providing refuge for the disinherited.[6]

If black religion is not truly Christian, then it follows, according to
Washington, that black religious institutions are not actually churches
in the classical Protestant sense:

> There is no Negro Protestantism, Negro Christianity, or Negro church.
> . . . Rarely is it admitted that Negro congregations do not constitute
> churches by any stretch of the theological imagination, but religious con-
> gregations. . . . In this perspective, Negro congregations are not churches
> but religious societies.[7]

If black congregations are not true Christian churches, then it follows that they cannot possess an authentic theology or comprehensive
interpretation of the meaning of the Christian Gospel:

> Negro congregations have been divided on every conceivable issue except
> that of theology — within the Negro communions virtually no theol-
> ogy has existed. . . . A church without theology, the interpretation of and
> response to the will of God for the faithful, is a contradiction in terms.[8]

A corollary to Washington's assessment of black religion as merely
"folk" religion, black churches as merely "religious congregations,"
and the dearth of an authentic theology in either is his negative evalu-
ation of the origins and centrality of that most visible manifestation of
black religion, the dynamism of black worship. He argues that "the
frenzy," or the emotional output, that characterizes much of black
worship is essentially the residue of those religious practices taught to
slaves by evangelical white preachers and that by abandoning this frenzy
black Christians will contribute to their full participation in European-
American Christian culture.[9] The final solution for the problems that
face the black church, according to Washington, is the dissolution of
separate black worshipping congregations and their absorption into
the white churches. "It is incumbent upon the Negro now to close his
houses of worship and enter the white congregations of his choice en
masse."[10]

The shortcomings of Washington's analysis have been widely discussed among African-American theologians since its appearance. He
fails to appreciate the African antecedents of black religion and he en-
gages in a reductionist social analysis of African-American religious
experience. The problem is not with what Washington observed in the
African-American religious experience, but that, due to his Eurocentric
perspective, he misinterpreted those observations. His uncritical allegiance to the classical Protestant notion of the relation between faith

and religion in effect blinded him to the interdependence of faith and practice in black religion.

The first aspect of black religion is its praxiological function in which black religion serves as a guide to behavior for its adherents. This praxiological, ethical, and moral emphasis is clearly visible in the historical accounts of slave religion.[11] For African slaves religion could not be separated from the way in which their world was structured, and their beliefs always related closely to their behavior in that world. For instance, the slave belief in the righteousness of God was directly related to the belief that God would inaugurate a revolution in the conditions of white people and black people. African slaves demonstrated the uniqueness of their religion in the way that they shaped their moral universe. They saw through the hypocrisy of white preachers who lectured them on the wrongness of stealing from the master, and many of them rejected the contradictory ethical norms of white religion by claiming that because they, as slaves, were stolen property, the commandment against stealing did not apply to them.[12] They would not be put into the position of having to condemn themselves as sinners simply because they did not want to starve to death.

Therefore, many slaves constructed their own ethical codes that responded more sympathetically to the physical and spiritual conditions of the slave community. Other slaves took pleasure in exposing the hypocrisy of white slave-holding Christians by devoting themselves to a life of virtue and moral superiority over their masters. They took no small pleasure in reminding their masters that their questionable business dealings and their sexual improprieties were contrary to God's law. In slave religion the praxiological emphasis of black religion is evident.

The fertile ritual and emotive drama of African-American worship are perhaps its most misunderstood aspects. The creative play and imaginative combination of aesthetic elements, singing, chanting, dancing, handclapping, and shouts of praise may give the casual observer the impression that African-American worship is primarily a cultural performance. In a sense, this impression is accurate. The relationship between the "cultural" and the "religious" is quite intimate in black experience. The poetic quality of black preaching and the secular spirituality of rap music, the bluesy sound of traditional black Gospel music and the deeply religious dimension in soul music, lithe bodies dancing on Saturday night and then swaying to the metronomic rhythm of divine inspiration on Sunday, suggest the fundamental inseparability of the cultural and the religious perspectives in black experience. (Thus Paul Tillich was not far from being correct when he asserted that "culture is the form of religion, and religion is the content of culture.")

This is not to say that there are no boundaries between what is acceptable in black churches and what is not. Rather, one must look closely at the roots of the criteria that are used to make such a determination and ask whether they simply reflect the degree to which a given congregation has adopted Protestant evangelical norms, or whether there is a significant theological statement being made. While black worship may be seen as a cultural performance, it is also more than that. However, to make that determination one must partake of the reality to which that symbolic performance points. The noted anthropologist Clifford Geertz speaks directly to this issue:

> Of course, all cultural performances are not religious performances, and the line between those that are and artistic, or even political, ones is often not so easy to draw in practice, for, like social forms, symbolic forms can serve multiple purposes.... Where for "visitors" religious performances can, in the nature of the case, only be presentations of a particular religious perspective, and thus aesthetically appreciated or scientifically dissected, for participants they are in addition enactments, materializations of it — not only models of what they believe, but also models *for* the believing of it. In these plastic dramas [people] attain their faith as they portray it.[13]

Thus the flaw in Washington's analysis of black religion was his failure to "participate" in the ethos of that religion and thereby assess the points at which the cultural performance became a religious one. That is, he did not engage black religion on its own terms and failed to ask, "What faith is suggested by the unique religious praxis of African-American Christians?" An Afrocentric perspective on the phenomenon of black religion looks for the connections between its faith and its practice, its worship and its theology.[14]

The second aspect of black religion is its hermeneutical function in which the search for truth on the part of its adherents is advanced. Passion needs to be balanced by a critical consciousness and every praxis seen in relation to its cognitive complement. It should be noted here that the hermeneutical and praxiological functions of religion are distinct but inseparable. One must begin with the praxiological aspect and then move to the hermeneutical aspect because there is a kind of cognitive value to praxis. What one knows as the truth is very much conditioned by the reality in which one participates. This is especially true in reference to African-American religion. The style, aesthetics, and creativity evident in the visible manifestations of black religion are not merely the products of the artistic imagination of black folk; they are also the attempt of the worshippers to envision new ideas, concepts, and cognitive paradigms for the interpretation of the world in which they live.[15] That is, black religion is more than an epiphenomenon; it has an ontological status.[16] Black religion does more than provide space for an alternative mode of existence for people who are downtrodden; it also asks and answers the questions related to "why things are the way they are." A source of the radicalism of historic black religion is precisely this questioning. The spirituals and their counterpart, the blues, often sound a familiar refrain, asking why the humble suffer and the wicked prosper.

Hermeneutics refers to the act of interpretation. Most often this activity is directed toward a written text, but a broader view of human experience recognizes the textuality of that experience and the need to interpret the meaning not only of written texts but also of one's experience and social practices. All religions have a hermeneutical aspect to them, but not all religions are engaged in the same kind of hermeneutical tasks. Susan Sontag in her classic essay "Against Interpretation" describes two kinds of hermeneutical activity:

> Thus interpretation is not (as most people assume) an absolute value, a gesture of mind situated in some timeless realm of capabilities. Interpretation must itself be evaluated, within a historical view of human consciousness. In some cultural contexts, interpretation is a liberating act. It is a means of revising, of transvaluing, of escaping the dead past. In other cultural contexts, it is reactionary, impertinent, cowardly, stifling.[17]

A reactionary hermeneutic attempts to "possess" the truth, ignore its own limitations, and protect its own privilege by masking reality rather than letting it come to light. A liberating hermeneutic allows one to be grasped by the truth, in full consciousness of one's limitations and in deep awe and respect for the reality that is being revealed. While the reactionary hermeneutic is what Sontag calls "the revenge of the intellect upon the world," the liberating hermeneutic is the submission of the questioning personality to the irruption of God's truth in a troubled world. The connection between truth and liberation is reflected in Jesus' words to those who would become his disciples: "You will know the truth and the truth will make you free" (John 8:32).

In its hermeneutical aspect, African-American Christianity brings into view the epistemological break between white Christians and black Christians in America. That "break" consists of the fact that though both the black and white churches proclaim to profess Christ, their religious visions of the world are radically different. This was evident in the practice of white preachers exhorting black slaves to "be obedient to your masters," while slave Christians were simultaneously celebrating the liberating presence of God in their lives. Black religion attempts to help African-American Christians to sense the world as God senses it. A second hermeneutical task of black religion is to dismantle the misinterpretations of themselves and the world that undergird American Christianity. That is, black religion is a protest against those portrayals of African-Americans as less than human or outside the providential care of God. A third hermeneutical task is for African-Americans to promote an authentic and essential knowledge of themselves. Charles Long observes that "every adequate hermeneutic is at heart an essay in self-understanding. It is the effort to understand the self through the mediation of the other."[18] Black religion attempts to provide a self-knowledge for African-American Christians by helping them to see themselves as God sees them.

The praxiological and hermeneutical aspects of black religion are ideally held in perfect balance. Wherever and whenever black religion becomes distorted and a caricature of itself, the balance between these dimensions is lost. On one side, the devaluation of the hermeneutical aspect can lead to a rampant anti-intellectualism in black religion that not only destroys its critical edge, but abandons its historic radical intellectual tradition. On the other side, a rejection of the praxiological aspect can lead to a dispassionate sterility in black religion that blunts its imaginative and emotive creativity. When the perfect balance is approached black religion succeeds in responding to the needs of both the head and the heart.

### Narrative and African-American Theological Discourse

African-American religion is not a static phenomenon, but is the result of a dynamic interaction of the remembered past, the experienced present, and the anticipated future. It reflects the changeable character of African-American experience in the world. Even the form of black religion, then, must suit the variable spiritual, emotional, and physical needs of its adherents. This is why the essence of black religion is expressed in the form of story. By telling the story of African-American faith, the past is preserved and kept alive in the collective memory of the community, the enigmas and puzzles of contemporary life are demystified, and the future is suggestively inferred and hinted at. Moreover, a genuine story initiates some kind of transformation in the life of the hearer and requires a response to its truth.[19]

African-American theology, simply defined, is the explanation, defense, and critique of the religious practice and interpretation of the black community. This theology must be intimately related to the cultural religious form from which it springs. If the form of black religion is story, then the form of black theology must be narrative. The two aspects of black religion, the praxiological and the hermeneutical, can be held together only by a form of discourse that reconciles the two types of human activity — praxis and criticism — that have been separated by Enlightenment thought. Traditional metaphysics is no longer an adequate base for doing theology because it depends on a common vision of "reality as such" and a common notion of "general human experience." These assumptions have become suspect in a world where disagreements about "reality" and what constitutes "common human experience" erupt into tribal, racial, and international strife. What one makes of the world cannot be separated from one's cultural bias, class interests, and political allegiances. Further, traditional metaphysics (with the possible exception of process thought) normally begins with some static notion of reality. Narrative, on the other hand, suggests in a variety of ways an unfolding, historical idea of reality. African-American theological narrative is a retelling of the black religious story with an emphasis on intellectual clarity and existential commitment.

What then does it mean to claim that African-American theological discourse must take narrative form? How does its narrative structure relate to its function? First, African-American theology must be responsive to the contemporary experience of African-Americans. It has been observed that "the formal quality of experience through time is inherently narrative."[20] That is, human beings make sense of their apprehensions of the world around them in relation to the passing of time, the dynamic interplay of the past and future brought together in the decisive tension of the present moment:

> Narrative alone can contain the full temporality of experience in a unity of form.... Only narrative form can contain the tensions, the surprises, the disappointments and reversals and achievements of actual, temporal experience.[21]

Black religious experience is story-shaped; therefore black theology must be experiential narrative.

Second, the African-American story is not only contemporary, but is part of a continuous discursive tradition outside of which it cannot be fully understood. Therefore, African-American theology must turn again and again to the historical material, both oral and written, that documents the black struggle for freedom. It must continuously dialogue with that "great cloud of witnesses" whose grit and determination have oiled the wheels of the black liberation movement. It must be in conversation with the African-American communion of saints whose works and faith continue to edify black Christians. Black theology must be both a personal testimony and a collective testament; it must be historical narrative.[22]

Third, the black religious story is an attempt to integrate both the inner, personal and the outer, political life of its hearers in the midst of moral chaos. As James Cone notes, "the easiest way for the oppressed to defy conceptual definitions that justify their existence in servitude is to tell stories about another reality where they are accepted as human beings."[23] Thus stories about justice serve as refutations of the political immorality that threatens the black community.

The black story also addresses the lives of African-Americans at the personal level. It has a crucial role in character formation and the honing of one's moral judgment. That is, the stories in which one lives, so to speak, do not only reflect what kind of individual one is, but also shape one's identity and sense of values.[24] Thus black stories about compassion, loyalty and faithfulness provide a sense of integrity that counters the specter of personal moral disintegration. African-American theology should reflect this struggle in its own formal dimensions; it must be integrating narrative.

Fourth, stories have the capacity to uncover truth and expose falsehoods when the hearer is willing to enter into the discursive world of the tellers. Stories can both convict and convince, comfort and terrify. (The biblical account of Nathan and David demonstrates how the truth of David's greed is revealed and how he convicts himself through a story.) Stories allow people of one culture and history to enter, however provisionally, that of another people.

The black religious story is not exclusive in the sense that other people are, by definition, incapable of understanding it. But the truth of the black story will elude anyone who is unwilling to entertain its revelational potential. The black religious story provides opportunities for people to break out of their ideological prisons and to see that the roles of oppressed and oppressor are not the ultimate categories of human existence. Black theology must contribute to the liberation of people from the false stories that enslave them; it must be critical narrative.

Finally, and perhaps, most importantly, stories are aimed toward the transformation of the hearers. When the black religious story is told among African-Americans the truth is revealed:

> It is difficult to express this liberating truth in rational discourse alone; it must be told in story. And when this truth is told as it was meant to be, the oppressed are transformed, taken into another world and given a glimpse of the promised land.[25]

When the black religious story is engaged by those from other cultures a *metanoia* may occur:

> Finally, what may happen is that hearing another story can force us to tell our own story in a different way, transformed to such a degree that we can properly call the experience one of *conversion*.[26]

The transformation of the oppressed and the subsequent conversion of the oppressor through a turn toward the truth is the goal of the black religious story. Black theology must reflect this teleological dimension of the black story; it must be redemptive narrative.

## Narrative and Method in African-American Theology

The narrative forms of African-American theological discourse are not simply convenient constructs that render the religious infrastructure of black religion accessible and intelligible. Rather, they are inherent to the entire process of "doing" African-American theology. That is, the customary components of any discussion of theological method — the sources and norm — should be understood as narrative in character, and the central problematic of theological method — assessing and determining the truth of theological affirmations — should be framed in narrative terms.

The sources of African-American theological affirmations are the Bible, the traditions of African-American worshipping congregations, African-American culture, and the African-American worldview. The Bible is the primary document of the Christian faith, because it is a record of God's revelation to humanity. It is important for African-Americans because, in many instances, they were forbidden to read it, even as a distorted version of it was preached to them by slavemasters and white preachers. When possible, slaves taught themselves to read it in the belief that it held the key to their self-understanding. On a few occasions, slaves were allowed to read only the Bible because of the slavemasters' mistaken conviction that it would promote docility and quietism. It is an important source for African-American theology because, in spite of the contradictory nature of their introduction to it, African-American Christians are a biblical people. The Bible is a source of knowledge and inspiration.

The tradition of the black church is a response to the suffering of African-Americans. It is also an affirmation of the joy and freedom that they have intermittently and provisionally experienced. This tradition is a source of the truth about God in the religious experience of African-Americans. It is important to state that it is *a source* of the truth but not the truth itself. Therefore, African-American theologians have been both defenders and critics of this tradition. One aspect of this tradition is seen in the prophetic stance of the antebellum black church. This was the church that gave rise to revolutionary preachers like Henry Highland Garnet, who urged his compatriots to resist slavery, Nathaniel Paul, who declared that the Gospel and slavery are irreconcilable, and Nat Turner, who advocated open violent rebellion against slavery. The African-American church in this instance was the base for political and religious resistance, and the Christianity that sustained it was related to social justice in this world.

The postbellum black church, however, lost this zeal for freedom. In the disillusionment of the Post-Reconstruction period, many African-American ministers sold their prophetic birthright for fleeting material gains and promises of personal comfort. The tradition of the black church must be critiqued and defended in relation to God's revealed truth. Further, the tradition is rightly criticized because of its exclusion of black women and their contribution to that tradition. Jarena Lee, Amanda Smith, and Rebecca Jackson were women who were denied access to the pulpits of African-American churches despite their undeniable call to ministry. The tradition of the African-American churches is most true when it is a liberating tradition rather than an accommodating or constricting tradition, and, as the experience of African-American women suggests, it is a source of the truth but not the whole truth of African-American religious experience.

African-American culture is a source of theological reflection because the results of that reflection have to be expressed culturally. Because theology is a human act it is shaped, in part, by the cultural context of those whose faith and experience it addresses. European-American theology has always been expressed in forms and language drawn from European-American culture. An example is the "death of God" theology of the 1960s. The symbolic statement of the demise of God expressed a deeply felt loss of meaning, a diminishing of American hegemony in the world, and anomie among certain segments of the European-American theological intelligentsia at the time. At the same time, African-American theologians were expressing the awakening prophetic consciousness of the black church by declaring that not only is God alive and potent, but that God is black. The cultural context of this theological language was a resurgence of African-American cultural nationalism, the independence movements among African nations, and a sense of pride and self-worth. No theology is "acultural" or value-free. African-American theology is expressed in the symbols of and reflects the values of African-American culture.

In many discussions of theological method, reason is named as a source of theological discourse. In these discussions there is often confusion about what is meant by the term "reason" and about its role in the theological process. For some, reason refers to the whole complex of Western philosophical thought from Plato to Alfred N. Whitehead and beyond. In this instance, the subjects and themes of theology are enhanced or enriched by the contributions of classical philosophy. For others, reason refers to an epistemological style, a way of thinking that fits all of human experience into neatly defined categories; or it is a "normative gaze" in which the thinker objectifies and relativizes the central problems of human existence. In this instance, theologians are supposed to benefit from the style and stance of philosophy.

Reason defined in these two ways is not a primary source for African-American theology. The Western philosophical tradition — at least in the way that it is normally perceived — does not reflect the contributions of people of African descent. Reason understood as an uncritical reliance on the categories of formal epistemology or on the "objective" approach to the faith is not particularly useful to African-American theology because those categories cannot always adequately explain African-American experience, and the "objective" approach, besides being fallacious in and of itself, cannot account for the passionate character of African-American theological discourse. This does not mean that African-American theology is without coherence and integrity. Rather, it means that African-American theology is supported by an African-American worldview that defines the parameters and sets the themes of its discourse. It employs the African-American imagination to bring together the comfort and challenges of the Gospel and the sociopolitical and spiritual needs of black people. If "reason" is a source for African-American theology then its "look" is different for the African-American theologian and the European-American one.

It is through the norm of theology that its various affirmations are evaluated and assessed. The norm of Christian theological affirmations is the acme of God's self-revelation in some notion of the identity and mission or the person and work of Jesus Christ. Although a fuller discussion of Christology must await a later chapter, it is imperative at this point to examine the function of this norm in African-American theological method.

There are two major misconceptions regarding the theological norm that have limited the effectiveness of modern theology. The first is that theological statements are judged by a transcendent norm that exists somewhere outside of or above the discursive universe in which theological statements are made. An example of this is the theologies of the eighteenth and nineteenth centuries that "objectively" concluded that the enslavement of Africans was consistent with the will of God. In this instance, the norm is in reality the objectification of the cultural, political, and economic order of slavery. These theologies were the result of a "monological" theological methodology. They tolerated no dissent within their deliberations. They were not so much interested in the discovery of truth as they were in the establishment of theological authority. Authority is here defined as the power or right to give commands and enforce obedience. (The political corollary is the neglect of justice for the security of "law and order.") While these theologies claimed a kind of authority within the community of slaveholders, they could never claim legitimacy among African slaves.

The second misconception is that theological statements are evaluated and assessed by an immanent norm that is totally circumscribed by the discursive context in which theological statements are made. An example of this is found in various privatistic theologies that seceded from the cultural and political fray by focusing solely on the inner, spiritual life of the believer. These ascetic theologies were the result of the subjectification of the primacy of the individual in the socio-economic order and the primacy of the soul in the religious order of creation. These theologies were also monological in the sense that it was the inner voice speaking to the individual self that was most important. There was no dissent because the truth was whatever was consistent with the deepest desires of the inner self. In this case, theological affirmations were genuinely legitimate because they conformed to rules and standards arising out of the personal life. However, although they were legitimate, they lacked authority. (The Society of Friends, e.g., George Fox and John Woolman, were able to make legitimate affirmations of the humanity of the slaves because of their belief in the "inner light" given to them by their creator. However, the political and theological implications of their pacifism along with their marginality within American society diminished the authority of their pronouncements.) The point to be made here is that the norm of theology must both authorize and legitimate its affirmations.

In most contemporary theologies method is understood as dialogical. That is, method must relate the situational sources of theology (culture, reason, etc.) to the historical sources (Scripture, tradition, etc.). One can see this method operative in Paul Tillich's "method of correlation" in which the questions put forth by human existence must be correlated to the answers implied in the Christian message. John McQuarrie suggests that theological methodology is seeking a "rough coherence" between the data of human experience and the traditional sources of Christian faith. Karl Barth claims that it is in the dynamic tension between the situational and historical sources that truth resides. Although the dialogical model of theological method is a significant improvement over the monological model, it fails to avoid a kind of dualism that is foreign to the African-American sensibility.

When the sources of theology are grouped into the situational and the historical, what results are two norms, a situational one and a historical one. This occurs because the Bible and tradition are often seen as being of a different order than what we know of God through culture and worldview. Therefore, this normative split has been often contained in the phrase, "The Christ of Faith versus the Jesus of History" or the "universal Christ versus the particular Jesus." Because one is working with two norms rather than one, the theologian is ultimately forced to choose one as the dominant norm, thus resolving the theological conflict. However, the result is a theology that claims the authority of the Bible and tradition while denying the legitimacy of the situational norm, or a theology that claims the legitimacy of culture and reason, while denying the authority of the historical norm.

In African-American theology the sources of theology are not divided into the situational and the historical because they are all the result of the interpretation by the people of faith of the acts of God in their particular situation. Therefore, one cannot simply subject the biblical text to a literary analysis and the culture to a social scientific analysis. Rather, one must subject the biblical text to a social scientific analysis because it is the result of a certain mode of production and conditioned by specific institutional realities. Likewise, contemporary culture must be subjected to a literary (or hermeneutical) analysis because the culture is a "text" that must be read, deciphered, and decoded. The sources of African-American theology — the Bible, the traditions of African-American worshipping congregations, African-American culture, and the African-American worldview — are narrative elements that make up the discourse called theology. They are parts of the story of the Christian faith. Therefore, the primary task in African-American theological method is assessing that story. There may be tension but no conflict between these narrative elements because they are not vying to be the arbiter of truth; rather together they tell the truth (rather than depending on symbolic communication as much European-American theology has done). Stories grow out of and lead back to participation in concrete experiences and realities. Narratives are the result of and give rise to praxis. Narrative is the form of African-American theology because it is wholistic and praxiological. In African-American theology the sources of theology are narrative elements, and the norm is found within the narrative itself. In describing "the pragmatics of narrative knowledge" Jean-François Lyotard observes that

> Narratives... determine criteria of competence and/or illustrate how they are to be applied. They thus define what has the right to be said and done in the culture in question, and since they are themselves a part of that culture, they are legitimated by the simple fact that they do what they do.[27]

The norm that both authorizes and legitimates theological discourse is in the narrative itself. One discovers or has revealed to one the norm (the notion that the acme of God's self-revelation is the identity and mission or the person and work of Jesus Christ) not solely in the Bible, nor only through culture, but in the telling of one's own faith stories (affirming their legitimacy) and relating them to the stories of others in terms of the freedom struggle (affirming their authority). African-American theology emerges self-consciously out of the interstices of life and thought, faith and praxis, doctrine and culture.[28]

# 2

## THE BIBLE: A TEXT FOR OUTSIDERS

One cannot do theology in and for the African-American community without coming to terms with the influence of the Bible. It is necessary for the Bible to play an important, if not central, role in such theological discourse for it legitimately to be considered Christian theology. It is the primary, though not exclusive, conduit of the community's understanding of God's being and acts. It is the church's book in this sense, and it serves as a plumbline for the life and practice of the Christian community. However, there is another reason that theology in the African-American churches must pay particular attention to the Bible. Black people have had a unique and peculiar experience in relation to the biblical text. Their introduction to it, its varied influence on their existence, and the issue of its continuing relevance in their struggle for freedom and wholeness all signal the need to ask critical questions of the Bible. What should be its place in African-American theological reflection? In what sense is the Bible true? To what extent can it be trusted to accurately transmit something of the will and purpose of God? What is the relationship between the Bible and black experience?

While a full analysis of these questions and their implications would take us beyond the scope of this chapter, they do point to the need to consider the significance of the Bible and black experience as a prelude to a systematic exposition of the faith affirmations of African-Americans.

The canopy under which an examination of the Bible and African-American experience takes place is the "scripturality" of the American experience, that is, the pervasiveness of scriptural legitimation of American aspirations and the buttressing of the American consciousness by biblical mandates. It reveals the context in which African-Americans have had to read and study the Bible. That reading and study have not been uncontested. Throughout their sojourn in North America

33

African-Americans have been and continue to be involved in a struggle for canonical control. In a provocative essay, "The Biblical Basis of the American Myth," Sacvan Bercovitch argues that "the Puritans provided the scriptural basis for what we have come to call the myth of America. In this sense their influence appears most clearly in the extraordinary persistence of a rhetoric grounded in the Bible, and in the way that Americans keep returning to that rhetoric, especially in times of crisis, as a source of cohesion and continuity."[1]

This scriptural rhetoric rested on the pillars of the Puritan determination to conquer, through the forces of modernization, the vast untamed territory that lay before them and their obsession with Scripture, *sola scriptura*. The Puritan experience in the New World was sanctified and legitimated by interpreting the Bible figuratively and typologically. When faced with the presence of Native Americans and their aboriginal claim to the land, the Puritans looked to the Scriptures and "discovered America in the Bible."[2] America became, in the eyes of the New England immigrants, the fulfillment of prophecy, and to challenge manifest destiny of America was to challenge biblical authority. The result of this view of the Bible was "an imperialism of the word unrivaled in modern times."[3] It laid the necessary groundwork for subsequent biblical justifications for the extermination of Amerindians and the enslavement of Africans.

This scripturality is not confined to the past, but continues to define, in large degree, contemporary American culture. Martin Marty has observed that "scripturalism" is one of the major continuities of American life.[4] Although scripturalism, as Marty argues, is not necessarily biblicism, the Hebrew and Christian Scriptures continue to occupy a privileged place in the American consciousness.[5] The Bible has become the visceral vortex of deep-seated convictions about the nature of the American reality and the survival of its customs and mores. As such, it functions as a verbal icon whose power "has little to do with the *content* of ancient Scriptures but much to do with the *form* of modern American life."[6] It solidifies a national identity forged by the biblical rhetoric of the Puritans. (As has been noted, that rhetoric defined the "American" reality as Eurocentric and verbally banished Amerindians and Africans from the arena of discourse.) While the Puritans could assume a populace familiar with the contents of the Bible to support their figural interpretations, contemporary biblicists can assume, at least for the present, that most Americans are aware of the Bible as a powerful symbol of authority and continuity. Marty concludes that "as for the future, it may be that our secular-pluralist culture is becoming so differentiated, its norms so diffuse, that each generation will see the Bible surrounded by an increasing number of icons, until it *loses centrality*."[7] To go a step further, it is quite possible that the Bible, in losing its privileged place in Eurocentric culture, may gain — or regain — its original status as a central text for outsiders.

The invisibility and vulnerability of Africans in Puritan America were largely the result of flawed interpretations of the Bible. However, within the black community alternate interpretations of the Bible were being rendered, often at the peril of those untutored exegetes. These interpretations were unmistakably shaped by the status of the interpreters as outsiders. It is still the case that the social, political, economic, and aesthetic marginalization of African-Americans — that is, the social dislocation of black people in the United States and elsewhere — conditions their approach to and use of biblical imagery, precepts, and motifs. Black churches and religious communities consistently proclaim that God's realm includes those who have been left out. The purpose of this chapter is to identify the hermeneutical "keys" used to decipher and decode hidden meanings within the Bible. An overview of the major issues in the relationship between the Bible, slavery, and freedom in African-American experience may provide clues to the distinctive slant of the Christian Gospel issuing from black churches and, further, illuminate the biblical foundations for black theology.

## The Bible and Slavery

African slaves in North America were introduced to the Bible at a point in history when the Bible was the main support in proslavery ideology.[8] From about 1772 until 1850 the Bible was the primary source of authority and legitimation for the enslavement of Africans.[9] Slaveholders turned to the Scriptures to prove that slavery was in no way contrary to the will of God. Of course, the abolitionists countered with exegetical salvos of their own, but while the proslavery forces appealed to the literal truth of the Bible, especially the Old Testament, as an infallible authority, the abolitionist forces appealed to the moral thrust of the Bible, especially the New Testament, as a guide to ethical behavior.[10] Thus the disagreement between the proslavery forces and the abolitionist forces was primarily over *how* the Bible should be read and only secondarily over *what* the Bible said on the subject of slavery.[11] However, the proslavery voices were more focused in their biblical defense of slavery as a part of Southern genteel culture, and, in addition, the proslavery argument provided an arena for alienated Southern intellectuals. The physical proximity of proslavery ideologues to the world of the African slaves and the residual influence of their racist arguments suggest that it is impossible to understand fully the African response to their scriptural bondage without noting how the Bible was used by their captors.

One of the biblical passages to which proslavery ideologues appealed in their defense of slavery was Genesis 9:25, "Cursed be Canaan, a servant of servants shall he be to his brethren. Blessed be the Lord God of Shem, and Canaan shall be his servant. God shall enlarge Japheth, and he shall dwell in the tents of Shem and Canaan shall be his servant." Although the passage speaks of a curse on Canaan, it is ostensibly for the sins of his father, Ham, that he was punished. Hence, this defense of slavery is most often referred to as the Hamitic hypothesis or the Hamitic curse. The Episcopal bishop of the diocese of Vermont, John H. Hopkins, wrote in 1864 that "the heartless irreverence which Ham, the father of Canaan, displayed toward his eminent parent [Noah] whose piety had just saved him from the deluge, presented the immediate occasion for this remarkable prophecy; but the actual fulfillment was reserved for his posterity."[12]

The Hamitic defense of slavery rested on the rather spurious assumption that all Africans were descendants of Canaan and that Jews and Gentiles were the progeny of Shem and Japheth. Thornton Stringfellow, a Baptist clergyman from Virginia whose scriptural defense of slavery was widely regarded as "the best" by the advocates of slavery, went even further than Hopkins. Stringfellow argued that God not only established the institution of slavery through the Hamitic curse, but that God thereby granted divine favor on slaveholders: "It is quite possible that [God's] favor may now be found with one class of men, who are holding another in bondage. Be that as it may, God decreed slavery — and shows in that decree, tokens of good-will to the master."[13] According to some scholars this text not only served as a defense of slavery as an institution; it was crucial to the proslavery Southerner's self-perception:

> Abolitionists did not fully understand why the Ham story captivated the Southern imagination. While they recognized its prominence in the proslavery arsenal of biblical texts, they never fully understood its symbolic persuasiveness.... The Southern versions of the Ham myth were rooted in the biblical story rather than controlled by it. In the Southern story, Ham and Jepheth became archetypes, respectively, for the black and white races in America; the relationship between these two brothers in the myth both validated and provided a model for the whites' treatment of blacks in the antebellum South.[14]

Thus the Ham story provided more than merely a defense for the repugnant institution of chattel slavery. It also rendered justification for an emerging Southern culture and an ascendent Southern economy, as well as explaining how humanity could, given a common ancestor in Noah, find itself divided into two classes of beings, subhuman slaves and superhuman masters. As the Ham myth grew and tore loose from its biblical moorings, it became a convenient vehicle for associating

sin, sex, and blackness in a way that put the African outside the pale
of humanity. Ham's transgression was most often interpreted in sexual terms. Cain Felder, an African-American biblical scholar, notes that
"uncertainties about the precise nature of Ham's error result in a fantastic variety of suggestions, which range from Ham's having possibly
castrated his father, attacked his father homosexually, committed incest
with his father's wife, or having had sexual relations with his own wife
while aboard the ark."[15]

Charles B. Copher, a renowned African-American biblical scholar,
observed that the Hamitic hypothesis served two distinct functions in
relation to people of African descent and the biblical narrative. First,
it provided a place — albeit subordinate — for African people in the
biblical story. They were mentioned in the Bible as those people who
were destined to be "drawers of water and hewers of wood." But after 1800, a new twist surfaced in proslavery biblical interpretation.
A "new Hamitic hypothesis" emerged that sought to expunge black
people from the Bible altogether by arguing that those black people
mentioned in the Bible were "Caucasoid Blacks who instead of being
regarded as Negroes are viewed as being white. . . . [This new hypothe-
sis] not only removes [Africans] from the biblical world but also views
[them] as incapable of civilization."[16]

The Hamitic curse provided the biblical rationale for slavery and
the patriarchal paradigm provided the biblical model for it. The Bible
did not supply the only argument for the view of slavery as a benevolent social system, but while sophisticated treatises on the nature of
bondage and the political economy might have eluded the grasp of the
average citizen, the Bible provided a simple, familiar depiction of the
virtue of slavery.[17] The Genesis account of Abraham was a mainstay
in the proslavery argument. In it was a pattern of relations between
masters and slaves that was, presumably, divinely approved. Hopkins
appealed to the fact that Abraham owned "three hundred and eighteen
bond-servants who were born in his own house as well as those who
were bought with his money" as proof of God's blessing of slavery.[18]
Stringfellow cites Abraham's great wealth and the magnitude of his
household, both slave and free, as evidence of God's favor on this social arrangement, and thus the bestowal of the appellation "father of
the faithful."[19] Samuel B. How, a nineteenth-century cleric, notes that
Abraham was commanded to circumcise his slaves, thereby bringing
them into the covenant relationship. This relationship, however, is not
egalitarian, and rather than being brought into the fold, ironically, the
slaves appear to be given the status of permanent outsiders.

Abraham was the biblical model of patriarchy that Southern slaveholders sought to emulate. The slaveholder was the descendent of the
feudal "protector" and the cornerstone of a stable political-economic

order. It was, therefore, necessary, given this connection, for the African slave to be considered as a class of property. Citing the Decalogue's prohibition against the coveting of another's property, How argues that

> this precept establishes the right of property, and forbids not only the unjust depriving the owner of lawful property, but even the secret desire to do so. It strikes down at once into the dust Communism and Socialism. It teaches us that there is a division, and that there are rights of property.... God therefore commands us to respect the right of property, to leave the lawful owner of it in the undisturbed possession of it, even though it be a man-servant or a maid-servant.[20]

The Abrahamic model, along with the paradigms suggested by other biblical patriarchs, gave American slavery a structure that was consistent with a neo-feudal emerging capitalist society.

The Old Testament provided the biblical rationale and the biblical paradigm for slavery. The New Testament provided whatever ethical principles were to be operative in the relation between slaves and masters. Slaveholders were quick to support their position by pointing out that the Scriptures nowhere recorded Jesus' condemnation of slavery. The point was made that Jesus did not allude to slavery at all, in spite of its ubiquity in his time and place. Therefore, the argument goes, one must assume that it was not contrary to the will of God. This argument is supported by focusing on Jesus as the continuation of the work of God in Israel, and therefore the fulfillment of the patriarchal tradition rather than the destroyer of it. In other words, any new dispensation by Jesus was not incompatible with the old Law. Abolitionists argued that, carried to its logical conclusion, the Gospel of Jesus established *principles* that would divest all oppressive systems of their moral claim.

For the proslavery ideologues, Jesus established *no new principles* but simply restated the Old Testament social arrangement for his own era.[21] This restatement, presumably, involved a focus on the soul of the person rather than her physical condition and established the ethical parameters of the master-slave relationship as spiritual rather than political. Of course, the spiritual condition of slaves could make no difference in their physical condition. Because the proslavery advocates could see no protest against slavery in the life and death of Jesus and because their skewed reading of the New Testament provided no critique of the patriarchal arrangement of the Old Testament, the epistolary writings of the New Testament were mined for every possible reference that might appear to condone or support the system of slavery. Many of these pericopes became the texts of sermons preached by white preachers to black slaves ad nauseam. Among the most widely used were Ephesians 6:5–9 and Colossians 3:22.

A central New Testament text for slaveholders was Paul's letter to Philemon. This letter supplied what was called "the Pauline mandate" for slavery. In it Paul converts and then returns a fugitive slave, Onesimus, to his master, Philemon, with the admonition that they should treat one another kindly within the confines of their social arrangement. The influence of this epistle can be seen in that at least one proslavery writer saw it as biblical support for the Fugitive Slave Law of 1850.[22] African slaves were able to resist the contorted biblical interpretation of their masters to some degree. Indeed, many rejected outright the letter to Philemon as revelatory. What should not be lost in the proslavery use of the New Testament is that the ethical mandates fell almost exclusively upon the slave, while leaving the master free from any constrictions. Further, the ethical norms never jeopardized the privileged status of the slaveholder or altered the social condition of the slave.

The biblical arguments for slavery rested on a core assumption about both the nature of slavery and the identity of those who were enslaved. Many proslavery ideologues noted that there were Hebrew slaves among the ancient Israelites, but their enslavement was regulated by the law of God. The tradition of the year of Jubilee cited in Exodus 21:2–4 meant that the Hebrew slave could anticipate being freed after serving six years. In a sense they were indentured servants and were protected by a humane code.

The core assumption on which the biblical defense of the modern enslavement of Africans rested was that Africans were outsiders and therefore beyond the pale of the God-humanity relationship. The text quoted in almost every proslavery defense and almost never refuted in the abolitionist response was Leviticus 25:44–46:

> Both thy bond-men and thy bond maids which thou shalt have, shall be of the heathen that are round about you; of them shall ye buy bond-men and bond-maids. Moreover, of the children of the strangers that do sojourn among you, of them shall ye buy and of their families that are with you which they begat in your land, and they shall be your possession; and ye shall take them as an inheritance for your children after you to inherit them for a possession. They shall be your bondmen forever.

Slaveholders saw the Africans whom they enslaved as "the heathens" who surrounded them and their progeny as "the children of the strangers." Unlike the European indentured servant (the Hebrew slave) the African slave was a slave for life. Before the barbarity of modern slavery could be justified, it was necessary to define the African as an outsider. The Hamitic rationale placed African slaves outside the pale of humanity. The patriarchal paradigm situated African slaves outside the covenant of favor with God. And the ethical norms of the

New Testament located African slaves outside the redemptive power of Jesus Christ.

Slavery was more than an economic system; it was both the symbol and support for the construction of a discursive world where the grammatical possibilities were controlled by the slaveholders. It was part of a narrative arena in which language about human freedom and the universal parenthood of God, forbidden by slaveholders, had to be ciphered by the slaves. The Bible was part of that narrative arena but certainly not totally circumscribed by it. The slaveholders' literalistic use of the Bible to defend slavery was, as we shall see, countered by slave interpreters who saw in it a proclamation of liberation in which the outsiders became insiders.

## The Bible and Liberation

African slaves constructed their own scriptural world on three pillars of biblical interpretation. These strands of African-American interpretation were responses to the major biblical defenses of slavery. They were the means by which African-Americans read the Bible with "new eyes." They were also forged in the context of the struggle for liberation. Virtually every intellectual activity of African-Americans was related to their condition of oppression and their desire for freedom. Thus the hermeneutical perspective that they brought to the Bible was inseparable from their determination to live as full human beings in the presence of God.

The first of these interpretive paradigms was based on the experience of the people of Israel as recorded in the book of Exodus. Key motifs were found in Exodus 1:12, in which the biblical writer asserts that the more the Israelites were oppressed the more they multiplied. The account of Moses' childhood, upbringing, and fateful decision to align himself with the suffering of his sisters and brothers (2:1–3:22), the delivery of Yahweh's message to "let my people go" (5:1), the crossing of the Red Sea (14:19ff), and the triumph song upon attaining their freedom (15:1ff), all found ready ears among the slaves. In fact, the Exodus experience was an archetypal myth that, while drawn from Scripture, became the lens through which the Bible was read. While the fact that the Exodus account was central and decisive in Israel's self-understanding played no role in the slaves' use of that paradigm in their biblical interpretation, it is, perhaps, an indication that their reading of the text from the perspective of slavery elicited its truth more clearly than that of the slavemasters. The Hebrew model of interpretation is most clearly seen in the sacred music of the African slaves. "Go Down, Moses" chronicles the liberating act of God on behalf of the oppressed. "Oh, Mary, Don't You Weep" celebrates God's defense of the oppressed against Pharaoh's army.[23]

The Hebrew model of biblical interpretation appears to have been more prevalent among slaves in the South. While there were certainly exceptions to this assertion, the peculiar configuration of the condition of African slaves in the South suggests several reasons why this might have been the case. First, the Exodus account reflected in a striking way the experience of the slaves. "It required no stretch of the imagination to see the trials of the Israelites as paralleling the trials of the slaves, Pharaoh and his army as oppressors, and Egyptland as the South."[24] The tale of the liberation of Israel provided a narrative explanation for their condition. Second, the Exodus motif furnished an acceptable expressive vehicle for the slaves' yearning for political emancipation. While the sustaining resources of traditional African religion had been driven underground by the system of slavery, the Bible, read in this way, provided the means for asserting that freedom was a central thrust in the biblical narrative. Third, the low literacy level among slaves, which was enforced by law, made the oral transmission of biblical material the primary means of sharing the riches of Scripture. Moreover, when slaves taught themselves to read, the Bible was the most available text to them. Thus Martin Luther's principle of *sola scriptura* emerged in a distinctive fashion in the slave community. Fourth, by identifying themselves with the Hebrews, African slaves declared themselves as insiders in the scriptural drama. The Hebrew model of interpretation placed the slaves squarely in the center of the salvation narrative. While slaveholders focused on ancient Israel as a slaveholding society, the African slaves saw ancient Israel first as a nation descended from slaves. In this sense, slave interpreters were able to reverse the patriarchal paradigm of the slaveholders.

The second interpretive paradigm was based on biblical references to Ethiopia, Cush, and Egypt. Key motifs were found in Psalm 68:31, where the biblical writer declares that "Ethiopia shall soon stretch forth her hands to God"; Numbers 12:1, which describes Moses' wife as an Ethiopian; 1 Kings 10:1–10 and 13, which presents evidence that the Queen of Sheba was a black woman; and Song of Solomon 1:5, in which the unnamed bride states that she is "black and beautiful." These texts and others struck a responsive chord in the hearts of black Christians in a manner different from the Exodus theme. The Psalms passage became central in the restoration and maintenance of racial pride among oppressed Africans in the United States. Albert J. Raboteau observes that

nineteenth-century black Americans identified Ethiopia and Egypt with their own African origins and looked to those ancient civilizations as exemplars of a glorious African past, surely as legitimate a fictive pedigree as American claims of descent from Graeco-Roman civilization.... From the Egyptians the torch of civilization passed on to the Greeks, from them to the Romans, and from the Romans, finally, and belatedly, to the Europeans.[25]

Gayraud Wilmore concurs, noting that early black interpreters, unimpressed by

...the testimony of many books and pamphlets arguing for black inferiority, stubbornly relied upon what has been an ineradicable feature of black religion in America: an interpretation of Scripture rooted and grounded in the corporate experiences and perceptions of blacks. They identified themselves with the Canaanites, who built great cities across the Jordan and resisted the invading Israelites for centuries; with the Carthaginians, who produced Hamilcar and Hannibal and were related to the descendants of the Canaanites; with Nimrod, the great Cushite hunter and warrior whose might founded cities and conquered others from Babel to Nineveh; but most of all they identified themselves with Egypt and Ethiopia — the two great African monarchies that were the incubators of much of what is called Western culture and civilization.[26]

This Ethiopic model of interpretation continues to inform the religious perspective of groups like the Rastafarians for whom Ethiopia has become a foundational symbol linking their history and their hope.[27] The passages concerning the ethnicity of Moses' wife and the nationality of the Queen of Sheba were also evidence of the presence and power of black people in the biblical narrative. The conclusion reached by African-American interpreters regarding the identity of these women was, and continues to be, hotly disputed by European scholars. Hailu Habtu concludes that "Afro-phobia and Eurocentrism" have led the majority of white interpreters to either deny that Moses' wife was truly an Ethiopian, or to deny that she was indeed his wife and not a concubine.[28]

Confronted by the reticence of European and American interpreters to acknowledge that the Queen of Sheba was a black woman, Cain Felder asks, "Why have Josephus, a number of the Church Fathers, and the Ethiopians themselves claimed that the Queen of Sheba was an African woman?"[29] The confession of the unnamed bride in Song of Solomon 1:5 is perhaps the quintessential statement of the Ethiopic motif in African-American biblical interpretation. The key phrase has been translated as "I am black but beautiful" in many instances, but Frank M. Snowden, Jr., among others, has concluded that this is a mistranslation of the text, the correct rendering being "I am black *and* beautiful."[30] The difference is a crucial one, but nineteenth-century African-American interpreters intuitively grasped the true meaning of the text in relation to their condition.

David Walker, in his *Appeal* published in 1829, identifies African-Americans not with the Israelites but with the Egyptians in the biblical story:

> Some of my brethren do not know who Pharaoh and the Egyptians were — I know it to be a fact that some of them take the Egyptians to have been a gang of devils, not knowing any better, and that they (Egyptians) having got possession of the Lord's people, treated them nearly as cruel as christian Americans do us, at the present day. For the information of such, I would only mention that the Egyptians were Africans or colored people, such as we are — some of them yellow and others dark — a mixture of Ethiopians and the natives of Egypt — about the same as you see the colored people of the United States at the present day.[31]

Walker anticipates the possibility that his observations could strengthen rather than weaken the argument against slavery by noting that because the Egyptians were a highly civilized people, "the condition of the Israelites was better under the Egyptians than ours under the whites.... [No one can show] that the Egyptians heaped the insupportable insult upon the children of Israel by telling them that they were not of the human family."[32]

The Ethiopic model of interpretation appears to have been more prevalent among free black people in the North. While, as is the case with the Hebrew model, there were certainly exceptions to this premise, the peculiar experience of African-Americans not under the immediate pale of slavery provides several clues to the ascendency of the Ethiopic model of biblical interpretation. First, African-Americans could identify with the Egyptians, Ethiopians, and Cushites in the biblical narrative because they saw parallels in their own experience. Americans of African descent saw themselves, like their biblical counterparts, as a maligned people, robbed by usurpers of their rightful place in the history of civilization. Second, identification with the Ethiopians set aflame a nationalistic yearning and a desire for cultural integrity. Having attained a precarious physical manumission, African-Americans encountered disdain in a society that not only did not recognize their contributions, but also rendered them invisible. Third, the literacy level among black people in the North was generally higher than among their sisters and brothers in the South. Access to other writings on world history and civilization meant that the Bible was often read as one among many sources of insight. Thus the Bible was seen as a text with a definite historical context.[33] Fourth, by identifying themselves with the Egyptians and Ethiopians in the Bible, African-American interpreters proclaimed themselves as insiders (as African people rather than just as an oppressed people) in the scriptural drama. In doing so, they effectively "decentered" the salvation narrative.

The cumulative effect of the Ethiopic model of biblical interpretation among nineteenth-century African-Americans was the rebuttal of the Hamitic curse. By identifying with the grand achievements of the descendants of Canaan, African-Americans managed to demystify the Hamitic myth. The African biblical scholar Modupe Oduyoye argues that the Hamitic myth was a slanderous tale "told by the Hebrews to ridicule nations against whom they harbored a grudge,"[34] among them being Egypt and Canaan. The Ethiopic model of interpretation allowed black Christians to turn what was meant to be a curse into a blessing.

When African-American interpreters turned to the New Testament, they did not find the social sanctions for oppression that the slaveholders saw. Instead, they found personal affirmation. That affirmation was first and foremost manifested in Jesus' stance toward the downtrodden and oppressed. His ministry among the marginalized persons of his day was seen to be the key to the Gospel. When African-American Christians asserted that "his eye is on the sparrow, I know he watches me," they were acknowledging God's personal attention to their plight. When African-Americans turned to the Pauline corpus they found an autobiographical narrative rather than an infallible guide to social behavior. Paul was seen as a human being whose struggles with the requirements of his faith were illustrative rather than definitive of the Christian life. The apostle's wrestlings with wanting to do the good rather than the evil that so easily beset him, his secret "affliction" that constantly reminded him of his inadequacy, his willingness to suffer for the cause of Christ were indicators of the humanity of Paul. While slaveholders found in Paul a mandate for slavery, African-Americans saw in him an example of struggle and ultimate victory.

The Hebrew motifs in the biblical narrative spoke to the struggle for political emancipation in African-American experience, thereby reversing the patriarchal paradigm espoused by biblical defenders of slavery. The Ethiopian/Egyptian motifs addressed the need for cultural integrity and racial pride, countering the Hamitic argument for the inferiority and invisibility of African-Americans. The affirmation of self-worth found in the New Testament gave sustenance to the struggle for survival and freedom in a hostile society. Because their oppression and suffering were multifaceted, African-American interpreters, of necessity, found the Bible to be a polyvalent narrative. One of the keys to understanding the role of the Bible in African-American life is the relationship between the multivocality of the biblical narrative and the multidimensionality of African-American experience. This means that interpretation becomes an act of human appropriation, finding or constructing meaning where it is not readily apparent. The ambiguity of the biblical text and of the African-American presence in America suggest that Scripture must be read as an imaginative text and a historical narrative.

## Dismembering the Text: Remembering the Story

To those observers whose perspectives have been shaped by the critical approach to the Bible regnant in the Western academic tradition, it might appear that African-American biblical interpreters have "taken liberties with the text." The issue is not whether one should take liberties with the biblical text, but whether the taking of those liberties can be justified in relation to the text itself. One of the persistent paradoxes of African-American religious experience is the resistance of black Christians to the results of historical-critical methods and the centrality of the Bible in black faith. Perhaps one explanation is the tendency for African-American Christians to read the Bible as a unified text. "Once one begins to wander in the wilderness of historical study, is there any way back to the wholeness of the unified text?"[35]

The need to see the Bible as a unified text has been recognized more by literary scholars than traditional biblical scholars. Northrop Frye argues that one cannot understand the role of the Bible in Western culture if it is seen as simply a collection of Near Eastern texts. "What matters is that 'the Bible' has traditionally been read as a unity, and has influenced Western imagination as a unity.... It has a beginning and an end, and some traces of a total structure. It begins where time begins, with the creation of the world; it ends where time ends, with the Apocalypse, and it surveys human history in between."[36] For the poet the Bible must be read as a unified text because she or he must be able to isolate some unifying principle. "That unifying principle, for a [literary] critic, would have to be one of shape rather than meaning."[37]

This propensity toward the unity of the biblical text has also been acknowledged by liberation theologians. J. Severino Croatto argues that "the Bible is a single text, especially from the moment it constituted a fixed canon of literary composition. This closure establishes new relationships among its different parts, and among its distinct literary collections — legal, historical, prophetical, sapiential, evangelical, epistolary, apocalyptic, and so on. Like any structured work, it has a beginning and an end — and an ordered progression between them. It runs from Genesis to Revelation along a particular route."[38] Here the propensity to see the Bible as a single text is grounded in the need to isolate an "axis of meaning" in the Bible. One of these semantic axes — or I would argue, the primary axis of meaning — is the liberation of the oppressed.

In the African-American religious community the Bible continues

to be read as a unified text whose central thrust guides the interpretation of its individual parts. Katie Cannon recounts what she learned
from discussing the Bible with African-American Christians who are
removed from academic debate about the text. "The second lesson
I learned from Black storefront clergy and laity is that every passage
of literature does not have the same importance. These women and
men understand the Bible to be a divinely inspired book but not every
jot and tittle has the same significance. In explaining the full meaning of God's revelation, Bible study leaders give consideration to the
whole Scripture and its unfolding movement. Afterward, they decide
the priority which should be given to selected texts."[39]

African-American Christians have seen and understood the Bible
as a whole text, at the center of which is the Exodus myth, the cornerstone of the Hebrew model of interpretation. They have exercised a
theological imagination that, like a prism, first focuses and then refracts
the biblical text. Or to put it another way, African-American Christians have generally refused to dismember the biblical text without
first remembering the biblical story.

Aesthetic, theological, and liturgical impulses among African-
American Christians all seem to require that interpreters exercise a
certain freedom in relation to the biblical text. But one must go further
and ask whether there is anything about the Bible itself that permits that
freedom. Robert Alter has argued that the writers of the Hebrew Bible
employed certain fictive techniques in their presentation of the material of the tradition, and that the creative license of those literary artists
has had an indelible impact on all subsequent readings of the text. By
examining several key biblical stories Alter proposes that the writers
were engaged in the paradoxical activity of *deception* and *unmasking*.
This process resulted in a kind of indeterminacy within the text:

> Indeed, an essential aim of the innovative technique of fiction worked
> out by the ancient Hebrew writers was to produce a certain indetermi-
> nacy of meaning, especially in regard to motive, moral character, and
> psychology. . . . Meaning, perhaps for the first time in narrative literature,
> was conceived as a *process*, requiring continual revision — both in the
> ordinary sense and in the etymological sense of seeing-again — contin-
> ual suspension of judgment, weighing of multiple possibilities, brooding
> over gaps in the information provided.[40]

This indeterminacy of meaning in the text means that there is a kind
of interpretive play inherent in the text that requires an equally imaginative response if the true meaning is to be apprehended. Therefore,
Alter concludes:

> The Bible presents a kind of literature in which the primary impulse
> would often seem to be to provide instruction or at least necessary in-

formation, not merely to delight. If, however, we fail to see that the creators of biblical narrative were writers who, like writers elsewhere, took pleasure in exploring the formal and imaginative resources of their fictional medium, perhaps sometimes unexpectedly capturing the fullness of their subject in the very play of exploration, we shall miss much that the biblical stories are meant to convey.[41]

Frank Kermode finds within the Christian Gospels a similar situation with regard to interpretation. He argues that the Synoptic Gospels of the New Testament display a dialectic of concealment and proclamation. Further, this bivocality of the text is the key to its *secret sense*. Kermode, however, extends his analysis to include the effect of one's social location on one's interpretive praxis:

> The power to make interpretations is an indispensable instrument of survival in the world, and it works there as it works on literary texts. In all the works of interpretation there are insiders and outsiders, the former having or professing to have, immediate access to the mystery, the latter randomly scattered across space and time, and excluded from the elect who mistrust or despise their unauthorized divinations.... Sometimes it appears that the history of interpretation may be thought of as a history of exclusions.[42]

The secret sense of the text is created by the distance between creative and conventional interpretations, between those interpretations that are institutionally supported and those that arise out of a more personal encounter with the text. Thus there is a difference between the insider's view of the biblical text, which seeks to destroy or banish all indeterminacy within the text, and the outsider's view, which sees the indeterminacy of the text as evidence of its divine origin in the experience of the holy. Those whom Kermode describes as supposed "insiders" are those who already know what the Bible means in its entirety and are therefore the only ones who are capable of a correct interpretation. Biblical literalists fall into this camp because their desperate fear is not that the Bible may contain error but that it may have a secret sense resistant to their manifest explanations. Outsiders, according to Kermode, are those whose station in life renders their interpretations of the biblical text illegitimate. However, it is precisely those outsiders who are capable of "standing under" the secret sense of the text and exploiting the hermeneutical potential of its indeterminate nature. As Kermode suggests, any fruitful reading of the Gospels will, of necessity, render all insiders as outsiders, thus bringing them before the awe, mystery, and interpretive freedom that the text demands.[43]

Elisabeth Schüssler Fiorenza, who argues for the feminist reconstruction of Christian origins, suggests that the biblical text should not be jettisoned by feminist scholars as a hopelessly patriarchal document, precisely because there are intermittent traces of testimony to women's presence and power in the narrative. This means that despite the sexist context in which the experience of the early Christian communities was canonized, the material can be viewed another way. "The task, therefore, involves not so much rediscovering new sources as rereading the available sources in a different key. The goal is an increase in 'historical imagination.'"[44] This means that one can take as truly revelatory only those texts which are not totally defined by their patriarchal frameworks; or, to turn this statement around, those texts that provide evidence of the egalitarian nature of the early Christian communities and affirm the membership and ministry of women within those communities are indeterminate and display a secret sense. Full apprehension of the religious experience to which the biblical text bears witness, albeit imperfectly, requires the free exercise of the hermeneutical imagination of those who are outside (women) of traditional schools of interpretation.

Approaching the Bible with respect for its secret sense and acknowledgment of its indeterminate character so long hidden from them was almost natural, and its message filtered through the sociopolitical interests of their oppressors gave it a mysterious aura. Therefore, the hermeneutical process developed by the slaves centered around what one might call the "divinization" or the "conjuring" of the text. In African traditional religions diviners are religious leaders who attempt to read the experience of the people, and thereby render spiritual interpretations of that experience. Diviners are moral analysts, cultural hermeneuts, whose ministry centers around laying open the secret sense of African religious experience for its devotees. These African priests typically undergo years of training during which they are introduced to the hermeneutical principles of decoding the mysteries of the divine and communicating that knowledge to the people. Among African-American slaves the role of the diviner was taken up by the conjure man or woman, who was more often than not a member of or descended from the African priesthood. "Conjure" also referred to an act of interpretation, but instead of only opening up the spiritual realm to the slaves, conjure was the attempt to explain evil, and further, to change the very situation that it interpreted.[45] The clandestine context of African-American biblical interpretation and the ferocity with which that interpretation was resisted indicate that stealth and violence were characteristic of this type of interpretive praxis.[46]

Not only is the Bible an imaginative text, it is also a historical narrative, or as Hans Frei has suggested, a "history-like" narrative.[47] Not only does it fire the imagination, it speaks truth to us as well. Erich Auerbach, in a stunning philological analysis of secular Greek and biblical Hebrew narratives, shows that even the shape of biblical narrative supports its claim to realistically represent human experience. By comparing the narrative structure of a section of Homer's poem the *Odyssey* and the Old Testament account of the sacrifice of Isaac, he observes that the former narrative lacks the element of suspense, hiddenness, surprise, or ironic reversals that mark human experience in the world. In Homer's poem everything is known and nothing is "left fragmentary or half-illuminated, never a lacuna, never a gap, never a glimpse of unplumbed depths."[48] All human motivations are presented in what Auerbach calls the "foreground." In the Isaac account the reader is left in the dark about Abraham's past, about the voice of God coming from somewhere beyond the purview of the reader. God's reasons for demanding the sacrifice are never stated; we are told precious little about Isaac himself; in fact everything is unexpressed:

> God gives his command in direct discourse, but he leaves his motives and his purpose unexpressed; Abraham, receiving the command, says nothing and does what he has been told to do. The conversation between Abraham and Isaac on the way to the place of sacrifice is only an interruption of the heavy silence and makes it all the more burdensome.... Everything remains unexpressed.[49]

Auerbach argues that the narrative context of this biblical story makes it mysterious and "fraught with background." Moreover, biblical characters are presented as complex or "multilayered." All of this means that biblical narrative, like one's historical experience, must be painstakingly interpreted. Thus while Homer's poem can be analyzed, it cannot be interpreted, because its narrative structure does not demand a personal investment in excavating its meaning. The biblical narrative, on the other hand, lays claim to the interpreter in a distinctive way:

> It is all very different in the Biblical stories. Their aim is not to bewitch the senses, and if nevertheless they produce lively sensory effects, it is only because the moral, religious and psychological phenomena which are their sole concern are made concrete in the sensible matter of life. But their religious intent involves an absolute claim to historical truth.[50]

For African-American interpreters the Bible was understood as a historical narrative because it provided insight into their experience. For them life's journey was "like a silent progress through the indeterminate and the contingent."[51] The nature of their historical reality, the irony of the experience of slavery, the mystery of their oppression, they found mirrored in the biblical narrative. What Auerbach describes as the terse syntactical connections that hold the parts of the biblical narrative together were like the sheer faith and dogged determination that held the slaves' world together. What made the Bible come alive as a historical narrative was the sense of being addressed by God through it. Perhaps this is the reason that for African-American Christians, like their counterparts in the early Christian communities, the essence of the Bible is preserved and transmitted orally.

William A. Graham suggests that it is impossible to understand fully the concept of "scripture" apart from recognizing it as spoken as well as written word.[52] In the early church the contents of the Scriptures were transmitted through the delivery of sermons and through the practice of reading from the Scriptures in worship. The Christians of the early church knew the power of the spoken word in effecting change and centered their liturgical life around telling and retelling the story. Among African-American Christians much of their hermeneutical largesse is the result of hearing the Bible interpreted in distinctive ways from the pulpit. The fact that most black biblical interpretation begins in the pulpit means that the biblical narrative is more than distant history; it is also their personal story. Interpretation from the pulpit also means that African-American Christians are constantly reminded that, to use a phrase of Walter Ong, the voice is the summons to belief. Again, this is why African-American Christians take the Bible seriously, as a historical narrative, but they do not take it literally. It is the voice of God that speaks through Scripture that requires allegiance. Interpretation is more than analysis; it is a personal investment in the unearthing of meaning in a given text.

Therefore, the preacher cannot be content simply to tell the people what the text says. She or he must embody the voice of God, enflesh the Word of the Lord, provide from her or his own depth of being the personal motivations and innermost thoughts of the biblical characters that the biblical writers providentially left unexpressed. The preacher must be able to show or make a place in the biblical world for those who have historically been outsiders. This is why "the preacher who consistently fails to enter this spiritually charged symbolic universe and to awaken these dormant cultural values runs the risk of being publicly held up as one who cannot preach."[53] The homiletical context of African-American biblical interpretation also points to the fact that the authority of the Bible rests primarily with the community of the faithful. When black preachers hear "Amen," they know that they have correctly, or authoritatively, interpreted the Bible or some aspect of human experience. "A text becomes 'scripture' in active, subjective relationship to persons, and as part of a cumulative communal tradition. No text, written or oral or both, is sacred or authoritative in isolation from a community."[54] The Hebrew model and the Ethiopic model of interpretation among African-Americans were the result of a communal tradition, a tradition forged in the need to transform their reality through an imaginative reconstruction of the biblical world and to participate in God's salvific activity by finding one's place in the biblical world.

## Biblical Foundations for Black Theology

African-Americans were defined by slaveholders in the nineteenth century as outsiders with reference to the biblical story. In response, African-Americans sought to establish their place within the biblical story by identifying with the Israelites — with an emphasis on political freedom — or the Cushites — with an emphasis on cultural integrity. Both of these emphases were supported by their reading of the New Testament, which confirmed their personal worth in the sight of God. Finding their place meant that the African slaves and their descendants read the Bible as an imaginative text that served the self-revelation of God and as a historical narrative that confirmed God's active presence in human affairs.

It now remains to examine what these insights can contribute to the constructive task of the African-American theologian. What does the history of African-American biblical interpretation mean for systematic theology?

First, it means that social location conditions biblical interpretation. The status of African-Americans as outsiders within American society has shaped their perspective on the Bible. In fact, their very marginality has made them sensitive to the misuses of Scripture and has made them more open to its critical dimension. It is this sense of being in, but not completely of, a given society that makes social criticism possible. The power of the prophetic tradition in the Bible resides precisely in the marginality — not complete detachment — of the prophet.[55] Further, reading the Bible under these circumstances itself becomes a critical act. Apprehending the biblical message from the vantage point of the oppressed in a society where the Bible has been used as an instrument of oppression is an act of cultural criticism.[56]

Second, what the Bible means takes priority over what the Bible meant. This does not mean that there is no value to rigorous historical-critical study of the Bible, but that historical-critical investigation and reconstruction of the *Sitz im Leben* of the text is not, in and of itself, enough. Certainly, faithfulness to the historical witness of the faith demands attention to the central documentary record of the experience of the early church. Thus there is a distinction of convenience between determining what the Bible meant in its original context and what it means today.[57] The priority of the contemporary meaning of the Bible simply recognizes that the Bible is a "reservoir of meaning" (J. Severino Croatto), whose full bounty is granted only to a living community of faith.[58]

Third, the story takes priority over the text. The conditions of the introduction of the Bible to African slaves, the circumstances of their existence as people to whom the skill of literacy was denied, and their

own cultural heritage made the telling and retelling of the stories of
the Bible more important than the criticism of the text.[59] This does
not mean that the text of Scripture is to be treated loosely or without
care. It means that in the religious experience of African-Americans
the text serves the story and not the other way around. Materialist or
deconstructionist approaches to the biblical text may indeed provide
insight into its internal symmetry or the mode of its production, but
it must be remembered that the Bible is primarily a record of the address of God to the faithful. The text is not a talisman, but simply a
visible, tangible gift through which the story of God's liberating and
reconciling presence in the created order is continually retold.

Fourth, the African-American theologian must articulate the liberating hermeneutic that grants authority to Scripture in the experience of
black Christians. The history and, to a great degree, the contemporary
experience of African-Americans' encounter with the Bible in Western
culture has been a struggle for canonical control. The Bible has continually ignited their creative energies and sustained their determination
to live in ways consistent with their understanding of themselves as
creations of God. This means that African-American Christians have,
throughout their history, brought to the Bible *a priori* interpretive
principles through which the meaning of the Bible was validated.

Peter J. Paris observes that "whenever Scripture is interpreted from
the perspective of some tradition other than the black Christian tradition, it fails to speak meaningfully to black people. In fact, it is
experienced as alien, irrelevant, insignificant, and even false. Thus the
interpretive framework is more basic than the Scriptures themselves
because it alone guarantees meaning. In fact, there are no sacred Scriptures for blacks apart from the hermeneutical principles by which they
are received and transmitted."[60] The theologian must recognize that
the Bible has been used both to oppress and liberate African-Americans
and others. The theologian must recognize that the Bible itself received
its final canonical shape amid the conflict between oppressive and liberating forces in the early Christian community. Thus appeal to Scripture
in and of itself cannot resolve the conflict of interpretations within
Christian communities today. What the theologian can do is remember
that the Bible in the African-American community achieved its status
as "Scripture" in the heat of a liberation struggle, and that it is only
within the contemporary struggle of the oppressed for liberation that
the continuing authority of the Bible can be validated.

# 3

## THE UNGIVEN GOD

How can the untutored African conceive God? ... How can this be? ...
Deity is a philosophical concept which savages are incapable of framing.
— Emil Ludwig

They seemed to be staring at the dark, but their eyes were watching God.
— Zora Neale Hurston

The idea of God is rooted in concrete human experience. This means that any discussion of God must begin with a people's recollection of their encounter with God. It is one of the ironies of theological discourse that God is the one reality for which we have no referent outside human experience, but the doctrine of God in systematic theology is most prone to abstraction and speculative conceptualization. Yet to speak of ultimate reality is, at the same time, to speak of the transcendent dimension of human experience. Metaphysical language about God has always been more satisfying to academics in their debates and casual conversation than to people who were simply looking for a way to express the inexpressible in their daily lives. In the long run, however, the only meaningful language about God is experiential, metaphorical, analogical, and functional. The functional dimension of God-talk has not been emphasized in traditional theological discourse because theologians have been more concerned about the philosophical legitimacy of their work than about its own integrity. Both the medieval and modern attempts to prove the existence of God and the general viability of the idea of God are evidence of this concern.[1] Thus a cursory overview of mainline Protestant systematic theologies written in the modern era reveals an overriding concern with "hypothetical" discourse about God, rather than with "confessional" testimony.

Of course, the danger of language about God that claims immunity from criticism and questioning is that of idolatry. Militarism, a debased view of human sexuality, blind consumerism, ideas of racial supremacy, and xenophobia disguised as patriotism are among the contemporary idols that have asserted an indisputable divine mandate. Therefore the possibility that Feuerbach was correct in observing that talk about God is, in reality, only talk about humanity on a grander scale cannot be easily dismissed by theologians. At the same time, however, the inadequacy of our language about God cannot obscure its corresponding necessity. The experience of God is as compelling as it is ineffable. In the Christian faith the experiential encounter with God demands both public and private expression.

As it turns out, Feuerbach was not wrong in his observation of a connection between talk about God and talk about humanity, but was mistaken in his reduction of the former to the latter. Centuries earlier John Calvin noted that one could begin the systematic theological task either with God and proceed to humanity, or with humanity and proceed to God. This fact is unmistakably clear in African-American theological discourse. Black theology is both theocentric and humanocentric. In situations where their humanity is called into question in subtle and not so subtle ways, African-Americans cannot talk about God without talking about what it means to be black in the United States. In situations where African-Americans affirm their humanity in spite of dehumanization they cannot talk about what it means to be black without talking about God as the arbiter of human worth.

## The Problem of God in African-American Experience

In spite of the common assumption that African-Americans are inherently a religious people, the idea of God among black Christians is problematic. One way of expressing that problematic is to say God is "ungiven" in African-American experience. This "ungivenness" is not the result of the same disenchantment with the "holy" that gave rise to the death of God movement among European-American theologians in the middle decades of the twentieth century. There the issue was admitting that for many European-American Christians the notion of God as a supreme being was no longer necessary or desirable. For African-American Christians the issue is much more complex and essentially grounded in their history of victimization and despoilment.

The African writer Kamuyu-wa-Kang'ethe recounts that his first exposure to the death of God ideology triggered the recognition that the Christian notion of God had lost its meaning for him. However, the more significant insight was that while the insurgency of postmodernism announced the divine demise for many Europeans, it was the sheer brutality of colonial conquest that rendered the idea of God problematic in African experience. He describes the relation between the God

whom white people brought to Africa and "Ngai who is alone Ngai,"
Ngai being the name for God among the Gikuyu, Masai, and Wakamba
peoples of East Africa:

> God who is Jesus, the God who was brought by the white Westerner,
> was *nothing other than the white Westerner*. What we thought was God
> was nothing but a shadow drawn very artistically in the form of Jesus,
> the white man. That "shadow" gave us the meaning and purpose of life.
> It gave us goals to pursue and directions to follow. But it was a mere
> shadow. It was not Ngai who is alone Ngai. When that shadow disap-
> pears, and it has happened to some of us, it leaves a terrifying darkness
> and void. It also brings theological anger.[2]

Idris Hamid, an African-Caribbean theologian, reached a similar conclusion after examining the notion of God in his own context:

> The formal god of the major religious groups is not one whom we have
> come to see as related to our everyday-ness. That god is not seen as one
> who enters our everyday experiences. What it boils down to is that we
> were trained to worship God through somebody else's experience....
> God is really foreign to us. In the religious imagination of our people
> he is a...foreigner....Even the categories of our religious experiences
> are imports which do not reflect our cultural and native experiences. We
> experience God as an outsider.[3]

Mokgethi Motlhabi, a black South African theologian, has expressed
this idea in even more striking language:

> When a man's mind is prevented from thinking on his god, God dies
> because he no longer manifests himself in the life of this man as its sole
> author, and so as its sole director. But as a man's mind is by nature
> God-oriented and God-inspired, and as his entire life and being is in-
> conceivable without God, the death of God means for him the birth of
> idols. Now these may be a fabrication of man himself or they may be
> what those who rule his mind present to him as "God."[4]

   This sense of God as foreign in the experiences of the people of
the African diaspora could possibly be construed as part of the general problematic of revelation in contemporary theological discourse.
Ronald Thiemann has argued that one must admit the possibility that
"God's reality is not a self-evident assumption of modern or postmodern culture."[5] Theologically, this means that one must recognize
that our ideas of God are as much the result of imaginative vision as
they are of a "given" reality in our experience.[6] However, it is more
likely that the "ungivenness" of God in African-American experience
grows directly out of the peculiar configurations of that experience
itself.

   There are two fundamental reasons that the idea of God in African-
American experience is not readily apparent. The first is the impact of

racist judgments about the theological capacity of people of African descent. The citation from Emil Ludwig, a twentieth-century missionary to Africa, that serves as one of the epigraphs for this chapter captures the basic mindset of Europeans and European-Americans when confronted with African ideas of God.[7] The assumptions were that Africans had no clear concept of God, and that whatever notions of deity that did exist among them were inchoate and incoherent. Of course, African ideas of God were couched in terms of African experience and did not readily fit into European theological categories. African peoples have many names for the Supreme Being. These names affirm God as "unchanging, holy creator" among the Yoruba, "transcendent origin of all things" among the Gikuyu, and "Lord of the sky" among the Zulu.[8] It is likely that Europeans mistook the variety of names for God used by Africans to mean that Africans had no idea of one Supreme Being. While European theologians tended to conceptualize God as a noncorporeal, ahistorical, impassive entity, with active attributes or characteristics such as love, wrath, and omnipotence, Africans tended to speak of God by referring to God's characteristics as indicators of God's true being.[9]

But the most important aspect of African notions of God with respect to the "ungivenness" of God in African-American experience is a mythopoetic description of divine-human relations that is nearly universal among African traditional religions. According to this constellation of stories, God and humanity once lived in close proximity. Various descriptions of this Golden Age include accounts of God's provision of all human need so that labor was not required and God's intimate relations with the human community.[10] According to these stories, through some ingratuitous and accidental human act, God withdrew from humanity to dwell in the sky.[11] Thus African peoples lived and continue to live with the sense of both the presence and absence of God.[12] In light of the ubiquity of this notion of the withdrawn God in African religions it would appear that its influence might be helpful in the analysis of African-American ideas of God.

Tracing the influence of African religion on the development of African-American Christianity is a highly complex and controversial venture. The conflicting positions of Melville Herskovits and E. Franklin Frazier have for decades framed the debate around African retentions upon the black population of the United States.[13] Herskovits argued that Africans maintained many of their traditions, customs, and beliefs in spite of the ravages of slavery. E. Franklin Frazier, on the other hand, believed that the experiences of the Middle Passage, the brutality of slavery, and the irresistible influence of European-American culture prohibited the retention of the essential elements of indigenous African culture. These two positions currently represent the extremes on the spectrum rather than positions that can be defended in an absolute way. Thus the truth, in all probability, lies somewhere between them. African ideas of God did not survive unaltered in African-American religious communities. Albert J. Raboteau points out that the unique circumstances of African slavery in the British colonies mitigated against the survival of African theology and ritual. He notes that the unusually high rate of increase among North American slaves as well as the resistance of Puritan Protestantism to syncretism contributed to what he calls "the death of the African gods."[14] The cultural and religious milieu in which African-Americans found themselves meant that they had to alter the object of their devotion. This change is expressed in a poem by Jean Toomer called "Conversion":

> African Guardian of Souls,
> Drunk with rum,
> Feasting on a strange cassava,
> Yielding to new words and a weak palabra
> Of a white-faced sardonic god —
> Grins, cries
> Amen,
> Shouts hosanna.[15]

Although African ideas of God did not survive intact among people of African descent in the United States, the alterity of African-American religious experience suggests that African slaves were not completely divested of their indigenous culture and religion. Raboteau concludes that "even as the gods of Africa gave way to the God of Christianity, the African heritage of singing, dancing, spirit possession, and magic continued to influence Afro-American spirituals, ring shouts, and folk beliefs. That this was so is evidence of the slaves' ability not only to adapt to new contexts but to do so creatively."[16]

The opacity of African-American experience is the second reason that the African-American idea of God is not readily apparent. The citation from Zora Neale Hurston, the second epigraph at the beginning of this chapter, captures this aspect of God. In a world where African-Americans were defined primarily in terms of their "otherness" their identification with the God who created them required that God be seen as embodying that otherness. In addition, when African-Americans found themselves faced with survival in a world seemingly dominated by greed, rapaciousness, and brutality, the God who would redeem them had to exist, in some sense, beyond the corrupting reach of oppressive structures. Theo Witvliet refers to this aspect of African-American Christianity when he observes that "[African-American] slaves have been aware of God's otherness, of the fact that he is a stranger in a world of death and oppression. . . . Black history confronts theology with a fundamental epistemological insight: God's otherness or exteriority ('the vertical from above') is not a theological metaphysic but is indissolubly connected with the fate and struggle of those for whom there is no place in his world. Their otherness represents his otherness."[17] The ungiven character of God in African-American experience is the product of traditional African orientations toward the divine and European-American Christian influences under the pressure of slavery and oppression. The idea of God for African-Americans is rooted in the concrete realities of their experience.

## The Idea of God

Benjamin Mays's 1938 study, *The Negro's God*, examined in depth the idea of God in African-American experience. Mays sought to show how the idea of God is related to the social situation in which African-Americans found themselves. In this work, he analyzed "mass" and "classical" literature of African-Americans, the former term referring to sermons, spirituals, and Sunday School literature, while the latter term referred to formal addresses, treatises, poetry, and fiction. Mays examined this literature during three distinct chronological periods, 1760–1865, the Civil War period to 1914, and 1914–1937. He concluded from his study that there were three basic attitudes toward God present among African-Americans. The first was God as *compensatory*, referring to those ideas of God that promised divine recompense for earthly suffering; the second was God as *a support for social adjustment*, referring to those ideas of God that served as "apologia" for the liberation struggle; and the third was the notion that God was *"no longer a useful instrument"* in the African-American quest for justice and freedom.[18]

   As Mays canvassed the mass literature in the period from 1760 to 1860 he observed two different ideas of God. The first was otherworldly and compensatory, promising to the faithful a better life in the hereafter. He confirmed, however, that the matrix of this God idea is the peculiarity of African-American historical experience and not the arena of traditional theological intellectual jousting:

> History bears testimony to the fact that compensatory, otherworldly ideas of God are usually developed at the point of social crisis — at the point where justice is denied, hopes are thwarted, and plans shattered....The otherworldly idea of God, therefore, finds fertile soil among the people who fare worst in the world.[19]

While this idea of God is often cited as a dominant theme in African-American religious thought of this period, Mays argued that a second motif in the understanding of God is evident. The situation of slavery meant that the idea of God had to be related to the experience of those slaves and their "free" kinfolk. This second idea of God affirmed that God was opposed to slavery, and that the idea of God compels the true believer to work vigorously for its abolition:

> Since God is just, slave holders will be punished. Since all men are made in the image of God, slavery is wrong and it is against God. Since God is against slavery, it cannot last. God is love: therefore, the slave must be kindly disposed toward his master. God is no respecter of person, and to discriminate on the basis of color is ungodly. God is to be obeyed above all others; it is, therefore, all right for slaves not to obey their masters, particularly since slavery stands in the way of divine grace.[20]

It is possible that the otherworldly idea of God was more apparent among the slave population and that the idea of God that demanded the abolition of slavery was more apparent among the African-American population in the North. In both cases, however, the idea of God is firmly rooted in the social situation of its framers.

In the mass literature of the period 1860 to 1914, the idea of God reflects the overriding question of African-Americans at the time. Can black people ever claim America as their home? The fact that former slaves found themselves landless as well as homeless and the fact that more reactionary segments of American society were hatching various schemes either to remove black people from the land or at least to limit their participation in society meant that the idea of God among African-Americans would take a distinctive shape. In this period, the idea of God was formed as African-Americans attempted to forge their relationship to Africa, on one hand, and to America, on the other. The God who had given a special destiny to black people was heard to call African-Americans to evangelize Africa for the sake of the Gospel. In some instances, this God was heard to call African-Americans to repatriate to their ancestral homeland. At the same time, the God who treats all people equally was heard to call African-Americans to demand their God-given rights to justice, freedom, and equally in America, their new hard-won homestead.[21]

In the mass literature of the period from 1914 to 1937, otherworldly, compensatory ideas of God were, as Mays observed, prevalent among African-Americans. God was seen as one who takes care of the unfortunate, providing shelter and sustenance. The collective experience of African-Americans during the period of mass migration to the Northern cities, the subsequent disillusionment with the urban promise, and the resultant anomie of ghetto life are part of the explanation for the emergence of otherworldly ideas of God. However, in this instance, the idea of God seemed to be disengaged from the struggle for freedom. Mays notes that these ideas of God

> ... savor of the belief that although times are hard God will take care of us. In some way, God will supply the food and shelter. Man's task is to praise Him. These ideas tend to encourage people to take a *laissez-faire* attitude toward their poverty.[22]

God's demand for "clean hearts" and righteous personal lives became the hallmark in African-American religious experience. As a result, "the masses, on the whole, [saw] no connection between God and social and economic reconstruction."[23]

Turning to the classical literature in the period between 1760 and 1860 Mays noted that compensatory, otherworldly ideas of God were present, especially in the writings of the poets Phyllis Wheatley and Jupiter Hammon. Hammon urged his sisters and brothers to be content with slavery, not because God sanctioned their bondage but because there was very little they could do realistically to change their condition. Slaves would have to wait upon the Lord to bring an end to their misery.[24] Wheatley did not relate God to the situation of slavery and indeed publicly thanked God for bringing her from "ignorant" Africa to "civilized" America. The God idea, for Wheatley, had more to do with establishing beauty and the "sweet affections" of divine grace in the believer than with changing one's social conditions and thus was similar in tone to typical religious treatises coming out of Puritan New England. Mays correctly observed that both Hammon and Wheatley were fortuitously spared the normal barbarities of slavery, and this had a great deal to do with the way that their ideas of God developed.

Although these otherworldly, compensatory ideas of God were present in this period, they were not dominant. Mays turned to the writings of Benjamin Banneker, Gustavus Vassa, Frances Ellen Watkins, and Frederick Douglass as more representative of the African-American understanding of God. Here the idea of God is inextricably bound to the issue of slavery and emancipation. Frances Ellen Watkins's view is particularly illustrative of the notion that to believe in God is to fight for freedom. At one point she uttered that "it may be that God himself has written upon my heart and my brain a commission to use time, talent and energy in the cause of freedom."[25] Mays concluded that in this period ideas of God among African-Americans ran counter to what might have been expected:

> The great revelation is that so few Negro writers were compensatory and other worldly in their emphases. One might expect the Negro writers, during these times, to use God as an escape from reality, as a means to make the Negro complacent under the stern realities of slavery by

looking away to the rewards that awaited him in Heaven. . . . But most of them were prophets of social righteousness and they developed their ideas of God in keeping with the social needs of their time.[26]

The dominant idea of God here is one that relates the divine will to the quest for liberation.

In the classical literature in the period from 1865 to 1914 the idea of God among black people in the United States reflects their altered social and legal status. As a dispossessed people the will of God is connected to their desire for a place where they can be free. In contrast to the emphasis found in the mass literature of this period, the focus here is not so much on Africa as it is on the Northern part of the United States. God was seen as the One who called black people out of the Egypt of the South to the Canaan of social and economic prosperity of the North. In addition, the idea of God prevalent during this time compelled African-Americans to engage in self-help and, in the vernacular of the period, social uplift.

While these ideas of God were dominant, two subordinate notions of God made their first appearance in these crucial moments in African-American history. The first was a kind of fatalism that resulted from a distorted view of God's providence. "This view of God sustains the philosophy, prevalent among some people, that it is useless to be vexed and worried over the tragedies of life because man cannot change what God has already decreed."[27] The second notion is that God may either not exist, or may no longer be useful in the struggle for freedom. While the seeds of African-American agnosticism, atheism, and fatalism were sown in this period, it was not until the third epoch that their force was fully felt.

In the third period in the classical literature, from 1914 to 1937, the central problematic is relating the idea of God to the need for self-acceptance for black people. The need for cultural integrity and the Washingtonian plea for economic self-reliance called into question the role of an all-powerful God whose sovereign presence blunted and devalued any human achievement on the part of African-Americans. Thus for some people it became necessary to reject the traditional idea of God in order to accept themselves as full, free, and competent human beings. A second factor in this problematic was the general disillusionment within the worldwide Christian community in the period after the First World War. Of course, 1914 was also the date that the liberal dreams of the evolutionary perfection of human society were dashed against the rocks of human cruelty and irrationality. At the same time, the hopes of African-Americans that America would finally accept them as full citizens were dealt a crushing blow by the lynch mobs and death squads who terrorized black people during this period.

Thus the juxtaposition of a social crisis and a crisis of belief leads inexorably to the theodicy question. In this instance, African-Americans doubted God's value to black people in their struggle for freedom, doubted God's usefulness in the modern world, or denied the existence of God completely. But even here, as Mays observed, these ideas of God are intimately connected to the historical existence of African-Americans. These ideas of God are not "unrelated to the growing demand for social change — not at all. But rather it seems to mean that these heretical ideas of God develop because in the social situation the 'breaks' seem to be against the Negro, and the authors are unable to harmonize this fact with the God pictured by Christianity."[28] So even "heretical" ideas of God among African-Americans emerge out of the anomalies in African-American experience.

The value of Benjamin Mays's work for an African-American theological understanding of God is significant. He demonstrated the extent to which African-American ideas of God are grounded in experience and confirmed the experiential authority of various God ideas among black people in the United States. The primary limitation of this work, however, is that it is a sociological study that is more descriptive than normative. While these insights are certainly important to the theological task, it does not ask the question of the legitimacy of these God ideas in light of the other sources of theological reflection. That is, it does not move from the ideational realm to the conceptual realm.

## The Concept of God

William R. Jones, in his classic 1973 text, *Is God a White Racist?*, begins where Mays left off, that is, with the theodicy question. Jones's treatise is intended as a "prolegomenon" to African-American theology and, as such, compels black theologians to examine their basic assumptions about God and the meaning of African-American experience. Jones is concerned to expose what might be called "methodological shortcuts" by which black theologians conclude that God is both benevolent and omnipotent. He is concerned that the possibility of "divine racism" has been ruled out in advance of any rigorous analysis of the experiential evidence.

The question that Jones raises, that of "divine racism," is not essentially new. It is the perennial question of the presumed righteousness of God. This question was given much attention during the Middle Ages by Duns Scotus, Anselm, and others, when unexplained human suffering was high on the theological agenda. Jones, however, addresses the question from the experience of the suffering of African-Americans.

He approaches African-American suffering as a theological problem and then relates it to the question of God.

The purpose of Jones's critique is to show that theodicy is at the heart of theology and to show how this fact should force the African-American theologian to consider the possibility of divine racism and to examine the relation between the theodicy question and the reality of black suffering.[29] His thesis is that the theodicy question must control the entire theological enterprise for African-Americans, because unless the apparent contradiction between the existence of God as traditionally conceived and their suffering and oppression is resolved, methodological inconsistencies will result in untenable theological assertions and faulty religious praxis. Either the African-American theologian must show that black suffering is not the will of God or it will be concluded that that suffering is sanctioned by God.[30]

In examining the works of several early black theologians Jones devises a test by which he assesses the viability of those theological positions with reference to African-American suffering and the character of God. "The critical test I utilize is whether the black theologian consistently disproves the charge of divine racism and whether his account of black suffering provides a coherent and sturdy foundation for the theology of liberation advanced as its explicit purpose."[31] To elucidate his thesis Jones presents five propositions related to the issue of divine racism: (1) that divine racism implies a two-category system, an "in" group and an "out" group, and that this division is sanctioned by God; (2) that the "out" group suffers more than the "in" group; (3) that God is responsible for the imbalance in suffering; (4) that God's favor or disfavor is correlated with the racial or ethnic identity of the group in question; (5) that God must, therefore, be a member of the "in" group. In this case, since African-Americans suffer disproportionately, God must be white.[32]

The logic of Jones's argument is heavily dependent on the insights of existentialist writers such as Albert Camus and Jean-Paul Sartre. Jones assumes that God is the sum of God's empirical acts, or that God is what God does. He also assumes that the essential characteristics of God are freedom and power, which, in different degrees, are the essential qualities of genuine humanity. If God is free and able to eliminate the negative suffering of African-Americans, then that suffering should not occur. The challenge to African-American theologians who claim that God is or has liberated African-Americans is to identify the actual events in which the benevolent and liberating hand of God is at work, not for humanity in general, but for African-Americans in particular. Unless the African-American theologian can show how the present situation of suffering is reversed by a concrete, historical, empirical "exaltation event," one must either conclude that God is *finite* and unable to eliminate suffering, or that God is *malevolent* and does not desire to eliminate that suffering.

It is the presence of disproportionate and unmerited suffering among African-Americans that, argues Jones, constitutes the fundamental challenge to traditional notions of God. The protest against God on account of this suffering is often muffled by the dominant ideas of God examined by Benjamin Mays, yet this does not blunt the force of black suffering in light of the presence of an almighty and benevolent God. Jones draws upon the verse of Countee Cullen, whose poem "Color" connects blackness and suffering, and whose poem "The Black Christ" raises doubt whether liberation will ever occur. The suffering of African-Americans forces the logic of divine racism and leads African-Americans to conclude that either God does not exist or is not active in the struggle for the liberation of people of African descent.

Thus African-Americans must face the possibility of affirming a kind of atheism as they look only to themselves as the source of their own salvation, realizing that the ultimate agents of African-American liberation are African-Americans themselves. The unwillingness to entertain the possibility that traditional notions of God are false or even illusory may be, according to Jones, "a fatal residue of the oppressor's world view.... Perhaps some of the cherished beliefs of black people are in fact part and parcel of their oppression!"[33] If an all-good and all-powerful God is an illusion then it also results in the faulty praxis of *quietism*. That is, if God has ordained the plight of African-Americans, then they will do nothing about their oppression. If African-Americans wait for God to do something, then they will, again, do nothing about their oppression.

The solution to this dilemma, according to Jones, is to adopt the stance of *humanocentric theism*. Humanocentric theism, as Jones describes it, is a theological position with three essential features.[34] First, it affirms that humanity is functionally the cocreator of the basic elements of human existence. That is, human beings have been given, by God, the freedom to create the kind of social existence they would have. (It is the view that this freedom is granted *by God* that distinguishes humanocentric theism from what is commonly called secular humanism.) Second, it places the primary emphasis on the activity, choice, and freedom of humanity, rather than God. Thus the African-American theologian, according to Jones, should be concerned foremost with how people actually engage in praxis, exercise choice, and express their freedom, rather than with questions of whether these or any other attributes might be correctly ascribed to God. Third, humanocentric theism offers a radical reinterpretation of divine power and sovereignty. God has chosen to exercise power in the form of persuasion rather than coercion. Further God's sovereignty refers to the fact that God is the transcendent source of humanity's being, rather than referring to God's miraculous intervention into history. Indeed, God has, in this view, left history and its fulfillment in humanity's hands. This position solves, for Jones, the problem of theodicy in black theology. It promotes human freedom as the essential framework for a theology of liberation, it absolves God of any responsibility for the tragic in history, and it disallows any claim of divine sanction for oppression by placing the responsibility for that oppression squarely on the shoulders of its perpetrators.[35]

The implications of this perspective for the African-American theologian are that African-Americans make the ultimate choice in regard to their suffering. Whether that suffering is to be resisted or endured is a human, not a divine, decision. Therefore, God must be understood as one who is not directly involved in the arena of history where human conflict occurs. Much like in the view of the Deists of the seventeenth century, God is seen as one who has withdrawn into the outer regions of creation in order to preserve the freedom that God has granted to humanity. Thus the initial task of black theology, according to Jones, is a "gnosiological conversion" of African-Americans, that is, a shift in concepts and beliefs, a fundamental reconstruction and reorientation of the African-American worldview and lifestyle. In sum, African-Americans must designate their condition of oppression as wrong. They must desanctify it by taking it out of the hands of God. African-Americans must rely only on themselves and seek their own liberation.

William R. Jones rendered a much needed critique of African-American thinking on the doctrine of God. He forced black theologians to come to grips with the question of suffering and the reality of God. There are, of course, objections that have been raised against Jones's proposal. One of the more obvious weaknesses of his position is his view of evil and suffering as synonymous.[36] More importantly, Jones emphasized the need for a *concept* of God that can provide a norm for believing and acting. The ambiguity — or what Jones calls "the multievidentiality" — of African-American experience requires a concept of God that is the result of logical thinking and methodological consistency. However, the major flaw in Jones's argument is the failure to note that rules of logic and methodological procedures are contextual, not universal. They are, as Wittgenstein observed, operative only in the vocabulary of the specific "language games" from which they were derived. Jones's work is more of a philosophical treatise than a theological narrative because it seeks to establish a norm for African-American theological discourse about God apart from the concrete historical experience and the religious affirmations of African-American Christians.

Benjamin Mays was, as a traditional black churchman, ensconced in African-American religious experience. The result of his analysis was a descriptive — and apologetic — account of the ideas of God in African-American experience. William R. Jones, while raised in the traditional black church, claimed to have rejected that experience as normative.[37] Thus his work is a prescriptive — and polemic — argument for a specific concept of God in black theology. One of the major frustrations of beginning students of systematic theology is the inability to discern the experiential roots of the various historical conceptualizations of God. The aseity of God, God as unmoved mover, prime cause, pure act (Thomas Aquinas), the supreme good (Augustine), wholly other (Karl Barth), the ground of being (Paul Tillich), as well as the various attributes or moral qualities of God, are all conceptualizations that, at one time or another, found their legitimacy and justification in the experience of specific Christian communities. Therefore, only the most cursory grasp of the significance of these concepts will be achieved unless their experiential authority is uncovered. At the same time, advanced students of systematic theology will find it necessary to move through the emotionally charged atmosphere of the experience of "the holy" to a point where reflection can lead to action. If one is content with privatized and idiosyncratic ideas of God, then the potential of these ideas to change one's personal and social existence is lost. The experiential matrix will generate ideas of God that are important to the community in question, and disciplined reflection on those ideas will produce conceptualizations of God that make intercultural and intergenerational discourse possible.

The contemporary African-American theologian must chart a course between undifferentiated ideas of God and disembodied concepts of God, seeking to make clear their connections and interrelationships. African-Americans cannot embrace a concept of God that is divorced from their experiential matrix. Nor can they afford to be satisfied with idiosyncratic ideas of God that make no constructive or normative demands upon them. A genuine understanding of God requires that African-Americans apprehend *and* think about the Holy, that they experience *and* reflect on God. Or, to put it another way, whatever black theologians say about God must affirm the transformation of the religious consciousness in the believer, as well as the transformation of her or his social existence.

Unfortunately, nascent black theology did not draw as fully as possible on the spiritual narratives and religious experience of African-American women. In their writings an integrated understanding of God is often expressed more clearly than anywhere else in African-American literature.[38] These sources will have to be explored in depth and from a variety of perspectives if the notion of God in African-

American theological thought is to be fully explicated. While such an explication is beyond the scope of this chapter, there are in African-American theological thought three themes — or affirmations, if you will — that have been and should continue to be central to its understanding of God: (1) the relation among God, freedom, and impartiality; (2) the relation among God, love, and partisanship; (3) the relation among God, personhood, and creativity.

## God, Freedom, and Impartiality

African-American Christians have experienced God as an impartial judge of human character and motives. One of the major affirmations of God in the African-American Christian community is that "God is no respecter of persons" (Acts 10:34). The importance of this affirmation of the character of God becomes clear when set in its historical and political context. Black Christians claimed that God is impartial because they lived in a society in which European-Americans claimed the divine right of race, denied the humanity of African-Americans, and decided who would receive the benefits of that society based solely on the color of one's skin.

By asserting that God is impartial, African-American Christians were saying that God was the universal parent of all humankind and that all people were created from the same dust. This meant that European-Americans were not superior to their African sisters and brothers precisely because God made no such distinctions. (A corollary to the notion of the impartiality of God is the belief that there is only one God. It is interesting that when yoked with political might the idea of monotheism has historically fueled the most barbaric conquests of so-called heathens, while among oppressed peoples the idea of monotheism suggests, first and foremost, the brotherhood and sisterhood of all people.)

It could be argued that this idea of the impartiality of God was more prevalent among those African-Americans who were most insulted by the system of racial segregation, that is, those who were convinced that by virtue of their education, resources, or self-assurance, were it not for that system, they would undoubtedly succeed in America. Or, to put it another way, the black middle-class and those who aspired to middle-class status, having been convinced of Booker T. Washington's gospel of self-reliance and of Marcus Garvey's gospel of black pride, were asserting that God had blessed both races with talents and abilities, and that only an idolatrous use of power by European-Americans prevented African-Americans from being competitive in American society.

There was, however, another reason for affirming the impartiality of

God. Not only would this prevent oppressors from claiming a divine mandate for their actions and divine sanction for their disproportionate share of the society's wealth; it would dissociate God from the unjust and discriminatory structures of a racist culture, thereby accentuating one of the central biblical emphases on the nature of God, that is, God's freedom. Freedom is essential to God's character. Biblical writers of every variety sought ways to express the fact that God stands over and beyond human beings, their political arrangements, their civilizations, and their cultural achievements. Augustine, for example, agonized over whether by describing God as "Lord" he was implying that God needed human subjects to complete God's existence.

In African-American theological thought the emphasis is not so much on God's freedom as an abstract quality of God's being as it is on what that freedom means in relation to the struggle of black people for liberation and wholeness. By claiming the freedom of God African-American Christians can open themselves to new possibilities for human existence not necessarily tied to the existing social order and new definitions of themselves not tied to racist, sexist, or patronizing stereotypes. The radical freedom of God allows African-American Christians to completely reorient their existence and not worry whether European-Americans approve. This notion of God's freedom formed the basis of James Cone's iconoclastic attack on the idolatrous God-talk of white racists in the 1960s and 1970s:

> The God of black liberation will not be confused with a blood-thirsty white idol. Black theology must show that the black God has nothing to do with the God worshiped in white churches whose primary purpose is to sanctify the racism of whites and to daub the wounds of blacks.[39]

Cone's assault on the verbal icons of European-American theology culminated with the controversial claim that "God is black."[40] Although, like any highly charged metaphor, this statement is open to a variety of interpretations, one of its effects was to take the definition of blackness out of the hands of white people.

The traditional term for the freedom of God is God's transcendence. In African-American theology, God's transcendence refers to the fact that God is not limited by one's experiences of God or by the language one uses to refer to God. When God is limited to one's experiences or one's language, the experience or the language is sacralized and God is neither worshipped nor known. What keeps the faith of African-American Christians from becoming absurd is the belief that, in spite of the contradictions, reversals, and disappointments of their experience, God is able to do "considerably more than one could ask or think" (Eph. 3:20). Transcendence refers to the *infinite* within the *finite*, that critical remainder of God that is not contained or even anticipated within our experience. In black theology, the transcendence of God means that God is not subject to the evil that people do or to the suffering that the innocent endure, but is victorious over it. The transcendence of God means that though God participates in the historical struggle for liberation, God is also "transhistorical," opening up history to radically new possibilities for human freedom. The freedom of God, like its derivative, human freedom, must be understood in relational terms. God is not free *from* humanity, the world, or the cosmos, but always and essentially free *for* us and the entire created order.[41]

## God, Love, and Partisanship

African-American Christians have not only claimed the impartiality of God, they have also affirmed what appears to be a contradictory claim, namely, that God is on the side of those who are oppressed in society. They recognized in the Exodus story and in the writings of the prophets of Israel a God who takes sides in human conflict. Not only does God render judgment on those who oppress (Amos 8:1–14), but God actually exercises what Latin American liberation theologians have referred to as "a preferential option for the poor." This affirmation, like the previous one, must be understood in relation to its social and political contexts. Black Christians asserted that God was on their side because they lived in a society where European-Americans made *absolute* claims on the divine legitimation of their dominance. Or, to put it another way, the oppression of African-Americans was often justified by implying that they were abandoned by God. However, the reality of the experience of God among African-American Christians convinced them that not only were they not abandoned by God, but that God had taken their plight as God's own.

Here it could be argued that the idea of the partisanship of God was most prevalent among those African-American Christians who were convinced that human sinfulness institutionalized in racist societal structures made just relations between the races impossible apart from the intervention of God. These were those for whom the doors to the American Dream seemed permanently closed. Further, the very fact of their poverty, oppression, and marginalization seemed to coincide with God's decision to champion their cause. In addition, God's choice of the oppressed appeared to be completely unrelated to their moral or spiritual disposition. That is, the poor did not merit God's partisan favor.

When one examines the slave narratives that recount conversions, for example, moral or spiritual devotion to God follows rather than precedes God's partisan choice of the slave. The effect of this state of affairs

is twofold. First, it counters the notion prevalent in the United States
and other capitalist societies that one can merit God's favor through
industry or moral striving. God's chosen people are chosen in spite of
rather than because of their moral worthiness before God. Second, it
surrounds God's choice with awe and mystery. Therefore, those who
are "chosen" in this sense are called to moral agency as a result of
rather than as a sign of their chosenness.

By affirming the partisanship of God, African-American Christians
expressed their faith that God had not abandoned them in their struggle for liberation. In essence, God's partisanship was a tangible sign of
God's care for the lowly. In traditional theological terms the partisanship of God is the political and historical manifestation of God's love.
God's love for the world and for humanity is a key theme in the biblical
witness. In the Hebrew Scriptures, God is seen as protector, nurturer,
guide, and provider. In the New Testament God's love is crystalized in
the life, ministry, death, and resurrection of Jesus Christ (John 3:16).
The love of God is the magnetic field that holds the created order
together. It is the glue of the universe.

In the formative stages of black theology as an academic discipline,
black theologian J. Deotis Roberts argued that the theme of God's
love was as important as that of God's freedom. This love, according to Roberts, "heals the brokenness between [people], it overcomes
estrangement, and it brings people together — it reconciles. Love is
compassion. Love is redemptive.... God is love; love is God."[42] Theologians have historically thought of God's love as the unconditional
acceptance of humanity even when people behaved inhumanely toward
one another. Therefore there appeared to be some necessary contradiction between God's love and God's periodic rejection, i.e., God's
wrath. One reason for this is that theologians have focused exclusively
on the *agape* motif as the paradigm for love. This meant that to love
was to sacrifice one's self, to endure all without complaint or murmur.
Certainly, self-sacrificial love is the modality of *agape,* but the purpose
of *agape* is justice. God's sacrifice of Jesus was certainly a free and unmerited act, but the purpose of Christ's cruel and bloody death was the
establishment of righteousness and the rectification of the just order of
creation. The force of the idea of self-sacrifice has not been without its
effects on the African-American religious community. Indeed, Martin
Luther King, Jr., based the philosophy of the civil rights movement on
this idea of *agape.*

Roberts, however, writing from a historical perspective cognizant of
both the strengths and weaknesses of the movement, notes that "even
Martin Luther King, Jr., was so captured by the agape motif... that
he was not able to forge a theological relationship between love and
justice, though he was deeply committed to both."[43] African-American

theologians have recognized that there is an essential connection between God's love and God's justice. God's love is prior to God's freedom in the economy of human experience. God's partisanship is the source of God's impartiality. It is in this context that the question often raised concerning the notion of God's preferential option for the oppressed can be answered, i.e., does not God care for everyone? God's love is the basis of God's freedom. Therefore, by being for a particular people God is for all people.

The traditional term used to express the loving presence of God is "immanence." For African-American theologians God's immanence refers to the fact that God is present in the experience of black people. Unless God is truly present in the lives and struggles of people, then the whole notion of an efficacious God is threatened with irrelevance. This is why even Karl Barth, who proclaimed God as "wholly other," found himself eventually compelled to address "the humanity of God" and finally to conclude that God's love is the basis of God's freedom. For African-American Christians, God is present and present with power in their lives. James Cone has noted that "the immanence of God means that God always encounters us in a situation of historical liberation."[44] Immanence, moreover, means that God suffers with suffering humanity, at the side of those seeking freedom and liberation when possible, and those seeking succor and survival when necessary.

In this view, the depth of God's choice, not only to champion the cause of the oppressed, but to make their condition God's own, is expressed in the theological affirmation that God is black. There is, of course, a tension or incongruity between immanence and transcendence. We cannot know, in full, the nature of the God who is beyond us, or rather the God who goes before us. However, having faith means taking the risk that what we do not know about God will be consistent with what we do know about God. It is a wager that the God who comes to us at the midnight of our despair is the same God who "sits high and looks low." The question of faith in God for African-American Christians has never been one of deciding whether the idea of a supreme being was feasible, but whether they could find the courage to believe in the God whom they already knew.

## God, Personhood, and Creativity

In addition to the impartiality and partisanship of God, African-American Christians have declared that God is personal. In traditional European-American theological discourse the understanding of God as personal has been set in opposition to the understanding of God as the ground of ultimate reality. The personhood of God has been seen

as a limitation of God's mode and manner of being in and with the
world. A primary spokesperson for the view of God as that power
that undergirds and sustains the created order was Paul Tillich.[45] In
the larger portion of his corpus Tillich argued that the only intellectually defensible concept of God is that God is the "ground" or
"power" of *being* itself. He argued that even the anthropomorphic
images used to describe God in the Hebrew Scriptures are symbolic
expressions of that benevolent power that calls into being and main-
tains in existence everything that is.[46] However, in a revealing essay
written in response to a critique of the idea of a personal God rendered by Albert Einstein, Tillich acknowledged the importance of such
a notion:

> But why must the symbol of the personal be used at all?...The depth
> of being cannot be symbolized by objects taken from a realm which
> is lower than the personal, from the realm of things or sub-personal
> living beings. The supra-personal is not an "It," or more exactly, it is
> a "He" as much as it is an "It," and it is above both of them. But
> if the "He" element is left out, the "It" element transforms the alleged
> supra-personal into a sub-personal, as usually happens in monism and
> pantheism. And such a neutral sub-personal cannot grasp the center of
> our personality; it can satisfy our aesthetic feeling and our intellectual
> needs, but it cannot convert our will, it cannot overcome our loneliness,
> anxiety, and despair.[47]

Although Tillich's time and circumstance blinded him to the possibility
that the "He" in God could well be the "She" in God, he recognized
the necessity of affirming the personal character of God.

Major J. Jones, one of the early pioneers of black theology in the
United States, argues that the notion of the personhood of God is
foundational in the doctrine of God in black theology. He observes
that a

> ...criterion for belief in a usable God in the Black theological tradition
> is the affirmation that God is a personal being. Not only is God the
> supreme and ultimate source of all reality emanating from himself alone
> but also God is that being of goodness and love who fundamentally
> upholds the world, because he wants to, for his own good pleasure, and
> for the world's good....A usable concept of God must be the affirmation
> that the God who is, who is personal, and who is creatively free and
> independent, good and loving in his personhood, is also an ultimately
> responsive being. A personally responsive God-concept is deeply woven
> into the fabric of the Black Church.[48]

Jones's point is that the concept of God among African-American Christians is not an abstract idea but a concrete reality with ties to the

cultural, historical, and sociopolitical contexts of the people. It is this concreteness that funds the theological assertion that God is black. The limitations of personal concepts of God have been pointed out by Sallie McFague. She urges a reformation in the metaphors for God that theologians have traditionally employed; her critique of the Western theological understandings of God does not fall on the fact that personal images of God are used, but on *which* personal images are used:

> The problem, I believe, is not that personal metaphors and concepts have been used for God; it is not the personal aspect that has brought about the asymmetrical dualism. The problem lies, rather, in the particular metaphors and concepts chosen. The primary metaphors in the tradition are hierarchical, imperialistic, and dualistic, stressing the distance between God and the world and the total reliance of the world on God. Thus, the metaphors of God as king, ruler, lord, master, and governor, and the concepts that accompany them of God as absolute, complete, transcendent, and omnipotent permit no sense of mutuality, shared responsibility, reciprocity, and love (except in the sense of gratitude).[49]

Here one must keep in mind that metaphors — even metaphors for God — are, in part, the products of particular cultural contexts. They are also formative ingredients in a given culture. They are meaningful only to the extent that they are accepted as cultural currency. Therefore, while one cannot change reality without changing that language used to refer to it, one likewise cannot simply create new language without the ushering in of a new reality.

Although the concrete, personal images of God are the most common in the literature of black theology, they are not the only ones used to express the idea of God. One of the effects of the recovery of the distinctive contribution of African-American women to the theological enterprise is the emergence of the notion of God as spirit.

Throughout the personal narratives and literary works of African-American women the emphasis on the spiritual essence of God is a recurring theme. This motif is perhaps most poignantly expressed in Alice Walker's novel *The Color Purple* in the context of a conversation between two black women, Celie and Shug. There Shug affirms that God can be found only by "them that search for it inside." For her, "God is inside you and inside everybody else." Indeed, she believes that "God is everything ... that is or ever was or ever will be. And when you can feel that, and be happy to feel that, you've found it." So for Shug, metaphors and images of God are simply dispensable, because "God ain't a he or a she, but a It.... It ain't something you can look at apart from anything else, including yourself."[50]

Even in this brief exchange one can discern images of God that are not personal in nature. In this view God is that spiritual presence that manifests itself in the created order and especially in human relationships.

The idea of God as spirit in black theology is not the opposite of the idea of God as person. Rather, they are complementary. To speak of God as person affirms the human need to relate to God as a significant other, thereby contravening the objection that what one calls God is simply the glorification of human sentiment. To speak of God as spirit affirms the human need to understand God as that intimate force that buttresses the humanity of black folk, thus avoiding the pitfalls of alienation and objectification that have often accompanied the idea of theism in Christian theology.

The primary mode of expression of the spiritual personality of God is creation and providence. In black theology God is understood to be creator. The emphasis, however, is not on God's responsibility for, ownership of, or causal posture toward creation, but on God's relationship to creation, especially as it speaks to the experience of suffering humanity. James Cone argues that "though white theologians have emphasized that God as creator is a statement about the divine-human relationship, they have not pointed out the political implications of this theological truth for blacks. God as creator has not been related to the oppressed in society. If creation 'involves a bringing into existence of something that did not exist before,' then to say that God is creator means that *my being* finds its source in God. *I am black because God is black!*"[51]

Creation in African-American theology is not primarily concerned with the question of the origin of the universe. The doctrine of creation is the attempt of African-American Christians to understand their relation to God. Creation is ultimately related to soteriology because the former affirms a decisive and positive link between the human and the divine. Historically, black people in the United States have suffered under the claim that they were somewhat less than human in the order of creation. W. E. B. Du Bois often referred to the prevalent belief at the beginning of the twentieth century that between cattle and humans God created black people as a *tertium quid* (third kind). Thus the persistent conviction by African-Americans that they were fully human confirmed a special relationship to God as creator. To be human is to be created in the image of God and, at the same time, to claim God as the source of genuine being and worth.

God's special relationship to creation does not end with the breathing of life into the lifeless form of humanity or the framing of the cosmos. It continues under the aegis of providence. Traditionally, the question of the providence of God has addressed the issue of God's continuing activity and presence in the world. This theme has been problematic for at least two reasons. First, the evidence for God's continuing presence and activity in the world, or even the cosmos for that matter, is often ambiguous. Thus the Christian's search for God's providential presence in the world is often frustrated by the complexities of human experience and the complexities of the world and the natural order. Second, providence has traditionally been understood as some intrinsic quality of God. Statements about God's providence, including the question of God's omnipotence, can become abstract and not intimately or continuously related to the arena of human living and dying.

In African-American theology the reality of God's providence is understood to be mediated through the complexities of human experience, not all human experience, but the human experience of struggle against the forces of oppression. The theme of God's providence does not consist merely of abstract statements about God's inner being, but of concrete statements about God's being in the world, about God's position vis-à-vis the world, about God's relationship to a cosmos set askew by injustice.

God's providence in African-American theological discourse is intimately related to God's creative activity. God, then, is not only the source of the dignity and worth of humanity, but God also sustains humanity. Thus when African-American Christians declare that God cares for them, it is a corollary of the statement that God created them. Implied in African-American religious expression is the notion of creation and providence as God's *work* in history. Normally, a discussion of God's providence raises the question of the modalities of God's activity in human history. Does God intervene in history and human affairs through the intermittent use of miracles? Does God act in accordance with the forces of human history, refusing to dishonor physical and rational processes? An affirmative answer to the first question leads to deism, and an affirmative answer to the second leads to pantheism.

There is another way to express the relation of God to the cosmos that preserves the biblical emphasis on God's miraculous presence and God's intimate transcendence. Providence refers not only to God's *acts* in history, but more accurately to God's *work* in history. God as actor implies that the activity of God is an intrinsic, metaphysical quality of God. One can act without relating consciously to another being or without encountering any recognizable resistance to that activity. God, in African-American religious experience, *works* in history. To work is to accomplish something in spite of resistance. To work is to enter into a formative relation with someone or something outside of oneself. One can act in the abstract. One works in the concrete reality of history.

This notion of a God who labors also sheds a different light on the idea of creation. A striking image from African-American folklore is that of God toiling over the clay as God forms "adam." This image is further supported by the oft-cited biblical reference to Jeremiah's vision of the potter and the clay (Jer. 18:1–6). Here God's toil is a kind of production, the manufacture and conversion of resistant matter. This is essentially a male trope reflective of the presumably masculine task of the conquest of nature and the building of civilization. The mark of God upon humanity in this understanding of creation is the formal manifestation of the *imago Dei*.

The laboring God can be conceived in another way. God as creator can be understood as the one who gives birth, issuing forth the fruits of God's own being. It might be unusual, but certainly not heretical, to image God straining over the birthing stool to bring the cosmos to life, into being. In fact, a rereading of the Genesis 2:4–7 account of creation suggests a God who breathes the breath of life into the new-born cosmos, clearing the mucous from its air passages and enabling the created order to breathe on its own. This is a womanist trope for the bringing into existence that which did not exist before, of giving life, of bonding and caring. The mark of God upon creation in this understanding is the material manifestation of the *imago Dei*. An emphasis on creation and providence as God's work in history and in the world suggests a God who is not determined by the interests of the leisure class. It suggests a God who produces genuine faith and gives birth to liberating praxis.

The emphases on the freedom, love, and personhood of God in African-American theological thought are interrelated. Freedom without love is capricious, arbitrary, and despotic. Love without freedom is obsessive, possessive, and neurotic. The personhood of God does not mean that God is limited in any way, but it affirms an integrity to the Divine Will. God's "ungiven" character in African-American theology refers to the fact that one can never fully apprehend God, no matter how intimately the Divine manifests itself in human experience. At the same time, it refers to the fact that the reality of God is hidden in the experience and history of oppressed and marginalized peoples. In essence, the ungivenness of God suggests that we can only follow God, whose wake leads us through the labyrinth of life.

# 4

## JESUS CHRIST: LIBERATOR AND MEDIATOR

> But who do you say that I am?
>
> — Matthew 16:15

The christocentric character of African-American religious discourse has deep cultural roots and profound theological implications. Neither dimension of Christology can be adequately understood without attention to the other. The idea of Jesus is so deeply ingrained in the religious experience of African-Americans that some scholars have claimed — within the context of a negative assessment of black religion — that the Christianity of African people in the United States is, in essence, *Jesusology*.[1] Implicit within this criticism is a rather curious dichotomy between the humanity and the divinity of Jesus the Christ, which is inconsistent with African-American theological thought.

This chapter will address the question "Who is Jesus Christ for African-Americans?" The response to this question requires an examination of the cultural configuration of Jesus Christ in African-American experience, an assessment of the major theological positions that have emerged in the development of black theology in the United States, and the identification of the problems and issues on the cutting edge of African-American christological discourse.

### The "Figura" of Christ in African-American Experience

In an important but often overlooked essay, Erich Auerbach traced the history of the term "figura" from its earliest appearance in Greek and Roman thought, through its adoption by the theologians of the early church, to the dawn of the Middle Ages.[2] Part of the importance of the appearance of this term is the desire of its users to refer to "the changing aspect of the permanent."[3] The word also allowed the writer to move between the ideas of "model," on one hand, and "copy," on the other, in ways that the traditional terms of "form" and "image" did not. That is, "figura" referred to both the reflection of something that already existed, as well as the projection of something yet to be. It did not take long for Tertullian and other Patristic theologians to recognize the usefulness of this term in expressing the complexity of their christological beliefs.[4]

Jesus Christ was a figura in the sense that he was a cosmic reflection of Adam, the firstborn, the image of God, as well as the historical reflection of Joshua, who led the Israelites into the Promised Land. Jesus Christ was also a figura in the sense that he was a cosmic projection of "the new Adam," the image of God restored to its original state, as well as the historical projection of liberated humanity, evident in the mystical/concrete notions of the church as the "body of Christ" and "the people of God." The central value of the notion of figura for the early church was its historical concreteness. As Auerbach observes, "Moses is no less historical and real because he is an *umbra* or *figura* of Christ, and Christ, the fulfillment, is no abstract idea, but also a historical reality."[5] Thus figura, with its connotations of the changing aspects of the permanent, its ability to refer to novelty and continuity, and its capacity to embrace both the spiritual and the historical dimensions of persons and events, proved an apt vehicle for expressing the relation between the Mosaic roots of Israel's faith, the messianic expectations of the prophets, and the christological claims of the early Christian community.

Figural interpretation, then, "establishes a connection between two events or persons, the first of which signifies not only itself but also the second, while the second encompasses or fulfills the first. The two poles of the figure are separate in time, but both, being real events or figures, are within time, within the stream of historical life."[6] Thus the notion of figura provided an interpretive trope that, unlike symbol or myth, held together the physical and spiritual dimensions of the central events and personages of biblical faith. Unfortunately, this emphasis was largely lost in the subsequent interpretive strategies in Western Christian theology. However, the importance of figural modes of interpretation in relation to black theology lies in the fact that they are the nearest approximation in European theological thought to traditional modes of interpretation in African-American religious thought. Therefore, figural interpretation, while unable to explicate the full complexity of Afrocentric interpretive paradigms, is helpful in approaching the significance of Jesus Christ in African-American theology. The key to understanding who Jesus Christ is for African-Americans is the relation between the biblical notion of the Messiah and the various heroic figures that populate their cultural landscape.

It can be argued that the idea of the Messiah is a subordinate theme in those biblical texts peculiar to the Christian faith. The term "Messiah," or "the anointed one," occurs only twice in the New Testament, both times in the Gospel of John.[7] The notion of the Messiah in the Hebrew Scriptures is intimately connected with the covenant established between God and the chosen people. The Messiah embodies the nationalistic hopes and dreams of an oppressed people. Although much of the messianic material is found in extracanonical texts, significant indices are found within the prophetic writings in the canon. The prophet Isaiah speaks of a Messiah descended from David who shall reestablish the reign of justice and peace (Isa. 9:2–7, 11:1–5). It is noteworthy that continued oppression and travail did not destroy the messianic dream but intensified it. Indeed, the more evil abounded the more powerful the idea of the Messiah became. As the actual historical liberation of Israel seemed to recede into the remote provinces of probability, the Messiah became one capable not only of transforming the historical situation of the people, but of transforming history itself.

The Messiah, then, was vested with the power to usher in a new age in which the powers of this world would be vanquished, sinners punished, and the righteous rewarded. This messianic age included the "in-gathering of Israel." The children of Israel, whether dispersed forcibly or by choice, would be reunited in their ancestral home. In essence, the Messiah was the embodiment of the nationalistic fervor of Israel and the evidence of divine favor for an oppressed people. The Messiah was intolerant of sin, but saw sin primarily in its concrete, historical manifestations. The Messiah was the sign of the revolutionary intentions of God in a world gone awry.

The relation between Jesus of Nazareth and the Jewish Messiah has been and continues to be the hub of theological controversy. William Barclay, a representative of the liberal strain of traditional Christian thought, argues that the very features that mark the Messiah are diametrically opposed to the New Testament understanding of Jesus as the Christ.[8] David F. Strauss, in his massive work on Christology, also explores the ambiguity of Jesus' messianic claims. He implies that bestowing the title of Messiah to the Nazarene carpenter might lead to "an unwarranted ascription of national bigotry to Jesus."[9]

Although it is fairly obvious that there are political considerations involved in the desire to separate "the gentle Jesus" of the New Testament from "the strident Messiah" of the Hebrew Scriptures, one cannot overlook the "messianic secrecy" urged by Jesus in the Gospel of Mark.[10] The interpretation of the life of Jesus in the early church seems to suggest that Jesus both fulfilled and frustrated the messianic hopes of Israel. Gunther Bornkamm argued that while Jesus never claimed the messianic title for himself, "the Messianic character of his being is contained in his words and deeds and in the unmediatedness of his historic appearance."[11] It is quite possible that the relation between Jesus of Nazareth and the Messiah can best be understood and expressed, not through any direct correlation, but through a kind of figural connection in which difference and similarity are refracted, yielding new insight.

Given these characteristics of the notion of the Messiah, it is not surprising that African-American Christians laid hold of messianic themes in Scripture in the formulation of their christological beliefs. African-American slaves and their descendants saw themselves as an oppressed people and a distinct nation. Thus the Bible supported nationalistic ideas in African-American thought. The idea of the in-gathering of the people of God was entirely consistent with the pan-Africanism that has been indigenous to progressive African-American thought, especially the notion of repatriation to Africa. The theme of the historical transformation of a sinful order meshed neatly with the radicalism that is laced throughout African-American religious and political thought. It now remains to consider those historical figures that embodied the messianic hopes of black Christians.

At the heart of African-American culture is a pantheon of heroes. This is evident in the references of African slaves to the figure of "High John the Conqueror," who wielded significant spiritual powers, as well as in the many exceptional performers in the fields of sports, politics, and the arts. In a particularly poignant account in her autobiography, *I Know Why the Caged Bird Sings*, Maya Angelou described the cathartic effect on the black community of the victory of boxer Joe Louis over a white opponent. As she related it, a victory by Joe Louis was tantamount to a victory by the entire race. Of course, heroes are not unique to African-American culture, but in a situation of oppression one's heroes take on added significance.

In his book *From Trickster to Badman*, John W. Roberts discusses the African-American heroic tradition.[12] According to his definition, a hero is "the product of a creative process and exists as a symbol of our differential identity. As such, our heroes act within boundaries defined by our perception of immanent social needs and goals which are, in turn, determined by historical and emergent realities of which we, as individuals and groups, may be only dimly aware."[13] Heroic actions are those that a group "perceives as the most advantageous behaviors for dealing with an obstacle or situation that threatens the values that guide action within specific temporal or social, political, and economic contexts."[14] According to Roberts there are several major features to heroic actions. Heroic actions function to bind and preserve the group culture; that is, these actions express group solidarity. Heroic actions are not suicidal or self-destructive to the community; that is, they never jeopardize the existence or well-being of the group. The actions of the folk hero must be assessed as normative against the backdrop of the heritage and traditions of the group; that is, the hero cannot appear "out of character" with the morals and values of the group.

The major issue in analyzing the heroic traditions of African-American people is the source of the criteria by which they are assessed. While some scholars have argued that the heroic traditions of African-Americans should be seen as derivative of European-American heroic traditions, Roberts argues that these traditions can only be fully understood in light of their African origins.[15] An Afrocentric perspective rests not on the presence or absence of specific African retentions in African-American culture, but on a common conceptual continuity between African and African-American cultures.[16]

To get to the root of christological thinking among African-Americans, we must examine the formation of the African-American spirituals.[17] In fact, these musical forms are the richest available historical resource for a black Christology. The copious research on these musical forms confirms that biblical persons and events formed the subject matter for these songs. However, the question remains whether the slave artists were merely copying and popularizing biblical sagas, or whether there was a prior hermeneutical grid that functioned to select and transform the biblical material in a way that guaranteed its significance for African slave Christians. That is, was there any conceptual relationship between the African understanding of the epic hero and the African-American understanding of the place of Jesus in the biblical saga? Roberts argues:

> To uncover the function and meaning that enslaved Africans derived from the biblical heroic tradition embodied in their songs, we must attempt to understand the factors that influenced their transmitting in spirituals a conception of biblical figures as folk heroes whose characteristic actions reflected values guiding action important to them.... Therefore, it is essential that we consider the possibility that the types of actions performed by biblical heroes were not totally unfamiliar to enslaved Africans and, therefore, could function as a model for heroic actions based on African cultural values.[18]

The African heroic epic, as Roberts describes it, provided a model for the transformation of the biblical saga into a form of expression and action particularly suited to the needs and circumstances of enslaved Africans. The African heroic epic is usually a performed, extended poem in which the actions of an individual embody the heart and soul of the people. It is "multigeneric," encompassing prose, poetry, riddles, laments or jeremiads, as well as humor. "The African heroic epic, though overtly neither an historical nor religious narrative, incorporates and reflects the values of Africans in regard to both religion and history."[19] If one accepts the thesis that enslaved Africans read the Bible in light of the traditional African heroic epic, then one can understand why they never used the Scriptures as merely "a book of religious instruction," on one hand, nor as merely "a relic of the past" on the other. Rather, the Bible was seen as a story book whose truth is grounded in fact and authorized by contemporary experience.

At the center of the African heroic epic is the epic hero. This heroic figure bears some astonishing resemblances to the messianic hero of the biblical saga. Like the superhuman Messiah of the Hebrew Scriptures, "the epic hero is himself a superman empowered by the gods to restore the state to its deserved grandeur in the natural order of things."[20] Like the biblical Messiah who appears in the midst of the turmoil of the Israelites, "the advent of the [African epic] hero is an astonishing phenomenon which is sometimes connected with cosmic turmoil (rain or thunder) or with unusual social or physical situations."[21] But the similarities are not limited to those between the African epic hero and the biblical Messiah. The epic hero also displays characteristics that are strikingly like those of the New Testament picture of Jesus:

> The epic hero whose exploits are the subject of the narrative is a national hero rather than one celebrated by a segment or subgroup within a society. He is also usually distinguished by an unusual birth, threatened in his youth, removed from his home, and forced to undergo hardships and trials before returning to his people. Although the epic hero is invariably described as an exceptional person, he is not necessarily an individual possessed of extraordinary physical endowments or stature.[22]

It is clear that African slave Christians found within the biblical saga enough meaning to warrant its use in maintaining and developing the African heroic epic tradition under strange, new, and terrifying circumstances. This African mode of interpretation, for which we have used the term "figural," allowed enslaved African Christians to see in Jesus an epic hero who embodied the values that not only promoted the liberation of the oppressed, but also to see in him a mediator who was concerned about their daily survival. The values of concern for others, honesty, and forgiveness were of a piece with the demands for justice, equality, and freedom.

The dynamics of figural interpretation meant that Jesus was more than a Palestinian Jew who lived two thousand years ago. Jesus lived and lives in the countless figural manifestations in African-American culture. The messianic revolutionary, manifested in the angry Jesus driving the money changers out of the temple, was the backdrop to the interpretation of the significance of the revolt of Nat Turner. The

Mosaic liberator, manifested in the resolute Jesus standing over against the political forces of his day, was the backdrop to the interpretation of the significance of the exploits of Harriet Tubman. In addition, references to Jesus as the "balm in Gilead" and "the rose of Sharon" in African-American religious expression point to his function as a healer and to his very being as testimony to the beauty of creation. It is this epic heroic tradition, along with the biblical saga, that provided the raw material for the formation of an African-American Christology.

## Jesus and the Disinherited

In 1949 Howard Thurman's *Jesus and the Disinherited* appeared as a precursor to the more systematic articulation of Christology in black theology some twenty years later. Certainly, earlier writers had discussed the meaning of Jesus for African-American Christians. Alexander Young's "Ethiopian Manifesto," appearing in 1829, referred to the appearance of a black Messiah. One could point to Countee Cullen's poem "The Black Christ," as well as other references to the special relation between Jesus and the black race scattered throughout the literature. However, Thurman's narrative is especially significant for two reasons. First, it is a transitional text that subtly draws on Afrocentric cultural motifs as well as systematic theological insights into the meaning of Christ. Second, in Thurman's text the biblical and historical ideas of Jesus as the Messiah are intertwined with the cosmic and mystical notions of Jesus as the Christ.

Thurman's discussion of Jesus is predicated on two key questions. First, what is the significance of the religion of Jesus for "people with their backs against the wall?" Second, why is it that Christianity is impotent in dealing effectively "with the issues of discrimination and injustice on the basis of race, religion and national origin?"[23] For Thurman, it is not a question of the moral obligation that Christianity lays upon those who have much, but the existential meaning of Christianity for those who have little or nothing. "The masses of men live with their backs against the wall. They are the poor, the disinherited, the dispossessed. What does our religion say to them? The issue is not what it counsels them to do for others whose need may be greater, but what religion offers to meet their own needs."[24] The crucial question is who is Jesus for the downtrodden.

From this perspective Thurman identifies three central features of Jesus in the biblical narratives. First, Jesus was a Jew. Jesus had a specific ethnic, racial, and religious identity. "It is impossible for Jesus to be understood outside of the sense of community which Israel held with God.... The Christian Church has tended to overlook its Judaic origins, but the fact is that Jesus of Nazareth was a Jew of Palestine when he went about his Father's business, announcing the acceptable year of the Lord."[25] Second, Jesus was a poor Jew. His condition of material want cemented his solidarity with the poor of his time. Further, his poverty takes on added significance in the light of his designation as *the human one*, or the Son of Man. "The economic predicament with which he was identified in birth placed him initially with the great mass of men on earth. The masses of the people are poor. If we dare take the position that in Jesus there was at work some radical destiny, it would be safe to say that in his poverty he was more truly Son of man than he would have been if the incident of family or birth had made him a rich son of Israel."[26] Third, Jesus was a member of an oppressed minority. He shared the sense of outrage that comes with domination. The oppression of the Jews of Palestine by the Roman Empire was the inescapable social and political context of Jesus' maturation. "It is utterly fantastic to assume that Jesus grew to manhood untouched by the surging currents of the common life that made up the climate of Palestine. Not only must he have been aware of them; that he was affected by them is a most natural observation."[27]

These conditions shaped the religion of Jesus. Thurman argues that the Israelites of Jesus' time had only two options in relation to Rome. The first was nonresistance, in which the oppressed Jews could either imitate the dominant group and assimilate their culture and traditions, or simply withdraw, as far as possible, from the oppressive group and be content with occasional displays of contempt. The second option was resistance, which manifests itself most often in armed struggle. This type of resistance has its appeal among the oppressed, but that appeal is often tragic in the sense that it must destroy part of what it seeks to preserve.

Thurman believes, however, that the religion of Jesus represents an alternate form of resistance. That religion is summed up in the statement "the kingdom of God is in us." This internal, or spiritual, liberation is not sought at the expense of social and political freedom. In fact, Thurman states that an otherworldly focus in religion is the Achilles' heel of traditional Christianity. "The desperate opposition to Christianity rests in the fact that it seems, in the last analysis, to be a betrayal of the Negro into the hands of his enemies by focusing his attention upon heaven, forgiveness, love and the like."[28] The religion of Jesus, on the other hand, is a direct response to the concrete sufferings of the oppressed.

> It seems clear that Jesus understood the anatomy of the relationship between his people and the Romans, and he interpreted that relationship against the background of the profoundest ethical insight of his own religious faith as he had found it in the heart of the prophets of Israel. The

solution which Jesus found for himself and for Israel, as they faced the
hostility of the Greco-Roman world, becomes the word and the work of
redemption for all the cast-down people in every generation and in every
age. I mean this quite literally. I do not ignore the theological and metaphysical interpretation of the Christian doctrine of salvation. But the
underprivileged everywhere have long since abandoned any hope that
this type of salvation deals with the crucial issues by which their days are
turned into despair without consolation. The basic fact is that Christianity as it was born in the mind of this Jewish thinker appears as a technique
of survival for the oppressed. That it became, through the intervening
years, a religion of the powerful and dominant, used sometimes as an
instrument of oppression, must not tempt us into believing that it was
thus in the mind and life of Jesus.[29]

The religion of Jesus was the product of the ethical fervor of the prophets, in the contexts of his life and times, under the pressure of the
kingdom of God clearly seen and magnified within him. Thurman concludes with two biblical references, each of which became central motifs
in the subsequent development of Christology in black theology. The
first is the aforementioned "the kingdom of God is in us." Here the
focus is on the internal dimensions of salvation or liberation, and Jesus
is the mediator or way to that kingdom. The second is the prophetic
manifesto from the prophet Isaiah read by Jesus in the synagogue,
"The Spirit of the Lord is upon me, because he hath anointed me to
preach the gospel to the poor."[30] Here the focus is on the external dimensions of salvation or liberation, and Jesus is the one who sets the
oppressed free for the glory of God. As we shall see, these two motifs
set the stage for the development of Christology in black theology in
its nascent and more mature stages.

### The Development of Christology in Black Theology

Early in the development of black theology two rather clearly defined
positions regarding Jesus and his work emerged. The first focused on
the idea of Jesus as "the Messiah" with all the Hebraic implications of
the term. One might say that Jesus is understood to be "the Son of
Man." In this case he is referred to as a liberator of oppressed humanity,
freeing them from the powers of sin as well as the social structures that
both bear and breed sin. Here salvation is essentially sociopolitical,
though it is not without spiritual implications. The proclamation of
Jesus quoted by Thurman, "The Spirit of the Lord is upon me, to
preach good news to the poor..." is a suggestive touchstone for this
position. The second position focused on the notion of Jesus as "the
Christ" with all the attendant Hellenized implications. That is, Jesus

was first and foremost understood to be "the Son of God." In this instance he is referred to as a mediator between the forces of evil, the effects of sin, and the forces of good, the powers of redemption. Here salvation is essentially spiritual, though it is not without sociopolitical import. Thurman's notion of "the kingdom is within us" is an apt summation of this position. Although most christological perspectives in black theology fall somewhere between these two positions, they are important because they each contain a germ of truth that virtually every black theologian must respect.

A representative of the first position is Albert Cleage's *The Black Messiah*. This collection of sermons and essays published in 1968 described the essential features of a doctrine of Jesus on what one might call the extreme left of the black theological spectrum. The essence of Cleage's argument is that the idea that Jesus was white was directly related to the fact that Europeans dominated the world. "That white Americans continue to insist upon a white Christ in the face of all historical evidence to the contrary and despite the hundreds of shrines to Black Madonnas all over the world, is the crowning demonstration of their white supremacist conviction that all things good and valuable must be white."[31]

According to Cleage, African-American people can never build the sense of dignity required to overcome oppression by worshipping a white Christ. In a radical rereading of the Bible Cleage argues that "the real Jesus" whose life is most accurately reported in the Synoptic Gospels is not the false "spiritualized Jesus" reconstructed many years later by the Apostle Paul, who never knew Jesus and who modified Jesus' teachings to conform to the pagan philosophies of the "white gentiles."[32] Perhaps the most controversial of Cleage's assertions was that Jesus was physically black:

> We know that Israel was a black nation and that descendents of the original black Jews are in Israel, Africa, and the Mediterranean area today. The Bible was written by black Jews. The first three Gospels, Matthew, Mark, and Luke, tell the story of Jesus, retaining some of the original material which establishes the simple fact that Jesus built upon the Old Testament. Jesus was a Black Messiah. He came to free a black People from the oppression of the white Gentiles. We know this now to be a fact. Our religion, our preaching, our teachings all come from the Old Testament, for we are God's chosen people.[33]

There are several emphases in Cleage's thinking that are important to the present discussion. First, he stresses the importance of the Hebrew Scriptures and their continuity with the New Testament. This affirms the relation between Jesus and his racial and cultural origins. Second, he stresses the importance of a national identity for the Israelites. This affirms Jesus' messianic role in solidifying that identity. Cleage's claim

that Jesus was physically black, a revolutionary leader, a Zealot actually, committed to leading Israel, a black nation, to freedom, met with
stiff resistance among traditional Christian groups. However, current
research seems to suggest that there is at least as much truth as there
is hyperbole to his position.

A representative of the second position is Tom Skinner's *How Black
Is the Gospel?* published in 1970. This work is located on what one
might call the right of the black theological spectrum. Skinner, an
evangelical, argues that though Jesus lived in violent and revolutionary times, he did not identify or support violent revolution. In fact,
Jesus was not a Zealot and therefore disappointed the hopes of Israel.
"Christ offered himself to Israel but was rejected because He refused
to accommodate His spiritual revolution to Jewish political ambitions.
His kingdom is not of this world, which explains His rejection of
militarism."[34]

Jesus' objective was not to redeem society but to save people from
sin. This focus on the spiritual dimensions of salvation, according to
Skinner, places Jesus above the cultural conflict over racial origins.[35]
"Whatever contemporary man decides about the 'color' of religion,
Christ stands outside that debate. Even a superficial reading of the
gospel reveals that Christ showed only one special interest — allegiance
to His Father and the Kingdom of God. He was owned by no man,
He belonged to no particular group, and He refused to sanction one
party or system over another. He was God in the form of man —
neither black nor white."[36] This meant that Christ did not take sides
in the Roman-Jewish conflict of his day, but called all people to a higher
righteousness through a spiritual revolution and transformation. The
true revolution of Christ was primarily moral and secondarily social,
economic, and political.

The important features of Skinner's perspective are the emphasis on
the New Testament and its discontinuity with the Hebrew Scriptures.
In other words, Jesus brings a new dispensation, the Gospel, which
renders the old dispensation, the law, null and void. Jesus, then, is
not to be understood as a product of Israel and its struggles. Jesus'
autonomy from his racial and cultural origins meant that he had no
constructive role in the nationalistic aspirations of Israel under Roman
rule. In this view, the work of Christ is the mediation between sinful
humanity and God to bring in the kingdom. That kingdom, however, is
not understood to be political, but essentially spiritual. Because even
in their struggle for social and political liberation African-Americans
are concerned about the spiritual dimension of their existence, this
perspective on Jesus found a home among certain segments of the
African-American church.

Between the positions of Cleage and Skinner lie the more centrist

positions in the early development of black theology represented by
J. Deotis Roberts, James Cone, and Gayraud Wilmore.[37] In his writings of the late 1960s and early 1970s, J. Deotis Roberts argues that
the black Messiah in African-American religious thought is primarily
symbolic and is not to be understood in any literal or historical sense.[38]
However, the notion of the black Messiah is important as a theological
symbol because it grounds the biblical teachings about Jesus in black
culture and the mythic configurations of black experience.

The central theme of Roberts's thought is the relation between the
black Messiah and what he calls "the Christ of faith." First, the black
Messiah is a *mythical* construct that is necessary because of the nega-
tivity associated with blackness. Because the blackness of the Messiah
is solely the result of the cultural milieu of African-Americans, the
black Messiah must ultimately point to and give way to "a colorless
Christ."[39] Second, the black Messiah is *particular*, while the Christ of
the Bible is universal. Therefore, "the universal Christ is particularized
for the black Christian in the black experience of the black Messiah, but
the black Messiah is at the same time universalized in the Christ of the
Gospels who meets all men in their situation."[40] Third, the black Messiah is a *formal* construct through which black people can comprehend
the traditional teachings of Christian thought: "The frame of reference is the black Messiah; the content will be 'the Jesus of history as
the Christ of faith.'"[41] Fourth, the notion of the black Messiah effects
a kind of psychocultural and experiential liberation for a people oppressed because of their color, but this liberation is only penultimate.
The ultimate goal is *reconciliation:* "The black Messiah liberates the
black man. The universal Christ reconciles the black man with the rest
of mankind."[42] Fifth, while the idea of a black Messiah may carry political overtones, the kingdom of Christ is primarily *spiritual:* "[Christ's]
Kingdom is not of this world. It is within. He reigns over a realm of
moral and spiritual ends."[43]

This basic position is continued in Roberts's later work with one
significant alteration. He adds an emphasis on the *difference* rather than
the relation between Christ and culture. "Jesus must not be locked
into a given cluster of political and cultural perceptions. We seek a
Christ above culture who is at the same time at work in culture and
history for redemptive ends."[44] In hindsight one might account for
this shift by arguing that the radical dimensions of African-American
culture, the exaggeration and denigration of black culture in the film
media — especially those films that depicted black heroes as pimps and
drug dealers — as well as the emergence of a secular spirituality, made
the notion of a culture-bound black Messiah untenable for Roberts.
In sum, for Roberts the notion of the black Messiah fills a psychocultural need created by the racism of white Christians, but in reality

the Christ to which the black Messiah points is above culture. It cannot be denied that the concept of the black Messiah answered a need in the beleaguered psyche of an oppressed people, but to place Christ above and beyond the cultural, meaning-making matrix of African-Americans risks, at best, an unnecessary dichotomy, and, at worst, the irrelevance of Christ to their struggle.

In James Cone's thought one finds a different emphasis. Cone argues that the notion of the black Christ, while not to be understood in only a literal sense, is not merely a cultural symbol. Rather, it is a theological statement of the truth about Christ among the oppressed. Cone does not deny the mythic function of the idea of the black Christ, but argues that the power of myth is always dependent on its grounding in history. Jesus' birth as one of the oppressed of the land certainly took on mythic features among the early church, as reflected in the highly stylized "birth narratives" found in the Gospels. Yet, as Cone states, those stories "undoubtedly reflect the early Christian community's historical knowledge of Jesus as a man who defined the meaning of his existence as being one with the poor and outcasts.... Focusing on the historical Jesus means that Black Theology recognizes history as the indispensable foundation of Christology."[45]

The central theme of Cone's thinking on this subject is the hermeneutical and theological potential of the concept of "the black Christ." First, the blackness of Christ refers not only to his victimization but also to his victory. "The concept of black...includes both what the world means by oppression and what the gospel means by liberation."[46] Therefore, blackness is a symbol in the Tillichian sense of the term; that is, it both points to and participates in a reality outside itself.

Second, the motif of blackness is the bridge between the Jesus who lived in first-century Palestine and the Christ proclaimed among the faithful. "Without some continuity between the historical Jesus and the kerygmatic Christ, the Christian gospel becomes nothing but the subjective reflections of the early Christian community."[47] Jesus' racial identity then becomes symbolic of his existential condition. "It is on the basis of the soteriological meaning of the particularity of his Jewishness that theology must affirm the christological significance of his present blackness. He is black because he was a Jew. The affirmation of the Black Christ can be understood when the significance of his past Jewishness is related dialectically to the significance of his present blackness."[48]

Third, the blackness of Christ is a comprehensive theological truth and not merely a cultural necessity for African-Americans. "Christ is black, therefore, not because of some cultural or psychological need of black people, but because and only because Christ really enters into our world where the poor, the despised, and the black are, disclosing that he is with them, enduring their humiliation and pain and transforming oppressed slaves into liberated servants."[49]

Fourth, the blackness of Christ does not only link the past and present manifestations of Jesus; it serves as a guide to the future coming of Christ. It means that the kingdom of Christ "strikes across all boundaries — social, economic and political"[50]; while appearing first among the oppressed, the kingdom will call all of creation to a point of decision, to choose the side of the oppressed or that of the oppressors.

It is important to note that while Cone's Christology is not without political implications, the structure of his argument suggests that the liberation of which he speaks is, first, liberation from the sin of racism, rather than from the political domination therein. Therefore, Christ's victory is a triumph over the forces of evil in the world.[51] Although Cone affirms the contribution of Cleage to his own thinking, he does not describe Christ in essentially messianic terms. Cone's major contribution here is his description of the black Christ as a challenge to the distortion of the biblical image of Jesus in European-American theology and as one who stands over and against the culture of which that theology is a part. The task of constructing a Christology based on a more detailed analysis of the morphology of African-American religious expression has been taken up by his successors.

The writings of Gayraud S. Wilmore on Christology, while not as extensive as those of Cone or Roberts, are representative of a third theological option.[52] Wilmore argues that African-American christological thought cannot be fully understood outside the complex color symbolism of Western culture. He notes that color prejudice against people of African descent is an ancient phenomenon with evidence of this fact being found in early Egyptian and Indian civilizations, for example. Because racism is not just a product of the modern, scientific mindset, one cannot ignore the impact of color prejudice upon the development of Christianity. First, the intensification of color prejudice

> in the Middle Ages irrevocably marked Christianity. During the Middle Ages Talmudic and Midrashic sources sought to explain Blackness with such suggestions as "Ham was smitten in his skin" or that Noah told Ham "your seed will be ugly and dark-skinned," or that Canaan was "the notorious world-darkener...." And if the Bible itself seems relatively free of this prejudice it is only because the Jews, after many years of residence and intermarriage in Africa, were themselves a dark-skinned people by the time the Old Testament was written.... It was not the Jews of the Old Testament period, but Jews and Gentiles of medieval Europe — especially of Northern Europe and Great Britain — who were repelled by black skin color and African physiognomy and gave renewed vigor to the color prejudice that had been sporadic and peripheral in the ancient world.[53]

Thus the Bible and its traditions have to be seen in the context of the issue of color in Western culture. Second, the truth in the claim that Christianity is a white religion must be addressed:

> God himself is white for Western man and the Christian faith, inextricably bound in its development to the history and culture of the great Western powers, is a white religion — a religion of, by and for white people. That is not a fantastic idea concocted by fanatical African priests and storefront preachers to persuade their people to resist white domination. It is not some wild allegation dreamed up by the Rastafarians or the Black Muslims. It just happens to be the simple, unadorned truth about what has been given to Black people as Christianity and something white people themselves believed.[54]

Third, the relation between blackness and suffering, or what Wilmore calls "color and calamity," in Western culture compels its victims to engage in a determined search for spiritual meaning and social coherence in their lives.

> Black color and calamity cannot be separated in the history of the West. . . . It forces us, in our search for a way out of the meaninglessness and absurdity of the inseparable connection between blackness and oppression, to discover at the most profound depths of our religious sensibility something that reinterprets that historic coherence. . . . We can create a new meaning for the coherence of color and calamity. . . . We can perceive blackness as a symbol of the human struggle against the sterile, oppressive "whiteness" of the principalities and powers. . . . A new structure of meaning is now possible for blackness that not only transforms the external or physical features of economic, political and cultural life, but can also transform the inner life of the people through a reinterpretation of Christian symbolism.[55]

It is in the context of color consciousness in Western culture that the importance of the black Messiah is to be seen for Wilmore. He does not mean that Jesus was physically black, though he does not rule out that possibility. Rather, the black Messiah is the singular trope for the quest for religious meaning among people of African descent, and ultimately it symbolizes a universal quest for religious meaning:

> To speak of Christ as the Black Messiah is rather to invest blackness in Western civilization, and particularly in the United States and South Africa, with religious meaning expressing the preeminent reality of black suffering and the historical experience of black people in a racist society. . . . To speak of the Messiah figure in terms of the ontological significance of the color black is to provide both black people and white people, if the latter are open to the possibility, with a way of understanding the relevance of the Person and Work of Christ for existence under the conditions of oppression.[56]

Thus for Wilmore, the black Messiah is both a concrete incarnation of God among people of color who cannot be understood apart from their experience, and a comprehensive symbol of the divine presence whose revelatory power is available to all. The primary contribution of Wilmore is his description of a black Messiah who critiques the racism in biblical religion and in the political order. Moreover, the work of this black Messiah is the redemption of the culture upon which both religion and politics rests.

## Conclusion

Efforts to formulate an adequate Christology for our times have not been peculiar to black theologians. Within progressive European and North American theologies, one can observe a similar struggle to make sense of Christian confessions of Christ. Schubert Ogden, for example, in his book *The Point of Christology*, argues that Christology should not be based on the historical Jesus because Jesus is representative of a reality larger than himself.[57] Tom F. Driver, in his book *Christ in a Changing World*, advances the idea that Christ should not be the center of Christianity, because the centrality of Christ fosters a kind of individualism that does not address the concerns or needs of the contemporary world. The focus of Christianity, he argues, should be the Christian community.[58]

Both Ogden and Driver present proposals that differ radically from that of Dietrich Bonhoeffer. In his work *Christ the Center*, Bonhoeffer argued that Christ is not only the center of existence for the Christian community, but that Christology demonstrates the problem inherent in all learning. Within the church it becomes clear that "christology is the centre of all disciplines. It is the unknown and hidden centre of the university of learning."[59] The focus of Christology, for Bonhoeffer, is the person rather than the work of Christ. "Christology is not soteriology.... Christology is primarily concerned with who he is rather than what he does. To put that into an academic formula: the subject of christology is the personal structure being of the complete, historical Jesus Christ."[60] The reason that Bonhoeffer gives for the centrality of the person of Christ is that sin makes it impossible for human beings to ever follow the example of Christ. Therefore, the perfect deeds of Christ elicit only despair among imperfect human beings. In essence he is reacting against the "moral exemplar Christ" of classical liberal theology. One might deduce, however, from the context in which he thought and wrote, that the situation of idolatry and the reign of demonic powers during his lifetime made the focus on the personal incarnation of God in history a crucial anchor in a social and political maelstrom.

Outside the arena of European and North Atlantic christological discourse, fresh approaches to the topic are also being developed. Rita Nakashima Brock, in her book *Journeys by Heart: A Christology of Erotic Power*, critiques classical Christologies, arguing that the "erotic power" that Jesus manifests cannot be contained in any one individual. Therefore, Jesus "neither reveals it nor embodies it, but he participates in its revelation and embodiment."[61] Therefore, she concludes, the power of Christ is not found exclusively in "the life of one heroic person who is singly identified as the Christ" but within the relationships that constitute the community. The idea that there may be other "christs" besides Jesus of Nazareth, an idea suggested by Paul Tillich many years earlier, is one of the more absorbing and controversial issues in contemporary christological discourse.

Kortwright Davis, a black theologian from the Caribbean, has developed a christological proposal that relates Jesus Christ to four levels of human liberation.[62] He argues that, at the personal level, Jesus liberates black people from a false consciousness by the respect he showed humanity by taking human form and calls them to a new awareness of what it means to be truly human. At the religious level, Jesus liberates the conscience of black people by calling them to repentance and a life of adoration of God. At the historical level, Jesus liberates black people from their condition of suffering by the responsibility he showed for others, therefore allowing the oppressed to anchor themselves in a redemptive existence. At the social level, Jesus liberates black people from the contempt with which they are held by others because of their race by his reconciling acts, thereby making possible among the oppressed the joyous affirmation that is the purpose of each human life.

The christological issues with which African-American theologians are struggling overlap, in many instances, with those mentioned above. However, the particular shape that a doctrine of Christ will take in black theology in the United States today will be related to those concerns closest to the hearts of African-American Christians. Two emerging issues for Christology in black theology in the twenty-first century are the mediation of traditional sources of sustenance and resistance in African-American religious expressions, understanding, and practice, and the liberation of persons oppressed by the distortions of religious expressions, understanding, and practice. The first issue, for example, is evident in the writings of many womanist theologians, and the second issue is central to the thought of many African Christian theologians.

The first twenty-five years of black theology in its academic form — because of various social and cultural factors — have been dominated by African-American males. This fact does not render all that has been done and said by black male theologians meaningless, but that "fact" should not be taken as a "given." The significance of the work being done by African theologians and by African-American women theologians is that it is the result of the meeting of the forces of tradition, on one hand, and the challenges of the contemporary world, on the other. That is, this work is being done where the past and the future meet. Among African-American women theologians, Delores Williams has articulated an understanding of soteriology that substantially revises classical notions of atonement. She argues that one must relate the ubiquitous experience of "surrogacy" among black women to their understanding of salvation.[63] Kelly Brown argues that a womanist Christology must "find a way to affirm that Jesus is Christ, that is, God incarnate, Resurrected Savior, while disaffirming a relationship between Jesus' maleness and his being the Christ."[64] Instead, she notes, a womanist Christology must focus on the sustaining and liberating activity of Christ and insist that "Christ can be incarnate wherever there is a movement to sustain and liberate oppressed people."[65]

Jacquelyn Grant in her book *White Women's Christ and Black Women's Jesus* argues that a womanist Christology must center on the humanity of Jesus and that this humanity, rather than Jesus' maleness, has been the primary frame of reference in black women's experience. She states that in the experience of African-American women "Jesus Christ thus represents a three-fold significance: first he identifies with the 'little people,' Black women, where they are; secondly, he affirms the basic humanity of these, 'the least'; and thirdly, he inspires active hope in the struggle for resurrected, liberated existence."[66] This three-fold significance of Jesus Christ points to what Grant outlines as the three major challenges for womanist Christology. Womanist Christology must (1) examine the relationship between theological symbolism and the oppression of black women, (2) ask the question of Jesus' relationship to the class structures in society, and (3) formulate a constructive understanding of Jesus Christ in the context of the struggle for wholeness and liberation.[67]

The common starting point in the writings of most womanist theologians is that of the historical, religious, and literary experience of black women. The primary material is the body of wisdom and spirituality found among the neglected voices of African-American women in history and literature. Katie Cannon, for instance, in her book *Womanist Ethics*, draws upon the writings of Zora Neale Hurston for the construction of an ethic suitable to the experience of African-American women.[68] The aim is the resurrection of traditional sources of strength and power.

In the case of Christianity and African culture, the limitations of Eurocentric christological understandings are thrown into sharp relief.

When one adds the coercive power of European intellectual, military, and economic dominance, those limitations easily become distortions. Therefore, African Christians have found it necessary to articulate for themselves an African understanding of Jesus Christ. John S. Pobee, Sigquibo Dwane, John S. Mbiti, and Mercy Amba Oduyoye are among those who have contributed to this task.

John S. Pobee, in his book *Toward an African Theology*, attempts to restate the traditional affirmations about Jesus Christ in the light of Akan religion. He argues that the humanity of Jesus can only be recognized as such if it has correlates in the experience of ordinary human beings. The humanity of Jesus, then, is seen in his kinship with his tribe and clan, in the ceremonial act of baptism that signifies one's solidarity with the rest of the community, in his very real fear of and desire to avoid death, and in his ultimate dependence on a power more sublime than himself.[69] The divinity of Jesus is evident in the claim that he was "sinless." The Akan understanding of sin, however, is that "sin is an antisocial act. It is not an abstract transgression of a law; rather it is a factual contradiction of established order."[70] The divinity of Jesus is also seen in the authority and power that he commanded, in his ability to heal the brokenness of the body, mind, and spirit, and especially in his function as "Nana," or "the great and greatest Ancestor." As ancestor, the presence and efficacy of Jesus persist beyond his physical manifestation. He is a spiritual being who both judges and nurtures the community. "To say Jesus is Nana is to let his standards reign supreme in personal orientation, in the structures of society, in the economic processes, and in political forces. It means in practical terms personal and social justice and re-creation."[71]

Mercy Amba Oduyoye and Elizabeth Amoah echo these themes from the perspective of African women. They expose the intricate relation between understanding Christ as ancestor, the mediating work of Christ, and the idea that there may be many Christs:

> Is Jesus our ancestor, the quintessence of a life of faith? If so, then one begins to formulate Christology in terms of mediation and of participation in the divine-human axis that links humanity to divinity. In Jesus of Nazareth we see the return to earth of the Divine Spirit of God; the source of life, as an individual — just as in African tradition the ancestors return in the birth of new babies. This would, of course, imply that there can be many Christs as the spirit of a grandmother returns to grandchildren in perpetuity as long as such children are named after her, that is, called by her name. Does Christianity have room for the concept of many Christs, persons in whom the Spirit of God dwells in all its fullness?[72]

The issue of one Christ or many Christs is far from being resolved in contemporary black theological discourse. However, it is possible

that the figural interpretation to which we referred at the beginning
of this chapter offers some promising possibilities in this direction.
In any case, it is the language of the experience of African women
that will provide the appropriate symbols for their Christology. Jesus
Christ, then, can be affirmed as "liberator from the burden of disease
and the ostracism of a society riddled with blood taboos and theories
of inauspiciousness rising out of women's blood."[73] Jesus Christ is
also the mediator, "the one who has broken down the barriers we have
erected between God and us as well as among us...thereby saving us
from isolation and alienation, which is the lack of community that is
the real experience of death."[74] Jesus Christ is the one who saves us
in both spiritual and material terms, in both the religious and social
dimensions of life.[75] The problem common to most African theologians writing on Christology is attempting to understand and affirm
Jesus Christ on one's own terms and in light of one's own experience
of salvation. This problem, along with that being articulated by womanist theologians, appears to be defining the agenda for christological
discourse in black theology for the years ahead.

In the first centuries of the history of the church in the West, the
issues confronting theological discourse were by and large preserved in
the creeds of Chalcedon and Nicea. The issue of whether Jesus Christ
was really God, or whether one could defend the affirmation that humanity and divinity were both — completely and without confusion —
present in Jesus of Nazareth, were burning issues for those times. It is
not that Chalcedon and Nicea have no relevance for African-American
theology, but rather that their relevance is indirect or illustrative. Both
Chalcedon and Nicea dealt with problems related to the interface between Christianity and Greco-Roman culture. One could argue that the
missionary or apologetic thrust of the church at that time was the redemption of that culture. African-American Christians have their own
Chalcedons and Niceas that grow out of the interface between Christianity and African culture. This is the locus of whatever christological
controversies that have occupied black Christians. African-American
Christians have claimed Jesus Christ as both liberator from social and
political oppression and as mediator of the goodness of God and as
victor over the cosmic forces of evil. Every black theological statement
about Jesus Christ is, like all creeds, a partial and contextual answer to
a pressing practical problem in the life of the believing community.

Black theologians have attempted to define the person and work
of Christ so that black Christians might be able to claim both their
personhood and their faith. Too often, however, the person and the
work of Jesus Christ have been framed as opposites between which
one must make a choice. A more fruitful approach is to see both the
person and the work of Christ pointing to the demand to live the

Christian life, or to "abide in him." The early Christian community referred to its faith as "the Way." It was the way of Christ rather than either the work or the person of Christ that provided the norms for the life of the community. The faith had not yet been codified into a set of rules, practices, and behaviors that rigidly defined the work of Christ. The faith had not yet been reduced to a cult of personality, limited to an exclusive preoccupation with the person of Christ. The community was concerned about "the way" of Christ and its demands for an interpersonal, relational, liberated, and loving witness in the world. The way of Christ means doing the work of Christ in the world, but it is more than functional. The way of Christ means emulating the person of Christ in the world, but it is more than existential. Beyond mere "being" or "doing," the way of Christ points to the praxis of faith. The essence of this christological praxis is relationship.

Relationship does not necessarily exist because of the physical proximity of persons. Nor can it exist without persons to whom one can relate. Relationship is a force-field generated by personal presence; it exists between persons but is not the possession of any one person. This is evident in the question who is Christ *pro me*, for me, or more appropriately in this case, *pro nobis*, for us. It is the point of Jesus' question to Peter, "Who do *you* say that I am?" Intellectually, the question "Who is Jesus the Christ?" might be addressed from a safe emotional distance. However, the question of who Christ is for us cannot be answered outside the context of a genuine relationship with Jesus Christ.

Jesus in his "way" with black folk has been described as a political messiah or liberator, and as a spiritual mediator or healer. Jesus of Nazareth mediates the goodness of God and creation. Through him the indigenous sources of spirituality and strength bequeathed to African-Americans by God the creator become visible. The goodness of God is revealed through Jesus, which is why, when the rich young man called Jesus "Good Teacher," Jesus replied, "Why do you call me good? No one is good but God alone" (Mark 10:18 RSV). The goodness of God is also embodied or incarnate in Jesus, which is why Jesus, responding to Philip's request to see God, says, "He who has seen me has seen the Father" (John 14:9 RSV).

Jesus the Christ also liberates humanity from the triple threat of evil, sin, and death. African-American Christians have historically affirmed that Jesus liberates them from personal and cosmic evil through the life of perfect obedience that he led. Jesus liberates them from sin, both individual and structural, through his death on the cross. And Jesus liberates them from death, both physical and spiritual, through his resurrection.

In essence, Jesus mediates the ungivenness of God, bringing God into the sphere of our existence. Jesus liberates us from the crushing burden of otherness and difference, bringing to light the God in us. In doing so, Jesus makes possible a way of life — a mode of praxis — grounded in faith, assurance, and obedience. The challenge of Christology in black theology is the development of an understanding of Jesus of Nazareth with its feet on the ground, or, as our African sisters have put it: "One thing is certain: whatever the age or place, the most articulate Christology is that silently performed in the drama of everyday living."[76]

# 5

## ON BEING BLACK

Who are we that you are mindful of us?

— Psalms 8:4

Here, then, is the dilemma, and it is a puzzling one, I admit. No Negro who has given earnest thought to the situation of his people in America has failed, at some time in life, to find himself at these crossroads; has failed to ask himself at some time, "What, after all, am I? Am I an American or am I a Negro? Can I be both?"

— W. E. B. Du Bois

The question of the nature and destiny of humanity is one that theology shares with the other human sciences. The query "Who are we?" can be answered by biologists, psychologists, sociologists, philosophers, anthropologists, and others. However, the second part of the question asked by the Psalmist requires nothing less than a theological answer. Who and what we are in the sight of God and what there is about us that merits God's attention are the proper subject matter of a theological anthropology. Indeed, no systematic theology is complete without a significant consideration of human nature and destiny as it relates to God.

African-American theology does not escape the requirement to explicate its understanding of humanity. However, the social, political, historical, and cultural contexts in which that theological discourse takes place give this question a distinctive cast. People of African descent in Europe and North America have not been able to address the question of what it means to be human without, first, wrestling with what it means to be black.[1] One could argue that the question of being black was separated from the question of being human by the elevation of the factor of race to a normative status in relation to the human being. Thus in preslavery, precolonial Africa, one might assume that the question of being black never arose. Within their caste-like and

99

neocolonial status, black people continue to struggle to answer the question of what it means to be black (and human), caught between the identity that their oppressors attempt to force upon them and the identity that is theirs by their own conviction and by divine decree.

The true nature of black humanity has been veiled by a litany of stereotypes endemic to western European culture. People of African descent have been described as inferior, savage, profane, and invisible; they have been called outsiders, intruders, interlopers, and subhuman beasts. Zora Neale Hurston, demonstrating how powerful these images can be, vividly described African-American women as "the mules of the world." It is unfortunate that, historically, the European-American Christian church has accepted and employed these negative images of people of African-descent in its own theology. Even in an enlightened society on the verge of a new millennium, the question of the humanity of black people and others is shrouded by racist associations.

Spanish-speaking people are characterized as lazy, Asians as untrustworthy, and black people as criminals. Members of these communities find themselves having to work through a myriad of preliminary issues in order to get to the central question of what it means to be human. A theological anthropology that would speak to the humanity of people of African descent in the contemporary world must also address what it means to be black. This chapter will examine the doctrine of humanity in black theology by treating the idea of humanity in African-American history and culture, investigating the relationship between racism and the Christian conception of humanity, describing the major positions on the doctrine of humanity in early black theological discourse, and in conclusion, briefly explicating the three dimensions of human existence in African-American religious thought.

### The Problem of Humanity in African-American Experience

The theme of the nature and destiny of humanity in African-American religious thought is, understandably, dominated by the issue of racism. However, it would be a mistake to assume that there is no positive content to an African-American understanding of humanity. In fact, one of the sources of resistance to the ignominious estimations of the humanity of black people was the African understanding of their humanity. It is ironic that the suffering and oppression of people of African descent involved the degradation of their humanity while their indigenous religious and philosophical thought is based on the elevation of their humanity. John S. Mbiti argues that humanity — more specifically, humanity in relationship to God — is the central theme of traditional African thought. "Man is at the very centre of existence, and African peoples see everything else in its relation to this central position of man. God is the explanation of man's origin and sustenance: it is as if God exists for the sake of man."[2] Another African scholar concurs, noting that "God is; hence man is — that is the core of African belief."[3]

A person is recognized as *possessing* a body but as *being* spiritual. This creates an ambiguity but not a dichotomy in Afrocentric thought on the human person. While the spiritual dimension is essential to human existence, there is very little of the European tendency to denigrate the body. The body is not a hindrance but a vehicle for the true expression of the spiritual. This spiritual essence is, for all practical purposes, inseparable from the body, because both make up the totality of the human person. Thus it is difficult to discuss or completely understand the ongoing essence or immortal aspect of humanity in African thought in terms of a "body" versus "soul," or "pneuma" versus "sarx," for example. The difficulty is more than linguistic: it is also ideational. In traditional theological thought the notion of the immortality of the soul is usually discussed in individualistic terms. In African thought, life, whether temporal or eternal, "is something communal. This is signified by the phrase 'our life' in which the plural is commonly used to designate the life of a single individual."[4] Another feature of African thought is the belief that that which is immortal in the human being is a vital force. "[It] becomes evident that we are dealing with a dynamic element, not a mere entity or static being. It is something very close to being the life-essence of man which draws from the very life-essence of the universe."[5]

The idea of humanity in African traditional thought is summed up in the phrase "existence in relation" and is undergirded by two principles: that of indwelling and that of interaction. Indwelling refers to the notion that the human being participates in the divine so completely that the boundary between the natural and the supernatural diminishes almost beyond definition. The remnants of this idea are evident in African-American religious thought in the absence of strict boundaries between the sacred and the secular. Interaction refers to the notion that no person can achieve the fullness of life apart from the group. "Within the one communal and dynamic existence, for good or for ill, every man influences the individual existence of the other man, and they influence his in the same manner."[6] One, then, cannot separate communal and individual existence. As John S. Mbiti puts it, "What then is the individual and where is his [or her] place in the community? In traditional life, the individual does not and cannot exist alone except corporately. He owes his existence to other people, including those of past generations and his contemporaries. He is simply part of the whole. The community must therefore make, create or produce the individual; for the individual depends on the corporate group."[7]

This emphasis on the group's role in the formation of the individual is a radical departure from the individualism that has marked European-American theological anthropology since the time of Augustine. However, it should be noted that the corporate understanding of the human person in African traditional thought is very similar to the understanding of the human person in the Hebrew writings of the Bible and may shed some light on why enslaved Africans found the biblical writings both familiar and compelling.

Slavery, and its theological justification, introduced a new set of issues for African thought on the human person. The physical color of the African became a way of marking the slave. It took on a symbolic significance and in time became associated with a defective religion, savage behavior (as defined by the captors), bestiality, and finally as the mark of unforgivable sin.[8] However, the negative assessment of their humanity foisted upon them by the slaveholding community did not prevent African slaves from affirming — in both direct and indirect ways — their innate conviction that they were fully human. Sojourner Truth's haunting question "Ain't I a Woman?" was not merely rhetorical, but continues to demand an affirmative answer in light of the historic and continuing struggle of African-American women.

Some slaves even found it possible to employ the tools of traditional theological discourse to display an understanding of the religious dimension of human existence as profound as any in the European-American theological tradition. One ex-slave wrote, "There is a man in a man. The soul is the medium between God and man. God speaks to us through our conscience, and the reasoning is so loud that we seem to hear a voice."[9] Mechal Sobel observed a distinctive affirmation of the existence of "a little me within the big me" in African traditional thought.[10] These examples are evidence of genuine theological reflection on the nature of humanity by African slaves. In fact, it should come as no surprise that the conundrum of the nature of the human person would give rise to thought among enslaved Africans because their very condition of bondage made the issue inescapable.

The end of legal slavery did not signal the end of the African-Americans' struggle to define themselves as human beings. Rather, that struggle took on a new shape at the beginning of the twentieth century. The person most responsible for the contours of contemporary thinking on what it means to be black in a white society is W. E. B. Du Bois. In his classic essay, "The Conservation of Races," Du Bois discusses the concept of race and its importance within a total understanding of human history. He begins by noting that, although their race is the marker by which their life-chances are assessed and their worth measured, black people are constantly urged to discount race and adopt the notion of the sisterhood and brotherhood of all humanity. "The

Negro has been led to deprecate and minimize race distinctions, to believe intensely that out of one blood God created all nations, and to speak of human brotherhood as though it were the possibility of an already dawning tomorrow. Nevertheless, in our calmer moments, we must acknowledge that human beings are divided into races."[11]

This emphasis on race — and Du Bois's subsequent and lifelong commitment to nationalism — stood in stark contrast to the direction of scientific thinking on anthropology. After freeing itself from dogmatic interpretations of human history found in the Bible, the scientific community in the nineteenth century moved toward the consensus that all human beings share a single ancestor, and that all, then, are related. At the same time, this same scientific community continued to develop theories of racial inferiority. Thus the major difference between quasi-biblical and scientific arguments for racial inferiority was that the former asserted that black people were inferior by some divine decree, while the latter asserted that black people were simply lower on the evolutionary scale than white people.

In light of the complexity and the ambiguity of anthropological thought at the end of the nineteenth century, Du Bois sought to define race in a way that would promote the dignity of African-Americans. He argues that

> the history of the world is the history not of individuals but of groups, not of nations, but of races, and he who ignores or seeks to override the race idea in human history ignores or overrides the central thought of all history. What, then, is a race? It is a vast family of human beings, generally of common blood and language, always of common history, traditions, and impulses, who are both voluntarily and involuntarily striving together for the accomplishment of certain more or less vividly conceived ideals of life.[12]

For Du Bois, the central issue in the concept of race is whether one is a member of a race by "blood" or by "history." In other words, do physiology and biology define the human person, or do history and culture? Du Bois argues that when it comes to races,

> no mere physical distinctions would really define or explain the deeper differences, the cohesiveness, and continuity of these groups. The deeper differences are spiritual, psychical differences — undoubtedly based on the physical, but infinitely transcending them. The forces that bind together [races] are, then, first, their race identity and common blood; secondly, and more important, a common history, common laws and religion, similar habits of thought and a conscious striving together for certain ideals of life.[13]

Du Bois defined race in terms of history and culture rather than blood or physical distinctions, because of the ambiguity of his own

racial background. His own mixed heritage forced him to ask himself
what it was that bound him so tightly to other people of African descent, although, physically, he had as much European blood as African
in his veins.[14] The distinction between blood and history in the definition of the human person and Du Bois's choice of the latter may be
rooted in an Afrocentric anthropology.

To define a person on the basis of his or her physical distinctions
tends toward biological determinism, undergirded by individualistic
assumptions, and leads to the conclusion that whatever a person is
or is to become is completely programmed in her or his genetic
makeup. To define a person on the basis of his or her historical and
cultural associations tends toward a spiritual dynamism, undergirded
by communal assumptions, and leads to the conclusion that whatever a person is or is to become, i.e., that person's destiny, is vital
and open. Although Du Bois did not explore the theological significance of his understanding of humanity, his ideas provided the context
for subsequent discussions of racism and the Christian understanding
of humanity.

### Racism and the Christian Understanding of Humanity

George Kelsey's classic work, *Racism and the Christian Understanding
of Man*, is a foundational text for the development of Christian anthropology in black theology. In this work, the author brings to bear
a scathing critique of the marriage between European-American Christianity and racism. His argument is that racism is a form of idolatrous
faith, a truncated search for meaning. He notes that racism did not
have, at the outset, the character of a faith, but acquired it by virtue of
the social, political, and economic factors associated with slavery and
colonialism.

Racism is a modern phenomenon, Kelsey argues, that is to be
distinguished from ethnocentrism. Ethnocentrism is a universal and
perennial characteristic of "tribal, territorial, national, religious, and
cultural groups" and refers to "the belief in the unique value and right-
ness of one's own group."[15] Divisions become racial when something
more than ordinary group pride is involved. "The line of demarcation
between groups is racial when the in-group seeks to keep its 'blood'
pure, no matter what the cultural state of affairs may be and no matter
where the lines of political jurisdiction may be located. Ethnocentrism
is not racial when it is based on religion, culture, class, or shared mem-
ories and experience."[16] Du Bois had argued earlier that an emphasis
on "bloodlines" as the marker for race was certainly impractical in the
U.S. context. Kelsey advances that argument by identifying the violence

associated with attempts to maintain racial purity. In addition, what Du Bois had defined as "race," that is, those persons sharing a common history, religion, and culture, Kelsey refers to as ethnocentrism. Ethnocentrism, religious intolerance, economic expansionism, and the power to suppress effectively those not of one's own group form the basis of modern racism. This racism soon evolved into a system of meaning and value complete with a theological infrastructure. The difference between ethnocentrists and racists, Kelsey argues, is that the latter have the political power to deny the humanity of the former.

Racism is also a perverted form of faith that alienates and divides human beings from one another. Its roots run much deeper than the cultural, political, or economic bases of human stratification. It is not the result, according to Kelsey, of faulty knowledge or ignorance. "Accordingly, the basic racist affirmation of superiority, on the one hand, and inferiority, on the other, is not an empirical generalization as is commonly supposed. Rather, it is an affirmation concerning the fundamental nature of human beings. It is a declaration of faith that is neither supported nor weakened by any objective body of fact. Racism is an expression of the will to believe."[17] Racism, then, is, by definition, suprarational.

Because racism assumes black people to be defective in their essential being, and because Christians believe that all being issues forth from God, God's creative activity is called into question. Because black people are supposedly the victims of a "double Fall," first into the human predicament of sin, and second into the peculiar plight of blackness, the question of God's goodness and power arises with respect to people of African descent. In other words, the theodicy question becomes paramount.[18] When race is elevated to the final point of reference for the decisions and actions of a group and is combined with the wherewithal to enforce those actions and decisions to the detriment of other groups, the notion of a God who can stand in judgment over the race is sacrificed:

> As the value-center, the race is the source of value, and it is at the same time the object of value. No questions can be raised about the rightness or wrongness of the race; it is the value-center which throws light on all other value. Criminals, degenerates, and even enemies have worth and goodness if they are members of the in-race. They have a goodness and worth which is not found in the most noble character of members of out-races, for goodness and worth are only secondarily qualities of behavior and character. Primarily they are qualities of being. Goodness and worth inhere in being that is worthy. If noble character inheres in a racially defective being, that person of noble character is nonetheless depraved, for the nobility he has achieved inheres in his unalterably corrupt humanity.[19]

Racism, then, in Kelsey's estimation, sets up a competition between the supremacy of the race and the supremacy of God. At best, this forces racist Christians into a kind of polytheism, and at worst the God of the Bible is jettisoned altogether, in material terms, leaving a thin, religious veneer for their self-adoration.

Kelsey concludes that racism is founded on three basic assumptions. First, racism is a form of naturalism. It assumes that

> man owes his existence to nature and nature controls his destiny. Nature had condemned inferior races and blessed the superior race. This means that the fundamental thing about a man is his body, specifically his genetic structure. Mental and spiritual qualities depend upon the natural quality, and are, in fact, but expressions of it. This naturalistic view of man is diametrically opposed to the biblical doctrine of the creation of man in the image of God.[20]

Second, racism is a plan of action. Racism may manifest itself in the concern for racial purity through segregating or quarantining those who are considered inferior or tainted, but because the flaw of the out-race is a defect in their very being, Kelsey argues that the end or goal of that plan is even more sinister:

> Despite the prevailing practice of segregation, the logic of racism is genocide. The logic of racism is genocide because that which is wrong with an out-race is its fundamental being. . . . The problem of defective humanity cannot be resolved by segregation and quarantine; it requires the final solution. The final solution is extermination.[21]

This political plan, argues Kelsey, is not simply an extremist fantasy or a twisted misconstrual of the aims of the racist. It is, in fact, what keeps racism alive. Thus the naturalistic view of humanity is the philosophical basis of racism, and the political plan is its vital impulse.

Third, racism is a philosophy of history.

> Racism teaches that the whole cultural superstructure rests on the genetic substructure. . . . [It teaches] that the quality of the superior race is the absolute determinant of history, and that quality is biological. The essence of man is his genetic structure. . . . [Racism] also elevates the alleged superior race to the status of lords rather than bearers of history. Meaningful history is identical with racial history.[22]

The power of Kelsey's argument is the result of his belief that racism is a distorted faith that contends with the true biblical faith. His thought has a distinctively "neo-orthodox" character and shares themes and emphases found in the methodologies of Karl Barth, Reinhold Niebuhr, and others. His description of racism as idolatry is reminiscent of the neo-orthodox critique of religion as misdirected faith, a faith directed toward humanity and away from God. Like the neo-orthodox theologians, Kelsey points to the subordination of reason to faith, in his assertion that racism is suprarational. Kelsey also argues that the racists' assumptions about humanity invariably lead to racists' conclusions about the nature of God. In this respect, he echoes the neo-orthodox refrain that humanity can be understood only in relation to God.

Kelsey's work, though dated, remains an influential text for black theological anthropology. A more contemporary, but brief, analysis of this same issue is provided by Cornel West in his book *Prophesy Deliverance!* Drawing on current philosophical thought on the nature of intellectual discourse, West argues that "the idea of white supremacy emerges partly because of the powers within the structure of modern discourse — powers to produce and prohibit, develop and delimit, forms of rationality, scientificity, and objectivity which set perimeters and draw boundaries for the intelligibility, availability, and legitimacy of certain ideas."[23] West convincingly demonstrates that racism cannot be adequately explained by means of social, political, economic, or psychological cause and effect. He concludes that "the emergence of the idea of white supremacy as an object of modern discourse seems contingent, in that there was no iron necessity at work in the complex configuration of metaphors, notions, categories, and norms that produce and promote this idea. There is an accidental character to the discursive emergence of modern racism."[24]

The views of both Kelsey and West reflect the major issues with which early black theologians struggled in their attempts to formulate a Christian anthropology for the African-American religious community. Kelsey's description of the profound, fundamental, basic, essential, fideistic character of racism points to the fact that racism affects almost every aspect of human existence for African-Americans. West's insight into the "accidental" character of the emergence of modern racism points to the fact that racism is not part of God's plan and that it is, in the final analysis, an unnecessary insult.

## The Doctrine of Humanity in Black Theology

Early black theologians were confronted with a dual task of asserting that African-Americans were no less or no more human than any other people. On the one hand, they faced the deep-seated belief that black people were especially predisposed to sin, and that this predisposition was related to the color of their skin.[25] Thus black theologians were compelled to break the historic association between sin and the stain of blackness. On the other hand, black theologians had to account for the persistent notion of the special destiny of African people in

Europe and the Americas and the related issue of African-Americans
as the "chosen people."

Although the claim to chosenness may instill a sense of pride and
self-worth in an oppressed people, the concept is often given to mis-
interpretation and distortion. One such distortion is discussed by the
British essayist Bertrand Russell in his suggestive piece "The Superior
Virtue of the Oppressed." He argues that

> one of the persistent delusions of mankind is that some sections of the
> human race are morally better than others. This belief has many different
> forms, none of which has any rational basis.... [People] tend to think ill
> of their neighbors and acquaintances, and therefore to think well of the
> sections of mankind to which they themselves do not belong.... A rather
> curious form of this admiration for groups to which the admirer does
> not belong is the belief in the superior virtue of the oppressed: subject
> nations, the poor, women, and children.[26]

In describing traditional liberal attitudes toward women and black
people, Russell argues that European-American men were quite willing to grant them a special kind of virtue, but at the price of political
equality. Women were virtuous because of their special role as mother
and nurturer, and only within the confines of those social parameters
could their special virtue be preserved. Likewise, "negroes" were virtuous precisely because of their "earthiness," and that virtue would be
destroyed if they were allowed to participate in the hard-edged business of the political economy. "The belief in their 'spiritual' superiority
was part and parcel of the determination to keep them inferior economically and politically."[27] In the long run, however, this strategy of
domination was doomed:

> The idealizing of the victim is useful for a time: if virtue is the greatest
> of goods and if subjection makes people virtuous, it is kind to refuse
> them power, since it would destroy their virtue. If it is difficult for a rich
> man to enter the kingdom of heaven, it is a noble act on his part to keep
> his wealth and so imperil his eternal bliss for the benefit of his poorer
> brethren. It was a fine self-sacrifice on the part of men to relieve women
> of the dirty work of politics. And so on. But sooner or later the oppressed
> class will argue that its superior virtue is a reason in favor of its having
> power, and the oppressors will find their own weapon turned against
> them. When at last power has been equalized, it becomes apparent to
> everybody that all the talk about superior virtue was nonsense, and that
> it was quite unnecessary as a basis for the claim to equality.[28]

The idea that African-Americans are distinguished from other people
because of their moral or spiritual superiority is extremely attractive and
even understandable in light of the moral and spiritual baseness of their
oppressors. Biblical notions of the "saving remnant" or "the chosen

people" must, however, be interpreted in the light of the concomitant claim that all people are created equal in the sight of God.

There is an almost universal tendency, when speaking of human equality in the context of the disparate experiences of the oppressed and the oppressors, to assume that the burden rests with the oppressed to find common ground with the oppressors. Or, more specifically, it is assumed that black people must demonstrate their equality with European-Americans. The implicit arrogance of this position often masks the fact that it is the task of those who have abused and misused their privilege to show that they are at least as human as those who have resisted their oppression with grace and determination. In this sense, the claims of Du Bois, Gayraud S. Wilmore, and others who argue for the aptness of the title "chosen people" for African-Americans can be understood to point to the gifts of black folk to the culture in which they find themselves. Thus chosenness, defined in this way, refers to the cultural and religious treasures that a people can share rather than the prerogative that they might forcibly take in their dealings with others.

At the same time, the idea of chosenness must be separated from the notion of any intrinsic superiority on the part of the oppressed. The term "chosen" is not one that a people claim for themselves, for that would lead to the kind of racial arrogance that was responsible for the establishment of apartheid in South Africa, for example. Chosenness is, rather, the name for the special quality and pattern of their experiences as human beings that the oppressed perceive as they look back over their sojourn. Ancient Israel could only claim the title "chosen people" in retrospect, by remembering what God had done for them. There was little in their culture or folkways that would warrant the claim to moral superiority. What made them special was not simply that they were chosen, but that it was Yahweh who chose them.

This point is convincingly made by Latin American theologian Gustavo Gutiérrez in a paper analyzing the results of the 1978 meeting of Latin American Catholic Bishops in Puebla, Mexico. In interpreting the phrase "a preferential option for the poor," Gutiérrez cautions against linking a preference for the poor to some idea of their moral superiority. "The preference for the poor is based on the fact that God, as Christ shows us, loves them for their concrete, real condition of poverty, 'whatever may be' their moral or spiritual disposition."[29] He goes on to note that the Beatitudes, especially those that speak of "the blessedness of the poor" are first and foremost statements that tell us who God is, and only secondarily refer to the nature of those human beings who are the poor. That is, while "blessedness" does refer to the openness that the poor may have to the word of God, the primary emphasis is on God and God's freely given and unconditional love for the poor.[30] If African-American theologians are to assert that God holds

African-Americans in special favor, then the basis of that favor must be found in God's freedom and love, and not in romantic assumptions about their moral or spiritual excellence.

In order to describe what is essential in human existence from an African-American perspective, it is necessary to move from a consideration of the virtue of black folk to a consideration of their power. To exist is "to stand out from something," but it is also "to stand within something." Existence, then, contrary to traditional notions, is not a passive state, but is a dynamic interaction — perhaps even a struggle — with one's environment. Thus power is necessary for human existence. Nathan Wright, Jr., writing on black power, argued that "all men need the power to *become*. Indeed, the Greek words for power (*bia*) and life (*bios*) reflect the essential interrelationship of power and life. Power is basic to life. Without power, life cannot become what it must be."[31] Power is the *animus* of human existence because people need the ability to individuate — that is, to exercise freedom — and the ability to relate — that is, to exercise love. If power is essential to authentic human existence, then the question with which early black theologians were faced was the function of that power. Is the function of power related to or aimed at freedom, individuation, and autonomy, or is it related to or aimed at association, solidarity, and community?

James Cone, in his early work, argues that freedom is the essence of the human being. The influence of Sartre and Camus, as well as Paul Tillich, is evident in his theological anthropology. However, his employment of the insights from these thinkers should not obscure the fact that this emphasis is indigenous to the African-American religious perspective. The idea that human beings were created for freedom surged forth in the eloquent, untutored testimonies of African slaves, as well as in the urbane writings of the black intelligentsia of the eighteenth and nineteenth centuries. This freedom manifested itself as a divine mandate. Simply put, salvation required the seizing of one's freedom from whatever and whoever hindered human beings from becoming that which God created them to be. Likewise, sin is defined as the rejection of that demand. This freedom is essential to humanity because it is the image of God pressed upon the human being in the moment of creation. When God set out to make humanity in God's own image, freedom became the guiding principle in human existence. As James Cone notes,

> The image of God refers to the way in which God intends human beings to live in the world. The image of God is thus more than rationality, more than what so-called neo-orthodox theologians call divine-human encounter. In a world in which persons are oppressed, the image is human nature in rebellion against the structures of oppression. It is humanity involved in the liberation struggle against the forces of inhumanity.[32]

For Cone, the great paradox of human existence is evident in that this intensely personal desire for freedom creates community among the oppressed. In their common quest solidarity is born. The devotion to freedom gives meaning to the suffering of the oppressed, yet it renders a critique of human suffering by declaring it to be contrary to the will of God. The paradoxical relationship of freedom and suffering is crystallized in the exemplary passion of Jesus Christ.

> The life of Jesus also discloses that freedom is bound up with suffering. It is not possible to be for him and not realize that one has chosen an existence in suffering. . . . Christians can never be content as long as their sisters and brothers are enslaved. They must suffer with them, knowing that freedom for Jesus Christ is always freedom for the oppressed.[33]

Freedom is related in a similar way to blackness. The quest for freedom among African-Americans affirms blackness as basic to their very identity, but at the same time it destroys the ability of the oppressor to define blackness in ways that are destructive to human dignity. Cone's central contribution here is a perspective on the complexity of human existence for the oppressed. As he puts it, "This is the paradox of human existence. Freedom is the opposite of oppression, but only the oppressed are truly free."[34] In this view, all people are endowed with the image of God. Whether that image is material or only formal is a theological question that has fueled some of the great debates in the history of European-American theology. More germane for African-Americans, however, is that without empowerment that freedom remains trapped in the unactualized realm of human capacity and potential. It is, then, the emphasis on power — in Cone's words, "black power" — that makes human salvation real.

J. Deotis Roberts, in his early theological writings, argues that human beings are meant for loving relationships. In his view, the pursuit of freedom is a necessary but not sufficient goal of human existence:

> A doctrine of man in black theology should begin with the human condition and aim at liberation through wholeness. Wholeness is related to a total view of man as body, mind, soul, and spirit. Theologies of the body are likely to be concerned primarily with carnal man and man's place in nature. Theologies of revolution aim primarily at the collective. The approach of black theology must be existential as well as political.[35]

Moreover, a black theological anthropology must move beyond traditional philosophical interpretations:

> We need an understanding of human nature that can bring to black people, under the conditions of their existence, sanity and wholeness. A perfectly rational interpretation of man, however much applauded by

white theologians, would be "dry bones" for the faith of the black masses
if it did not take seriously their life-and-death struggle in this society.[36]

This anthropological perspective is centered on the notion of
the collective dimension of human existence. Referring to African-
Americans, Roberts notes that "we are persons-in-community. Our
wholeness as persons depends upon a healthy group life in families,
communities, and nations. Our theological understanding of man is
concerned about the ethics regulating interpersonal relations."[37] Because relationship, community, and association are essential to human
existence, for Roberts, the image of God in the human person is described in terms of love, the ability to share the pain, burdens, sorrows,
and joys of others.

Freedom, according to Roberts, is experienced within the context
of responsibility to others. Therefore, it is related to the ethical dimension of human life. "Humans experience *relative* rather than *absolute*
freedom. But human freedom is sufficient to render man inexcusable
for his choices."[38] Sin, then, is the alienation from both God and the
rest of humanity that results from the misuse of the freedom that has
been granted by God. Sin is alienation precisely because humanity was
created for association. The overcoming of this state of sin is found in
reconciliation. Roberts centers the salvific work of Christ in the New
Testament proclamation that "God was in Christ reconciling the world
to Godself." The power, then, which makes this reconciliation possible is not a Nietzschean effort of the emancipated personality, but the
cooperation of God's gracious desire for reconciliation and the human
longing for association, "for we are heirs of a grace that *enables* as well
as *sanctifies*. To love those who love you is a human act, but to love
the oppressor and reject the oppression can be an act made possible by
the agency of divine power alone."[39]

For Roberts, as for Cone, power serves human need in theological anthropology. For Cone, the principal function of empowerment
is justification of the oppressed before God and the grounding of
true humanity in the freely given acceptance of the oppressed by
God. For Roberts, the main function of empowerment is the sanc-
tification of the oppressed in their relationships with God and the
human family. This is symbolized in the sacramental act of reconciliation with God and other human beings. Both writers recognize
that power is essential to human existence. Each emphasizes a different but crucial human need, the need for autonomy and the need
for community. Of course, in the final analysis, each must affirm
both.

## Three Dimensions of Human Existence

A common framework in many systematic theologies used in articulating the multidimensionality of human existence is to view humanity as created, fallen, and redeemed. In many cases the aesthetics and symmetry of this schema make it difficult to see that every statement one makes about the condition of humanity is contextual. That is, from what and by whom are we created? From what have we fallen? To what and by whom are we redeemed? These questions are not necessarily unique to the Christian faith, nor need they be construed as consciously religious questions. In fact, at the heart of every social philosophy is a distinctive anthropology. Every political and economic theory embodies a particular idea of humanity. Capitalism is driven by the profit motive because there is an implicit assumption that human beings are essentially acquisitive. Various forms of socialism are funded by notions of the ideal society because there is an assumption that human beings are naturally altruistic. Communism is based on the idea of a powerful state because human beings supposedly need centralized authority to keep their baser instincts in check. Most social theories approach the question of the nature of humanity from a general, abstract perspective.

From the perspective of the Christian faith, however, it is more appropriate to ask these questions in light of their immediate and personal dimensions. The question "Who are we that God is mindful of us?" is not merely the plea of anguished souls *in search of themselves*. Rather, it points to the autobiographical starting point of Christian anthropology. It is autobiographical because it is the key to the map of human existence. Jürgen Moltmann notes:

> What is needed then is to find a lively equilibrium between the fundamental self-questioning of man, and the answers by means of which he takes control of himself. Man cannot continue indefinitely in a radical attitude of questioning. He would then never succeed in giving form to his life. Nor can he tie himself down and be content with the external face which his time and his culture give to him. Then he would stagnate. He reaches an equilibrium if he respects the limits which make man's forms of living authentic, and recognizes that in the changes of cultures and of images of man there is, for all the seriousness and hope of the latter, a provisional element.[40]

Sallie McFague observes that "the theologian-autobiographer becomes not the vessel of an idea or belief (a spatial metaphor), but a map of the movement of a belief in a human life (a linear metaphor). Autobiographies are paradigms, as parables are; they are contemplative possibilities which can have an indirect effect on others; they give no rules and recite no doctrines but present us with some *possibilities* for living out."[41] Here it is evident that there is a connection between the existential and the ethical facets of human life. That is, one cannot answer the question "Who am I?" without also answering the question "How shall we live?" That much European-American autobiography is centered around these two questions and that European-American Christian anthropology is compelled to address the fact of human life and the possibilities for living out that life are intimately related.

The starting point of Christian anthropology in black theology is also autobiographical. Because the beginnings of the black autobiographical tradition are to be found in the slave narratives, there we might also find the emerging anthropology of African-American Christians. Examining the contexts in which the slave narratives were written, William L. Andrews observes:

> Traditionally, the Negro had been considered a kind of "Canaanite, a man devoid of Logos," whose low social status was "a punishment resulting from sin or from a natural defect of soul." Indeed, some apologists for slavery predicated their arguments on the idea that the Negro had not been endowed by his creator with a soul. Before the fugitive slave narrator could hope for success in restoring political and economic freedom to American blacks, the black spiritual autobiographer had to lay the necessary intellectual groundwork by proving that black people were as much chosen by God for eternal salvation as whites. Without the black spiritual autobiography's reclamation of the Afro-American's spiritual birthright, the fugitive slave narrative could not have made such a cogent case for black civil rights in the crisis years between 1830 and 1865.[42]

The same issues that concerned the slave narrator constituted the essence of theological inquiry into the meaning of human existence for people of African descent. When racism so distorts the cultural perception of a people, Christian anthropology cannot remain a quaint speculative affair. It becomes a necessary and consuming quest. As the African theologian Manas Buthelezi eloquently put it:

> Man suddenly discovers his humanity in caricature form: he realizes that he is neither what he thought he was nor what he would like to be. Out of this mental and emotional torture arise a number of existential questions: "After all, who am I?" "What is the destiny of my being and mode of existence?" "How can I so live as to overcome what militates against the realization of my destiny as a human being?" This in essence is the quest for true or authentic humanity. For a black man such as I am, this issue is loaded with historical accidents which project a peculiar dimension of the basic quest: "Can I realize my authentic humanity in the medium of my blackness?" Is my blackness some fatalistic road-block in life or a context within which God has made it possible for me to be an authentic man?[43]

The autobiographical starting point of anthropology in black theology requires that the two questions mentioned above be addressed:

"Who are we?" and "How shall we live?" However, there is one ad-ditional query that appears in African-American autobiography but is absent in most European-American autobiographical writing. That question has to do with *location*. The experience of being taken from one's homeland and placed in strange territory had significant conse-quences for the slaves' understanding of themselves. That geographical disorientation was often instrumental in increasing the slaveowners' control over the slaves meant that the question of identity had to in-clude a consideration of life's ethical dimensions but also the social location of one's life.

While a full explication of an African-American Christian anthro-pology based on the observations outlined in this chapter must await another occasion, what follows is a possible framework around which such an anthropology might be constructed. This schema addresses the question "Who are we?" by relating the quest for identity and the fact of human creatureliness. It addresses the question "Where do we belong?" by exploring the theme of social dislocation in light of the biblical notion of the fallenness of humanity. Third, this framework examines the question "How shall we live?" by treating the ethical dimension of human character in the context of the reality of God's redemption.

What does it mean to be a creature of God in African-American experience? The quest for identity in African-American experience leads to a consideration of one's relation to God. The Bible asserts that human beings are created in the image of God. We discover who we are only in relation to God the creator. The traditional norms of theological discourse described that image in rational and moral terms. That is, human beings are genuine human beings to the extent that they are demonstrably rational and manifest the moral capacity to love, obey, and express commitment. An unstated norm assumed that true human beings were also created in the *physical* image of God. Of course, most theologians would not ad-mit this because God was assumed to be Spirit and without need for a body. Yet in European and European-American art and lit-erature images of God were, more than not, reflections of their creators.

Thus Africans who were introduced to and victimized by Christian-ity in the last four centuries had both their identity as a proud African people and their status as beloved creatures of God called into ques-tion. The creation narratives in the book of Genesis describe God's act of bringing human existence into being, the giving of names to those first creatures of God, and the creative potential given to those creatures by allowing them to name the co-inhabitants of God's world. An anthropology for black theology must affirm the quest for identity in African-American experience and the status of African-Americans as creations of God.

What then is the meaning of the Fall in African-American experience? Traditional ideas include descriptions of the Fall as constituting a diminished, distorted, and misguided rational capacity, and a bankrupted moral capacity. Here also there is an implicit assumption that corrupting influence of sin is physically visible. For African-Americans skin color has often been construed as such visible evidence. From the perspective of African-American experience the Fall is more often associated with the experience of dislocation or alienation connected with abduction and slavery. In the nineteenth and twentieth centuries the persistent desire of black Americans to return to Africa was evidence of this feeling of alienation. George Kent, describing the autobiography of the kidnapped African Gustavus Vassa, states that his story captures "the chaos swirling at the root of transplanted black life."[44] The theme of dislocation and its relation to the Fall is also a neglected theme in the creation narratives themselves. The expulsion of the first woman and man from the garden of Eden is as much the evidence as it is the consequence of the Fall. Although the motif of dislocation is not unique to African-American religious experience, an anthropology for black theology must address the issue of the Fall in relation to the alienation of black people from the place they call home.

Finally, what is the meaning of redemption in African-American religious experience? In the history of European and European-American theology redemption has referred to restored rational capacity (Aquinas) or to the moral capacity rehabilitated by unmerited grace. However, redemption in African-American religious experience tends to involve the totality of the human person, something more akin to the character of persons rather than some combination of their attributes. The purpose of human existence is to glorify God in every dimension of one's existence. To be redeemed is to be enabled to live life thusly. This is why the testimony of African slave Christians often focused on redemption as both the freedom and the demand to live one's life for God and for others. James McClendon argues that

> to have character, then, is to enter at a new level the realm of morality, the level at which one's person, with its continuities, its interconnections, its integrity, is ultimately involved in one's deeds.... It is most important here to recognize that character, though by definition deep-seated, is not necessarily rigid or unchangeable. A man's character is formed by the way he sees things, by his vision, we say. It is shaped by the ways he does things, by his style.[45]

Both character and redemption are related the question of "how shall we live?" Part of finding out who we are and where we belong is determining what the Lord requires of us. This requirement is most perfectly present in the life of Jesus Christ. Erich Auerbach, discussing the idea of humanity in ancient European literature, offers an unexpected insight into the meaning of Christ in defining authentic human existence:

> The story of Christ revealed not only the intensity of personal life but also its diversity and the wealth of its forms, for it transcended the limits of ancient mimetic aesthetics. Here man has lost his earthly dignity; everything can happen to him, and the classical division of genres has vanished; the distinction between the sublime and the vulgar style exists no longer. In the Gospels, as in ancient comedy, real persons of all classes make their appearance: fishermen and kings, high priests, publicans, and harlots participate in the action; and neither do those of exalted rank act in the style of classical tragedy, nor do the lowly behave as in a farce; quite the contrary, all social and aesthetic limits have been effaced.[46]

The common foundation and goal of human existence are exemplified in Christ's example and ministry. For black theology this means that its definition of what it means to be human must be conceived in relation to both God and one's neighbor. The words of African theologian Mercy Amba Oduyoye express this truth most poignantly:

> As baptized people, our suffering is salvific when taken on voluntarily and our sharing of the gifts of others gives us the ability to thank God who made us male and female. Happy and responsible in my being human and female, I shall be able to live a life of doxology in the human community, glorifying God for the gifts I receive in others and for the possibility I have of giving myself freely for the well-being of the community while remaining responsible and responsive to God. It is only thus that I can say I am fully human. When we are all willing to see the humanity of the other, then we can begin the task of understanding a Christian anthropology.[47]

# 6

## THE COMMUNITY OF FAITH
## AND THE SPIRIT OF FREEDOM

For where two or three are gathered in my name, there am I in the midst
of them.

— Matthew 18:20

One of the most perplexing problems in black theology is that of
ecclesiology. Early black theologians articulated unique views of the
meaning of God, the person and work of Christ, and the nature and
destiny of humanity. However, no comprehensive theological statement on the identity and mission of the church found ready expression
in nascent black theology. This does not mean that black theologians
had nothing to say about the African-American church, but that the
distinctiveness of the black church as church was assumed and therefore its life and work were used in theological argument as warrant or
substantiation for black theology.

The question that lies at the threshold of any current attempt to
frame an ecclesiology for black theology is "Why has a comprehensive
ecclesiology of the African-American church not been developed?"

### The Problem of Community
### in African-American Religious Experience

There are at least two major factors that have made the ecclesiological task difficult for black theologians. The first is the heterogeneity of
African-American congregations. Here the question is "what are the
defining characteristics of the black church?" Some African-American
Christians see their denominational affiliation as, perhaps, the most crucial aspect of their ecclesial identity. In this instance denominational
loyalty, i.e., being Baptist, Methodist, or Pentecostal, is tantamount to

119

being a Christian. Other African-American Christians see their congregations as more representative of the "true" black church because they can trace their beginning to some African-American founding mothers or fathers. Hence, it is sometimes assumed that the members of the historically black Baptist, Methodist, Pentecostal and other groups represent the authentic black church. However, the presence of large numbers of African-Americans in the Presbyterian, United Methodist, Roman Catholic, and Anglican ecclesial communities poses a critical challenge to this notion. Still other African-American Christians associate the "true" black church with certain styles of worship. Thus it is sometimes assumed that a strident and energetic form of worship and preaching is more authentic than a more staid and subdued form. The unique context and the array of traditions, customs, and styles within African-American Christianity make the formulation of a black ecclesiology difficult.

The second factor impeding the ecclesiological task is that the notion of community is so basic to African-American religious experience that the normal doctrinal explanations for church formation are not sufficient. The black church was not born primarily of doctrinal disputes and heresy trials, but rather emerged out of deep-seated cultural tendencies toward solidarity and association among African-American Christians.

This second factor suggests that an African-American ecclesiology must take seriously, if not as fundamental, the black church in the United States in the eighteenth and nineteenth centuries. The establishment of African Baptist congregations in the southern part of the United States signalled the institutional emergence of distinctive forms of ecclesial life among African-Americans. When a group of African-Americans were pulled from their knees in St. George's Methodist Episcopal Church in Philadelphia, the forces that had been clandestinely pulling against one another finally resulted in the shattering of any notion of a unified church in America. These events have established enduring patterns in the social understanding of the churches in the U.S. In his classic work *The Social Sources of Denominationalism*, published in 1929, H. Richard Niebuhr argues that the segregation that has historically defined congregations is deeply rooted in the culture. "The sufficient reason for the frankness with which the color line has been drawn in the church is the fact that race discrimination is so respectable an attitude in America that it could be accepted by the church without subterfuge of any sort."[1] Howard Thurman, writing twenty years later, observed that "most of the accepted social behavior-patterns assume segregation to be normal — if normal then correct; if correct, then moral; if moral, then religious."[2]

As important as the social and political factors were in the formation of the African-American church, it would be a mistake to assume that there were no positive or constructive reasons for its emergence. The innate African religious sensibilities of black Christians affirmed the importance of the group, clan, or tribe to their survival and prosperity, and the sacredness of life in all of its dimensions. Because of the belief in the importance of the group early black Christians often thought of themselves as God's people. The conviction that they were the people of God did not descend on them all at once, but came through the unhurried and timely revelation of God. The commonality of their oppression drew them together, and along with this sense of cohesiveness came the revelation that they were also God's people. If the Middle Passage and slavery obscured their history as Africans, they found in the biblical story a sense of themselves as remembered by God. This aspect of the life of the black church is the reason for its tendency toward engagement with the world and social witness.

The sense of the sacredness of life undergirded the conviction of black slave Christians that they lived under a mandate to "be ye holy." In spite of the moral vacuum created by slavery and oppression, early black Christians knew the difference between sinners and the saved. One scholar observed that religious ceremonies among early African-American Baptists were very exclusive with regard to sinners and the saved. Those who were not demonstrably born again could have no part in the worship of the redeemed.[3] The emphasis on holiness is one possible explanation for the separatism that marked the emergence of the African-American church in the United States and the social criticism that that separatism implied.

Although a comprehensive theological treatment of the African-American church remains to be done, scholars from other disciplines have examined the genius of the black church from its inception in slavery through the first half of the twentieth century. In his classic work, *The History of the Negro Church*, Carter G. Woodson describes "the religious development of the Negro in the United States."[4] Woodson's text focuses on the biographical history of the African-American church. He describes pioneer preachers such as George Liele and Andrew Bryant, pillars of the early African Baptist church. He provides insights into the pilgrimages of Lemuel Haynes, an African-American Congregationalist minister, and John Gloucester, an early black Presbyterian minister. Woodson's treatise also examines the institutional history of the African-American church. He traces the rise of the independent black church movement in the United States. His insights into the relationship between Richard Allen and the St. George Methodist Episcopal Church give richness to the "ecclesiogenesis" of the black church. He also recounts the role of James Varick in the origins of the African Methodist Episcopal Zion church, and of Thomas Paul as the founder of the Abyssinian Baptist Church in New York City. Woodson takes note of the establishment of schools, colleges, and seminaries by these fledgling congregations. With the aid of those to whom Woodson refers as "northern white philanthropists" Shaw University was established in 1865 and Morehouse College in 1867, among dozens of others. African-American churches also established schools without the aid of outside philanthropy. These included Simmons University in Louisville, Morris Brown College, and Livingstone College.

Although its perspective is limited, Woodson's analysis does give the reader a sense of the African-American church as a political phenomenon. It is this political dimension of the African-American church's existence that, according to Woodson, is the locus of both its strengths and its liabilities. While acknowledging that a significant portion of the property owned by African-Americans was church property, he criticizes black Christians for spending an inordinate amount of their income on maintaining their churches and paying for their edifices.[5]

Woodson also acknowledges that many of the ministers in the African-American church were involved in the political arena. He notes that in many instances these ministers argued that their presence in the political sphere was advantageous for their people. However, Woodson concludes that ministers have been most effective when protesting the injustices of the political system from the outside. A more damning criticism is that the clergy have brought the banalities of secular politics into the church. Obtaining lucrative appointments in the Baptist conventions and powerful bishoprics in the Methodist churches have, according to Woodson, impeded the progress of the African-American church.[6] While it would be impossible to arrive at an ecclesiological statement on the African-American church without the perspective found in Woodson's work, it reflects a certain brand of historical discourse. By focusing on ministers, bishops, and priests, its view of the church is largely clerical. Also by focusing on the founding of churches and the establishment of church-related schools, its view of the church is also largely institutional.

A second treatment of the African-American church is found in E. Franklin Frazier's oft-cited study *The Negro Church in America*. Frazier's point of departure is the conviction that black people in the United States were robbed of any indigenous African resources for survival and prosperity. He argues that "one must recognize from the beginning that because of the manner in which Negroes were captured in Africa and enslaved, they were practically stripped of their social heritage."[7] Because the possibility of retaining significant elements of African culture was reduced to a minimum, African slaves experienced a subsequent loss of social cohesion. Factors in this loss were the alien-

ation of black slaves from the fruits of their labor, the transient nature
of slave life, and difficulty of communication between slaves because
of tribal language differences.

The most important factor, however, was the lack of community
in the slave quarters.[8] The absence of a viable community among the
slaves, according to Frazier, meant that there could be no continuity
between African religion and the African-American church. He argues
that "from the available evidence, including what we know of the
manner in which the slaves were Christianized and the character of
their churches, it is impossible to establish any continuity between African religious practices and the Negro church in the United States."[9]
Frazier goes on to state that Christianity made possible the social cohesion formerly provided by African traditional religions. The church
emerged then, in this view, as a response to slavery. The black church
served as an agency of social control, regulating the sexual mores of
African-Americans, which had been thrown into disarray by slavery.

The church also provided an opportunity for economic cooperation among African-Americans, allowing them to exercise a degree of
fiscal influence in spite of meager individual resources. When it came
to the attainment of higher education and political clout, the black
church, according to Frazier, was less than successful in empowering
its members. The desire of black Christians for higher education was
ambivalent because "there was no intellectual tradition among Negroes
to sustain colleges and universities."[10] Frazier also argues that the internal power struggles within the black church were the result of the
political frustration of its members in their attempts to determine their
fate in the wider society. He concludes that the black church served as
a means of social cohesion for African-Americans and as "a refuge in
a hostile white world."[11]

Frazier observes that because of the increasing social mobility of
African-Americans the church is losing its function as a refuge. He
also notes that the increased numbers of African-Americans who live
outside the sphere of the black church mean that it is losing its ability
to function as a means of social control. Frazier's most controversial
assertion, however, is that the degree to which the black church holds
on to the residue of African culture will be the measure of its unfitness
for a future racially integrated society. "The most important cultural
institution is, of course, the Negro church. It embodies, as we have
seen, the cultural traditions of Negroes to a far greater extent than any
other institution.... When one comes to the Negro church which is the
most important cultural institution created by Negroes, one encounters the most important barrier to integration and the assimilation of
Negroes."[12]

The notion of the black church as a cultural institution is the basis of the important but overlooked work by Zora Neale Hurston, *The Sanctified Church*. Hurston employs the methodologies of cultural anthropology and the study of folklore to examine the distinctiveness of the African-American church. She takes note of what Du Bois had earlier identified as the "marks" of the black church: the music, the preaching, and the frenzy. Hurston's analysis of the indigenous music of the African-American church emphasizes its improvisational character. She notes that the genre of music known as the spirituals "are unceasing variations around a theme.... Like the folk-tales, the spirituals are being made and forgotten every day.... The idea that the whole body of spirituals are 'sorrow songs' is ridiculous. They cover a wide range of subjects from a peeve at gossipers to Death and Judgement."[13] Further, these songs exemplify the uniqueness of the African-American church in several ways. First, their primary purpose is the creative expression of feeling:

> The truth is, that the religious service is a conscious art expression. The artist is consciously creating — carefully choosing every syllable and every breath. The dialect breaks through only when the speaker has reached the emotional pitch where he loses all self-consciousness.... All religious expression among Negroes is regarded as art, and ability is recognized as definitely as in any other art. The beautiful prayer receives the accolade as well as the beautiful song. It is merely a form of expression which people generally are not accustomed to think of as art. Nothing outside of the Old Testament is as rich in figure as a Negro prayer. Some instances are unsurpassed anywhere in literature.[14]

A second aspect of these songs is that while they are improvisational in many instances, they are not the expression of individual creativity. Hurston notes that "Negro spirituals are not solo or quartette material.... Negro songs to be heard truly must be sung by a group, and a group bent on expression of feelings and not on sound effects."[15] That is, they are the products of the collective genius of the race and reflect the African traditional emphasis on the group rather than the individual. Third, these songs are marked by what Hurston calls dissonance and irregular harmony:

> The jagged harmony is what makes it, and it ceases to be what it was when this is absent.... The harmony of the true spiritual is not regular. The dissonances are important and not to be ironed out by the trained musician.... Keys change. Moreover, each singing of the piece is a new creation. The congregation is bound by no rules. No two times singing is alike, so that we must consider the rendition of a song not as a final thing, but as a mood. It won't be the same thing next Sunday.[16]

In a sense, the dissonance and irregularity of the spirituals are a reflection of the contingent and bittersweet character of African-American experience.

The same creative energy that animates the music is at the heart of traditional African-American preaching and prayer. In form and content, sermons and prayers must exhibit the creativity born of the free flow of the spirit. They must evoke the appropriate response from the other worshippers, drawing the total group into a swelling crescendo. They must exhibit the poetic power to move listeners to new and deeper levels of spiritual awareness. Without these characteristics the speaker is said to be "lecturing" rather than preaching.[17]

The third feature of the black church is the "shout," or what Du Bois called the "frenzy." It is here that Hurston sees the clearest evidence of African traditional religions in the black church. She asserts that

> there can be little doubt that shouting is a survival of the African "possession" by the gods. In Africa it is sacred to the priesthood or acolytes, in America it has become generalized. The implication is the same, however; it is a sign of special favor from the spirit that it chooses to drive out the individual consciousness temporarily and use the body for its expression.[18]

Like the music and the preaching, the frenzy is rooted in the vitality of the group. Hurston observes that "shouting is a community thing. It thrives in concert. It is the first shout that is difficult for the preacher to arouse. After that one they are likely to sweep like fire over the church. This is easily understood, for the rhythm is increasing with each shouter who communicated his fervor to someone else."[19]

Hurston's accounts of this aspect of traditional African-American worship accurately portray what has become the zenith of ecclesial experience for many black Christians. In the shout, the believer transcends the constrictions and limitations that society imposes and is caught up in the spirit. In this state the believer is both completely subject to a force outside of himself or herself, and, at the same time, completely free from custom and convention. Moreover, the believer is often left physically exhausted, but almost always spiritually empowered.

Hurston's criticism of the black church lay in its tendency to abandon the fountainhead of its culture for the elusive goals of acceptance by the wider society, thereby losing its character as true black church. When this happens, Hurston argues, the "sanctified church" emerges in response. "The Sanctified Church is a protest against the highbrow tendency in Negro Protestant congregations as the Negroes gain more education and wealth."[20] While Woodson saw the black church as a political-historical institution embodying the aspirations of an upwardly mobile people and Frazier saw the black church as an ambivalent source of social cohesion for a psychologically disoriented people,

Hurston saw the black church as the locus of cultural expression and creativity for the genius of African-Americans.

As important as these perspectives are, they do not get at the heart of the existence of the African-American church. There are deeper reasons for the political activism, social solace, and cultural celebrations of black Christians. What is the essence of the community? What holds it together?

There are two concepts that come close to providing an answer to these queries. The first is Victor Turner's concept of "communitas." In his work as a cultural anthropologist, Turner observed among religious groups who made pilgrimages a distinctive type of social bond. During these pilgrimages, participants shared a special relationship, which Turner calls "communitas." One feature of communitas is the liberation from the normal social stratifications. According to Turner, communitas "remains open and unspecialized, a spring of pure possibility as well as the immediate realization of release from day-to-day structural necessities and obligatoriness."[21] Communitas seeks "to extend its influence throughout whole populations as a means of 'release' or 'salvation' from the role-playing games which embroil the personality in manifold guiles, guilts, and anxieties."[22] The situation that promotes communitas "liberates the individual from the obligatory everyday constraints of status and role, defines him as an integral human being with a capacity for free choice, and within the limits of his religious orthodoxy presents for him a living model of human brotherhood and sisterhood."[23]

Communitas is also antistructural. It is a spiritual power that, in its purest form, resists institutionalization. At the same time, however, it is possible for communitas to exist in latent forms within human religious institutions. In fact, the conditions of human existence require that the spiritual power of communitas interface with the structural elements of religious practice and life. "Thus social and cultural structures are not abolished by communitas and anamnesis, but the sting of their divisiveness is removed so that the fine articulation of their parts in a complex heterogenous unity can be better appreciated. Some might say that pure communitas knows only harmonies and no disharmonies."[24] This harmony, however, can never be compulsory, abridging the rights of persons to freely accept or reject participation in communitas. Communitas strains toward universalism but does not do so at the cost of its essential character. "When communitas becomes force rather than 'grace,' it becomes totalism, the subordination of the part to the whole instead of the free creation of the whole by the mutual recognition of its parts."[25] In sum, communitas is liberating, it exists in tension with the structural dimensions of religious practices, and it is gracious rather than compulsory. Turner concludes that in the creative tension between structure and communitas, participants experience "a forgiveness of sins, where differences are accepted or tolerated rather than aggravated into grounds of aggressive opposition."[26]

Turner's description of communitas bears a striking resemblance to the testimonies of African-American Christians regarding their experiences in the company of faith. The amelioration of the effects of oppressive social structures, the intense experience of solidarity, and the confirmation of unconditional acceptance referred to as forgiveness, suggest that Turner's concept might be helpful in an ecclesiological statement on the African-American church.

A second concept is Emil Brunner's notion of "ekklesia." Brunner, a neo-orthodox theologian, argues that the church cannot be understood primarily as an institution. The essence of the church, as depicted in the New Testament, is that spiritual community known as the "ekklesia." While the Greek word *ekklesia* is often translated as "church," Brunner observes that "if we wish to follow the New Testament, we cannot simply translate Ekklesia by the word 'Church,' and we have the right to say only of the Ekklesia and not of the Church that it is essentially bound up with faith in Jesus Christ."[27] While Protestant Christianity emphasizes the personal dimension of faith, the ekklesia is, according to Brunner, the social form of faith. Referring to the first generation of Christians, Brunner observes that

> the social form of the Ekklesia was a necessary consequence of their faith.... This means that the social character of the Ekklesia resulted from its spiritual character as an association of men through the Holy Spirit through the love of Christ. And that itself was the structural law of this social entity. There was no other law, nor was there need for any. The Ekklesia was a spiritual brotherhood, free from law.[28]

The heart of spiritual community for Brunner then is a solidarity among persons of faith. In this ideal community, the bonds are not formal or structured, but are free-flowing, other-centered expressions of *agape*. The real, flesh-and-blood manifestations of ekklesia, however, are found in tension with the institutional tendencies of the church. As Brunner puts it, "the brotherhood can *have* laws and institutions but it can never regard these as belonging to its *essence*. But, above all, it can never *understand itself as an institution*.... And this non-institutional character is much more evident still in the Ekklesia of the New Testament whose life-element is the Holy Spirit."[29] Here one can see striking parallels between Turner's notion of communitas and Brunner's idea of the ekklesia. Both refer to social manifestations of intense personal religious experiences. Both refer to the liberation of the religious participant from the deleterious effects of law, social stratification, etc. In addition, both refer to the necessary tension between the essence of human community and its institutional form.

In traditional theological terms, one might say that the notions of communitas and ekklesia point to the fact that the church presents the ambiguity of institutionalized religious life, residing between the existential dynamism of faith, which is the Holy Spirit, and the historical form of faith, which is Jesus Christ. Brunner did not base his observations on the experience of African-American Christians but on an intensive examination of the New Testament church. Turner did not focus on African-American Christianity, but it should be noted that he examined the religious practices of some traditional African societies, and he used the experience of Malcolm X and his pilgrimage to Mecca as illustrations of communitas.[30] While neither term fits exactly the phenomenon of the African-American church, they are drawn from the two sources from which the black church forges its identity, its African heritage and its encounter with the Bible.

At this point it seems clear that a comprehensive understanding of the African-American church requires the kind of descriptive studies undertaken by Woodson, Frazier, and Hurston.[31] It also requires, however, the kind of normative gaze that has been the traditional approach of systematic theology. This tension was the source of the risk encountered by early black theologians as they sought to address the church as it really existed as well as say a word about its mandate as the community of faith in the spirit of freedom. The task was to formulate an understanding of the African-American church that is sociologically accurate and theologically true.

## The Church in Black Theology

In its nascent form, rather than focus on the internal issues that are traditionally the subject matter of theological discourse on the church, black ecclesiology focused on the relation between the church and the world. A common element in the statements of black theologians on the church is the attempt to identify modalities that would elucidate and clarify that relationship. Although the creative and expressive traditions of African-American Christianity have provided numerous ways of speaking of the church, there appear to be three primary modalities around which most of the early ecclesiological discourse was centered. These are "the company of the elect," "the family of God," and "the nation of God."

In traditional theological terms, the company of the elect, or the *coetus electorum*, are those people who have been called together by God and whose lives truly, even if only fragmentarily, manifest the new redemptive reality that they proclaim. The bond that holds this community together is their chosenness. In this sense, the church is a chosen people of God, whose mission is to be the vanguard of the new redeemed order. An example of this first modality is found in James Cone's early writings on the doctrine of the church. In *Black Theology and Black Power*, Cone argues that the black church was the creation of black people. The impetus for its creation was the degradation that marked the lives of African-American slaves. "For the slaves [the church] was the sole source of personal identity and the sense of community. Though slaves had no social, economic, or political ties as a people, they had one humiliating factor in common — serfdom!"[32] This common factor of humiliation became the basis for their sense of community in a positive sense, because of God's choice of the oppressed as God's own people.

In the history of the company of the elect, however, there may be points at which God's election is refused or distorted. According to Cone, this is particularly true of the black church in the postbellum period. Following the Civil War the black church "lost its zeal for freedom in the midst of new structures of white power. The rise of segregation and discrimination in the post–Civil War period softened its drive for equality."[33] The loss of prophetic fervor among black preachers and the general quietism of the black church was, for Cone, a sign that the Kingdom was only fragmentarily present even among the elect.

In spite of human frailty, the church has a mandate to make public the redemption of Christ in the world. Cone notes that through its proclamation of the Word, its participation in the struggle of the oppressed for liberation, and the manifestation of that liberation in its own life and witness, the black church strives to live with its status as the company of the elect.[34] It is constantly reminded that "election involves service."[35] According to Cone, because of the relationship between election and service, the church must be understood primarily in terms of servanthood:

> If Jesus is Lord of the church, then the church is his servant. It is that congregation of people whose identity as the people of God arises from a definition of servanthood that is derived from Jesus' life, death, and resurrection.... The servanthood of the church is defined by the cross of Jesus, and nothing else.... Being a servant of Jesus involves more than meeting together every Sunday for worship and other liturgical gatherings. It involves more than serving as an officer or even a pastor of a church. Servant includes a political component that thrusts a local congregation into society, where it must take sides with the poor.[36]

In this view the church is understood to be the company of the elect who are chosen for service. They are to be, amid the evil of the world, a redemptive presence.

The second modality employed in addressing the church in black theology is the family of God. The family-type structure for the church has been described as one in which "all the members function as one family. Its main task is nurture of its members of all ages so that they may participate in God's mission in the world. Usually residential in character, the family-type structure serves a particular segment of God's world in which it is located."[37] In this modality, the emphasis lies on internal survival, psychological affinity between the members, and the nurturing of the community. An example of this motif is found in the writings of J. Deotis Roberts. Roberts, who has written more on ecclesiology than most of his contemporaries, argues that there is an intimate relation between the family and the church in African-American experience.

> The "family" is one of the few "images" that still has rich potential for communicating meaning to black people....Family life is universal; it answers to universal human requirements....The family is not only a social and economic institution — it is also a moral and religious school for children when it functions properly. The black church, as a social and religious body, has served as a kind of extended family for blacks.[38]

For Roberts, the family and the church serve the common purpose of haven and refuge. These two institutions are crucial for the development of health and wholeness among African-Americans. In the midst of oppression, both the church and the family, as forms of institutional life, can serve as bulwarks against the outside world. Yet the family and the church for Roberts are more than cognate institutions in African-American experience. The notion of family can provide significant clues to the theological meaning of the black church:

> A family membership is assumed and anticipated when there is a conversion of any member. In a similar manner a Jewish rabbi may reckon his membership in terms of families. This is, in essence, *the model* which the new black church style must follow. While we will take our cue from the practice of "familyhood" rooted in our African heritage, it will provide in the black church that reality of community which will make of it at once a family of God and a household of power.[39]

By examining the family as the model for a black ecclesiology, Roberts believes that the nature and the mission of the church will come into sharper focus:

> There is a need for [a] careful theological statement on the Black Church. The purpose of this theological enterprise will be to discern clearly the nature of the Black Church in order to understand more adequately its mission. The very nature of the Black Church involves it in the mission of liberation....The Black theologian has a great opportunity to make constructive use of "the family" as the people of God expressed through

the Black Church. Thus we speak of the Beloved Community, the Black Church as the Family of God.[40]

Employing the black family as a modality for understanding the African-American church results in a distinctive ecclesiological identity and mission. The identity of the African-American church, according to Roberts, is best expressed in the images of exile rather than exodus, of institute rather than only event, and in terms of its structure rather than just its dynamic.[41] This means that the political analogies of the black church are drawn from the Pastoral Epistles, as well as the Hebrew Scriptures and the Gospels. These images of the church connote the quest for stability. This is the mission of the church.

The black church in this view is in the world and must accept that fact. The missiological emphasis of the black church, for Roberts, must focus on solidarity, survival, and wholeness. Roberts observes that "the household of God refers, then, to the inner cohesion of this community called church. The understanding of the church as a household, a family, points to the reunification of all families."[42] The black family and the black church are not mystical unions or ethereal frames. They are real embodiments of Christ's presence among African-Americans. This means that African-American Christians must recover the image of *the Body of Christ* as a trope for their communal experience and the solidarity they seek. "This emphasis upon *unity* in the body of Christ is essential for the black church's self-understanding."[43] In this view the church is understood to be the family of God and the household of faith. It is to be a sustaining presence amid the distorted potential for good in the world.

The third modality used by black theologians to describe the church is that of nationalism. Nationalism refers to the bond that is created among a people based on a common history, common values, and common political aims. In European-American theology a major example of the use of this modality is found in the writings of Frederick Denison Maurice.[44] Here the relation between the nationalism of English people and the identity of the Anglican church is pronounced. For African-Americans, the roots of nationalism are found in the attempts of enslaved Africans to survive and overcome their bondage. The tribal divisions that were so important in traditional African life were superseded by the common values that they shared as Africans, their common experience of slavery, and their common political aim of liberation. This meant that

the nationalism of the slave community was essentially African nationalism, consisting of values that bound slaves together and sustained them under brutal conditions of oppression. Their very effort to bridge ethnic differences and to form themselves into a single people to meet the challenge of a common foe proceeded from an impulse that was Pan-African — that grew out of a concern for all Africans — as what was useful was appropriated from a multiplicity of African groups even as an effort was made to eliminate distinctions among them.[45]

This nationalism is the modality employed in Albert Cleage's view of the black church. In his early writings Cleage argues that the church must be part of the liberation struggle of African-Americans and that its theology must not have as its major concern situating itself within the dominant theological tradition and achieving formal symmetry. "Black theology is not a matter of putting together a pleasant jigsaw puzzle, making sure to use all the traditional white pieces, but of enabling the Black church to become relevant to the Black Liberation Struggle."[46] The animating power of the black liberation movement, as Cleage describes it, is the spirit of black power. In theological language this is the power of the Holy Spirit. "The Holy Spirit is the revolutionary power which comes to an exploited people as they struggle to escape from powerlessness and to end the institutional oppression forced upon them by an enemy."[47]

Cleage observes that when movements assume institutional form, their original dynamic is usually lost. It is imperative, therefore, that the spiritual thrust of the black church be kept at the forefront. This means that the black church must embody Black Christian Nationalism. Like Cone, Cleage posits a significant distinction between the "old" black church, a counterrevolutionary body, and the "new" black church, a progressive liberating movement. Cleage describes the old black church as "trivial, irrelevant, divisive, counterrevolutionary."[48] It was born of slave Christianity and grounded in the traditional neo-primitive individualist theology of the white church, which defined its basic task as that of calling sinners to repentance.[49] While this emphasis served a legitimate purpose it is, according to Cleage, unsuited to the present needs of black people. "This is the weakness of the [old] Black church. It was a survival instrument. It helped maintain sanity, but it destroyed the possibility of a united Black Liberation Struggle."[50] As such, it is completely alienated from the contemporary needs of African-Americans. The most regressive aspect of the old black church is its worship style:

> We see every aspect of worship in a traditional Black church contributing to Black enslavement.... [It is] an ecstatic orgy of spirit in which coherent words only serve to obscure rather than to clarify the message of a personal salvation through Jesus. This kind of worship is unquestionably a product of the Black experience, but totally unrelated to the Black Liberation Struggle. Because it diverts the Black man's attention from present ills and serves as an emotional safety valve, it is not merely irrelevant, it is counterrevolutionary.[51]

Within this kind of worship the sacraments are viewed as a means of escape, or, as Cleage puts it, "a ticket to glory."

The heart of Cleage's proposal is the redirection of the focus and emphasis of the black church through black Christian nationalism. This means that "we must change the church radically. We must make the church relevant to the Black Revolution.... Black Christian Nationalism seeks to chart new directions for the Black church because the Black Revolution needs institutional power and stability.... The Black church must seek to rediscover the original teachings of Jesus and the Nation Israel."[52] The concept of the black church as the institutional manifestation of black nationalism is the essence of Cleage's ecclesiology. He argues that

> instead of telling Black people about escaping from the world and going home to God on high, the Black church must begin to involve Black people in the Black Liberation Struggle by using the teachings of Jesus in the Synoptic Gospels, and the Old Testament concept of nation, to show Black people how coming together with Black pride and Black power is basic to survival. The Black church must become central in the Black Revolution.[53]

There are several significant features to the new black ecclesiology that Cleage proposes. First, worship is not the emotional catharsis that characterizes the old black church. Rather, "worship is the coming together of a committed people. We seek direction, power, and inspiration as the chosen people of God, and we see the power of God revealed daily in the life of the Black Nation."[54] Second, the new black church focuses on the education and evangelization of the masses in its mission:

> The Black church must undertake a total restructuring of the church and its educational functions. We must develop techniques which do not depend on trained teachers. We must learn to use tape recorders, filmstrips, and movies that can be sent out to small churches everywhere. Without trained teachers every church can convey the same basic message to Black people everywhere.[55]

Third, the baptismal celebration of the new black church is not an escape from the world but an immersion into it. Baptism is " 'baptism into the nation.' ... To be baptized into a Black church must symbolize a complete rejection of the values of a hostile white world and a complete commitment to the struggle of Black people."[56] Likewise, the eucharistic celebration of the new black church is not a "memorial" but the sacramental rite of the black nation. "When we take the sacrament of Holy Communion it symbolizes our total rededication to personal participation in the struggle of Black people and total rededication to the Black Nation. The sacraments and ritual of the church then become for Black people an intrinsic part of the revolutionary struggle."[57] The new black church for Cleage must be concerned with mission first, and only secondarily with Sunday morning worship. "The new Black church, moving in a new direction, is not going to be essentially a preaching church. It will preach and it will teach, but only because they make meaningful action possible."[58] What Cleage proposes is an ecclesiology of praxis rather than one of the proclaimed Word. In this view the church is understood to be the nation of God. It is to be a righteous remnant in an apostate world.

Early black theologians were compelled to speak of the church in its relation to the world in which African-Americans lived. This does not mean that there was no theological center to their ecclesiological statements. Their point of departure suggests, however, that concrete notions of community are the only legitimate avenue to the mystery and power of God's presence through Jesus Christ in human existence.

### Toward an African-American Ecclesiology

The central problem in ecclesiology is the tension between what the church claims to be and what it actually is. The major sources of theology — Scripture, tradition, experience, and culture — are employed to prevent that tension from becoming a rupture. Because of this tension ecclesiological statements are "contested" statements. That is, the complexity of ecclesiological claims is the result of the mystery of human-divine interaction. One of the primary manifestations of this tension is the perennial debate around who is in the church and who resides outside the realm of its safety. This was the issue between the apostle Paul and the "Judaizers" of Galatia, between Augustine and the Donatists, between Calvin and the Anabaptists. This tension is apparent in the contemporary claims by some officials of the Roman Catholic church and the Protestant fundamentalist churches that one must adhere to a specific body of doctrinal beliefs to be considered a true member of the Body of Christ. Indeed, it appears that this tension is part of the ecclesiological task.

One method of mediating disagreements is to appeal to the Bible as the final authority. However, here one does not even find unanimity about the origins and nature of the church. The Bible suggests at least three points at which the church originates. The church is sometimes described as the continuation of the ancient assembly of God, or the "new Israel." In this "ecclesiology of the first person of the Trinity," the church is the embodiment of God's covenant with Israel. At other times the church is said to be the result of Peter's confession at Caesarea Philippi. In this "ecclesiology of the second person of the Trinity," the church is the result of faith in and recognition of Jesus as the Christ. One could also claim that the church originated at Pentecost. In this "ecclesiology of the third person of the Trinity," the church is born in the power of the Spirit.[59] Ecclesiological statements are "contested" on several levels. In spite of the problems involved the theologian must describe and assess the church in terms of both its mission and its identity.

Liberation has been central to the African-American churches self-understanding since its inception. This liberation, however, is not just the missiological thrust of the church, it is the essence of the church's identity. Liberation is not just what the church *does;* it is what the church *is.* If human liberation is seen as secondary or tertiary to the center of the church's life, then the church at some point may be tempted to jettison this aspect of its mission in favor of something more closely related to its *raison d'être.* If human liberation is seen as central to the life of the church, then to lose sight of that center is to relinquish its claim to be the church. This liberation involves the liberation of the self and the liberation of the community. If the collective aspect is emphasized to the exclusion of the individual aspect, there is the danger of the tyranny of the majority. If the individual aspect is stressed to the exclusion of concern for the group, there is the danger of the anarchy of the minority. The African-American church is based on the African notion of "self-in-community." The self has no being apart from the community, and the community is an abstraction apart from the collection of selves. The liberation of one implies the liberation of the other.

Within this context it is possible to describe, however tentatively, the African-American church in light of two ancient claims. The first is that the identity of the church is summed up in the formula: the church is *one, holy, catholic, and apostolic.* The second is that the mission of the church is symbolized in its *kerygma, koinonia, diukonia,* and *didache.* These two claims, as well as an examination of the meaning of ministry and ordinances or sacraments within the life of the African-American church, will provide clues to its distinctiveness and its inherent possibilities.

Jesus is the center of the church. That is, the church is that community that is centered in Christ. It does not possess Christ, but is possessed by Christ. Thus the life, ministry, death, and resurrection of Jesus the Christ center and circumscribe the community called church. Because Jesus is the ground of human liberation, the church is centered in the project of human liberation. This is what is meant by the affirmation that "the church's one foundation is Jesus Christ her Lord." The emphasis on the singular position of Jesus in relation to the church points to the unity of the church. This is not a forced or artificial consensus, but a genuine commitment to the one thing for

which Jesus suffered, died, and rose from the dead. This one thing is
the content of the *kerygma* — the preaching and proclamation — of
the church. The kerygma is the Word around which the community
is gathered, and without this Word the community has no theological
reason for its existence. The kerygma of the African-American church
is the preaching that proclaims the past, present, and future liberation
that takes place in Christ. The centrality of preaching in the worship
of African-American churches is indicative of the power of the Word
to effect change in the lives of those who "labor and are heavy laden."

The church is animated and sustained by the power of the Holy
Spirit. While the church is centered in the communal memory and
ritual presence of Jesus of Nazareth, it is moved by the pentecostal
imperative to seek its *epicenter* in the world. Thus the church is always
involved in ushering in the reign of God. It is always seeking to establish peace and justice where they do not yet exist. This impulse points
to the meaning of the claim that the church is holy. Here holiness
has very little to do with asceticism, otherworldliness, or superhuman
perfection. Rather, holiness refers to the persistent discomfort of the
church with the unchallenged existence of oppression and exploitation
in the world. Holiness also points to the commitment of the church
to resist the defilement that toleration and complicity in human oppression bring. It is this commitment that cements the *koinonia* of the
community. Koinonia refers to the internal character of the church
community. It is the solidarity of that community in which a common purpose is strong enough to render all other stratifications among
human beings of only secondary importance. Thus in the holy community "there is no Greek nor Jew, slave nor free, male nor female."
The koinonia of the African-American church is its character as a community that has been liberated in Christ. The African-American church
is called to be that brotherhood/sisterhood in which "America's historic bowers and scrapers" (Maya Angelou) are affirmed as loved by
the God who created them, through the Christ who died for them.
Koinonia refers to the character of the church as the embodiment of
the reign of God.

The church — despite its sometimes lofty claims — is a social institution. It exists in the world, and therefore it must be constantly
aware of its relationship with the world and the implications therein.
Although the relation between the church and the world is often ambiguous, there is never a moment in which that relationship is absent.
Because the center of the church's life is the liberation and wholeness
manifested in the life and work of Jesus Christ, this center will define
the relationship between the church and the world. The church proclaims liberation from the world only to the extent that the church's
ultimate center of value is God and not the "things of the world."

This points to what is called the "vertical" dimension of faith, stressing communion with God. The church proclaims liberation in and for the world only to the extent that the church acknowledges that God is in the world, encountering the church as its neighbor. This points to what is called the "horizontal" dimension of faith, because it emphasizes solidarity with those who suffer.

The church's reach toward both the inner traumas and the outer troubles inherent in the Christian life is symbolized in the claim that the church is catholic or universal. The catholicity referred to here has nothing to do with the all too human tendency toward imperialism, even in the propagation of the Gospel. Rather, catholicity refers to the all-embracing care of God and its corresponding demand on the life of the church. Universalism, in this context, is not an abstraction of the particulars of human experience, but the result of the conviction that God can be found anywhere *and* everywhere.

The relationship between the church and the world is the essence of its *diakonia*. Diakonia refers to the external work or activity of the community of faith. It is the "service" of the church in society. This service includes caring for "the least of these," for the "widows and orphans," the poor and destitute. The diakonia of the African-American church is its participation in God's liberating work on behalf of the oppressed. The church is that community which serves the cause of freedom and love in the world.

The church has been entrusted with the safeguarding and perpetuation of the essence of the Gospel. It is, as such, the guardian of the faith. This means that the church and its traditions are not only measures of the responsiveness of the Christian community to changing times and circumstances, but that there is a positive content to what the church proclaims. Tradition is not to be thought of as "infallible" teaching, but is the record of the struggle of the church to be faithful to its calling. It must be recognized that the church has, at times, failed to live up to its own claim to embody the liberation and wholeness that God, through Jesus Christ, has promised to humanity. The traditions of sexism, racism, and classism, for example, stand alongside the traditions of self-sacrifice, prophetic valor, and martyrdom in the life of the church. Thus the church is not charged with the task of hiding its historic sins, but with recovering in every age the truth that anchors its preaching and praxis.

This struggle to remain faithful points to the apostolic character of the church. What makes the church apostolic is more than an unbroken ritual progression of leadership, or even the common practice of the "laying on of hands." Apostolic succession is the succession of faith. What is passed on is the substance of the Christian life as well as its signs. The passing on of the core of the Christian Gospel, both contemporaneously and to succeeding generations, points to the *didache* of the church. Didache refers to the process by which the community is formed in the faith. The teaching of the church, in this instance, is not the presentation of magisterial edicts, but a continual search for truth undertaken by the community as a whole. While clergy and theologians may possess a certain expertise in educational techniques and resources, the truth that the church seeks may come through anyone in the community. In the African-American church didache refers to the formation and empowerment of the community in faith and freedom.[60]

From the identity and mission of the church flows its understanding of ordained ministry. From the vast array of church styles and traditions it is possible to distinguish two major ways to understand ordained ministerial leadership. The first mode of ministry emphasizes clericalism and the hierarchy of gifts within the community. In this instance, ordained ministry is thought to be ontologically distinct from any other vocation within the church. Ordination in this case is often thought to effect, or to be a response to, a fundamental change in the person called to service. In essence, ordination is related to some basic aspect of the being of the minister or priest. The strength of this understanding is its emphasis on the distinctive character of the call to ordained ministry. Its liabilities can be seen in the use of this idea in arguments against the legitimacy of women in ministry. If the ordained ministry is related to the being of the person involved, it becomes possible to frame the argument against women in ministry in biological terms, i.e., Jesus was a man, therefore the biological distinctiveness of women makes them unsuitable for ministry, because women are in some way deficient in comparison to men. A danger in seeing the ordained ministry as constituting a distinct class of people is the possibility that recognition of the call of God may be reserved for some classes of people and denied to others on the basis of race, gender, or nationality.

The second mode of ministry emphasizes the common priesthood of the people and the variety of gifts present within the community. In this case ordained ministry is considered to be a functionally distinct form of service to the community. Ostensibly, any member of the community has the inherent capacity to perform the functions of ordained ministerial leadership. The ordained minister is one who has been singled out on the basis of innate gifts and abilities to serve the community as pastor. The major strength of this idea of ministry is its emphasis on the common life of faith shared by all members of the community and the solidarity of pastor and people. The major liability in this understanding of ministry can also be seen in its use in framing an argument against the legitimacy of women in ministry. If ordained ministry is related to specific functions within the life of the community, it is possible for the clergy to see themselves as a unique functional class, and as such, they may seek to maintain the prerogatives of leadership for themselves. One way to do this is to associate leadership functions with certain groups of people based on social convention and custom. Thus women can be denied ordination because "ordained ministry does not fall within the socially defined roles and functions of women to be subservient to men, and devoted exclusively to the care of home and hearth."

The vast majority of black Christians in the United States are Protestant; thus instances of the emergence of a priestly class, in the traditional sense, are rare. Yet because the Afrocentric sensibility makes no strict separation between form and function, both of these aspects of ministry with their attendant liabilities are present within the African-American churches. On one hand, clergy in the African-American community — whether they are respected or not — are seen to be a distinct class of people. (Indeed, the title "Reverend" often replaces the given name of the clergyperson and becomes part of his or her identity.) In literature and art they are sometimes revered and sometimes held up for ridicule. On the other hand, ministers are understood to be raised up from among the people and are confirmed in their leadership by the community. As such, ministers are allowed and even expected to involve themselves in the ordinary affairs of life. They are seen to be human, no more, no less. One of the most debated issues among the leaders of the African-American churches is that of the ordination of women and their full participation as leaders in the life of the church. Neither the assertion that "Jesus didn't call women to preach" (the formal argument) nor the claim that "women have no place in the pulpit" (the functional argument) can be justified in light of the pressing need of the African-American community for committed leadership. An African-American ecclesiology must address the social, cultural, and theological dimensions of this issue.

The heart of any Christian community is what it believes and practices in relation to baptism and the Lord's Supper, or the Eucharist. Baptism is crucial to the identity of the church. Through the act of baptism membership in the community of faith is confirmed. There are two basic ways of construing the function of baptism. The first is as an initiation rite. Here the person is included in the community by virtue of the initiative of the community. In this context, the church is a prerequisite for faith; that is, the community precedes faith. Thus in certain churches baptism is administered to children as a sign of their inclusion in the community of faith. The second way of seeing baptism is as an adult confession of faith. Here the person joins the community as the result of an inner personal conversion. In this context, the church is a collective response to a personal faith; that is, faith precedes community. In certain churches this means that baptism is restricted to "believers."

In African-American theological discourse on the church both aspects of baptism are present. In one sense, a person is initiated into the black church by virtue of being black. The black church claims all who have come through the trials and tribulations of the Christian journey. In another sense, a person consciously joins the black church by willingly assuming the burdens and joys of the Christian life. The black church is made up of those who have been converted to Christ's liberating work in the world. In sum, baptism in African-American ecclesiology is a sign of the historical solidarity of the believer with the community of faith, and thus with God.

The Lord's Supper, or the Eucharist, is basic in the life of the church. There are two ways of construing the function of this event. The first is as a memorial. Here the celebration is the recollection of the sacrifice and promise of Jesus Christ. It is the avenue by which the community collectively remembers the center of its existence. Thus the elements of the bread and wine are symbols of the death and resurrection of Jesus Christ. The second way of perceiving the eucharistic meal is as the actual presence of Christ in the community. Here the elements of the bread and the wine become the actual body and blood of Christ, broken and shed for the community. Thus the ordinary is transformed into the extraordinary and Christ is truly present.

In African-American theological discourse on the church both aspects of the Lord's Supper are evident. In one sense, the Lord's Supper is the occasion for the recollection of Christ's unique sacrificial act on behalf of the oppressed. Jesus Christ was "the crucified Jew who knew the writhings of the earthly damned" (Du Bois). That death was a concrete historical occurrence. In another sense, the Lord's Supper is the occasion for the celebration of Christ's contemporaneity with the community of faith. His death and resurrection were not simply first-century events. Through the Lord's Supper they become a present happening. This is the meaning of the African-American spiritual, "Were You There When They Crucified My Lord?" Jesus Christ is the liberator who is actually present in this celebration. In sum, the Lord's Supper is the celebration of the historical solidarity of Jesus Christ with the community of faith.

The key to understanding the ordinances, or sacraments, in the African-American context — it is also the key to understanding the distinctiveness of African-American ecclesial thought — is that they both derive their meaning in the concrete historical solidarity of the Christian and Christ with the community of faith in the Spirit of freedom.

# 7

## THE LAST SHALL BE FIRST

And the people of Israel went up out of the land of Egypt equipped for
battle. And Moses took the bones of Joseph with him; for Joseph had
solemnly sworn to the people of Israel, saying, "God will visit you; then
you must carry my bones with you from here."
                                                        — Exodus 13:18–19

But many that are first will be last, and the last first.
                                                        — Mark 10:31

Hope is central to the Christian faith. Although it is often the final
topic to be addressed in systematic theology, it would be a mistake to
consider hope as an addendum. It is rather the pinnacle of all Christian
theological discourse. The first epigraph cited above reminds us, however, that the hope of a people can never be separated from their history
without dire consequences. A hope that does not come to terms with
history can become unbridled optimism and idealism, or the cover for
unchecked expansionism. History anchors hope. Because history and
hope always belong to a specific community, they can mean different
things to different people. For example, hope takes on connotations
that reflect the social location of the community in question. Sociologist Max Weber noted that "the sense of honor of disprivileged classes
rests on some concealed promise for the future which implies the as-
signment of some function, mission, or vocation to them. What they
cannot claim to *be*, they replace by the worth of that which they one
day will *become*."[1]

In contrast, Weber notes hope takes on a different significance
among the non-poor. "Other things being equal, classes with high social and economic privilege will scarcely be prone to evolve the idea
of salvation. Rather they will assign to religion the primary function
of legitimizing their own life pattern or situation in the world."[2] For
the marginalized and disinherited, hope, as the second epigraph above

suggests, points to a reversal of fortunes. The Christian message declares that God in Christ is both our past and our future. Karl Barth suggested that "our memory of God accompanies us always as problem and warning. He is the hidden abyss; but He is also the hidden home at the beginning and end of all our journeyings."[3] Hope, then, is the recognition and affirmation that God is the beginning and the end, that Jesus is the alpha and the omega. Hope is the redemption of history.

### History and Hope in African-American Experience

Slavery is the watershed event in African-American thinking on history and hope. The experience of slavery demanded a reshaping of traditional concepts of time, human destiny, life, death, immortality, and so forth. Ironically, the exploration of the meaning of slavery for African-American eschatological thought has often been more thoroughly examined by African-American creative writers than by theologians. Toni Morrison's novel *Beloved*, for example, chronicles the attempts of African-Americans to work through the horrors of slavery so that hope might be rejuvenated.

Eschatology in African-American theological discourse has been so often misunderstood because its content is essentially the realignment of the history and hope of black Christians. African-American Christians have thought of eschatology not just in terms of impending future doom, but also in light of what Mircea Eliade called "the terror of history." Thus an adequate understanding of eschatology in African-American theological discourse requires a consideration of African notions of time and history and the adjustments that African slaves in the United States made in light of the Christian message and their situation of bondage.

In his groundbreaking work *African Religions and Philosophy*, John S. Mbiti examines the distinctive features of the notion of time from an African perspective. For the African mind, time is not a metaphysical concept. Thus there is no thought given to time as an academic concern. Africans think of time in relation to events that have occurred or that are likely to occur in the immediate future:

> The most significant consequence of this is that, according to traditional concepts, time is a two-dimensional phenomenon, with a long past, a present and virtually no future. The linear concept of time in western thought, with an indefinite past, present and infinite future, is practically foreign to African thinking. The future is virtually absent because events which lie in it have not taken place, they have not been realized and cannot, therefore, constitute time.[4]

The African mind, then, is focused more on the past than on the extended future. This is because time and events have to be experienced in order to be real. Time is not dissociated from events. Rather, it is a commodity or currency that owes its value to the coming and going of events. This, according to Mbiti, explains the absence of numerical calendars in traditional African societies. Time, for the African, is not to be lent or spent. The legendary and anecdotal resistance of African peoples to Western notions of punctuality and temporal expediency points to a different notion of time. Mbiti refers to this as "waiting for time" or "producing time" rather than wasting time.[5]

Because time is reckoned backward rather than forward, eternity for the African mind lies in the past rather than the future. The depth dimension of experience for the African lies in what has occurred rather than in what will occur. Whatever future there is for the traditional African mindset has to be virtually experienced to be real. Just as the immediate future is dependent upon the present, the present is dependent upon the past. The past, which Mbiti refers to as *Zamani*, is "the period of myth." This means that its meaning is not exhausted once its chronological life is over, but that the past continues to live in the present. The present, which Mbiti refers to as *Sasa*, is solidly founded on the past.

The thoroughly modern notion of historical progress, which has been so essential to the development of Western societies, is not part of traditional African thought.

> In traditional African thought, there is no concept of history moving "forward" toward a future climax, or toward an end of the world. Since the future does not exist beyond a few months, the future cannot be expected to usher in a golden age, or a radically different state of affairs from what is in the Sasa and the Zamani. The notion of a messianic hope, or a final destruction of the world, has no place in [the] traditional concept of history. So African peoples have no "belief in progress," the idea that the development of human activities and achievements move from a low to a higher degree.[6]

Whereas in modern Western societies *utopia*, or *the Golden Age*, lies in the yet to be realized future, in traditional African societies they lie in the past.

On the level of the individual, these notions of time reflect the relation between the person and the rhythm of nature. The rhythm "includes birth, puberty, initiation, marriage, procreation, old age, death, entry into the community of the departed and finally entry into the company of spirits."[7] Two of the more important aspects of this understanding of time are the meaning of physical death and the meaning of space and time. In traditional African societies, the death of a member of the community does not portend the end of life but the passage from one phase of participation in the community to another. When a person dies he or she lives on as part of the community as long as relatives and friends remember his or her name. These remembered ones, or ancestors, participate in a kind of personal immortality. When that person's name is no longer remembered — because there is no one left alive who remembers him or her by name — the process of dying is finally accomplished. However, the no-longer-remembered ones are not vanquished from the community. They are then referred to as the living dead and enter into a state of collective immortality. The participation of the ancestors and the living dead in the life of the community, along with the supreme value placed on procreation and the birth of children, means that the community in African traditional thought is held together by the power of ancient memory and immediate anticipation.

Mbiti observes that "space and time are closely linked, and often the same word is used for both."[8] This means that one cannot speak meaningfully of time in the African sense without also speaking of the meaning of sacred space:

> Africans are particularly tied to the land, because it is the concrete expression of both their Zamani and their Sasa. The land provides them with the roots of existence, as well as binding them mystically to their departed. People walk on the graves of their forefathers, and it is feared that anything separating them from these ties will bring disaster to family and community life. To remove Africans by force from their land is an act of such great injustice that no foreigner can fathom it.[9]

The traditional African, then, is linked to land and ancestors along a specific space-time continuum. Although there is a danger of idealizing traditional African concepts, Mbiti concludes his analysis with the observation that the impact of Christianity upon the African has been both profound and enduring. In terms of the influence of Christian ideas of eschatology on African concepts of time Mbiti suggests that the conflicting visions of time and history may be responsible for the political instability of African nations.[10] While the advent of the idea of a distant future may have great potential for the African, it can also be the harbinger of tragedy and disillusionment.[11]

Mbiti outlines the significance of African notions of time for Christian eschatology in his work *New Testament Eschatology in an African Background*.[12] He concludes that the absence of the idea of an extended future among Africans significantly affected the reception of eschatological preaching by missionaries. To say that Jesus was coming soon meant to the African that his arrival could be expected almost immediately. Since even the missionaries did not believe this, Africans had to make cognitive adjustments in their appropriation of the Christian faith.

With the onset of the slave trade traditional African notions of time and history ran headlong into European concepts. The crisis engendered by this encounter is described in such narratives as *The Life of Olaudah Equiano, or Gustavus Vassa, the African*. In essence, the African concept of cyclical time contrasted with the European concept of linear time. In order to make sense of the tragic and cataclysmic events of kidnapping and the Middle Passage, enslaved Africans were compelled to move "from a conceptualization of time that rejects change to one that is able to embrace change and thus potentially at least lend it order."[13] While the European emphasis on the unique and unrepeatable character of each moment provided a place, in the scheme of things, for the unspeakable horror suffered by the slave, the human relationship to time was quite different from that found in traditional African thought. In the Western mode, the human relationship to time "typically becomes one of individual ownership, a relationship reflected in idioms that show that, as the saying goes, time is money: the object of private ownership, it can be spent, wasted, lost, found, taken or stolen like so many gold doubloons."[14] Time, having become a currency of sorts, is taken out of the hands of the enslaved African. Thus in addition to a physical dislocation, the enslaved African also experienced a kind of "temporal dispossession." From that point on, African-Americans have lived with accusations of "bad timing" whenever their liberation struggle threatened the dominant order.

An example of this is found in Martin Luther King, Jr.'s, "Letter from a Birmingham Jail." In responding to his critics regarding the prudence of his nonviolent protests in the South, King observed, "I have yet to engage in a direct-action campaign that was 'well timed' in the view of those who have not suffered unduly from the disease of segregation."[15] In King's view the reason that his adversaries are unable to understand the urgency that African-Americans feel in their quest for the full rights of citizenship is rooted in conflicting notions of time. In answering the frequent refrain that the acquisition of equal rights by African-Americans would happen eventually, King states,

> I had hoped that the white moderate would reject the myth concerning time in relation to the struggle for freedom. . . . Such an attitude stems from a tragic misconception of time, from the strangely irrational notion that there is something in the very flow of time that will inevitably cure all ills. Actually, time itself is neutral; it can be used either destructively or constructively. More and more I feel that the people of ill will have used time much more effectively than have the people of good will. . . . We must use time creatively, in the knowledge that the time is always ripe to do right.[16]

This response reflects the seizure of time by the oppressed as part of the their liberation struggle and the adjustments that African-Americans made to alien conceptualizations of time. Black people in the New World were able to hold in a necessary tension both traditional African and newly encountered European ideas regarding time. As Bonnie J. Barthold observes,

> The balance that has been achieved between traditional African culture and Western influence reflects an essential facet of African culture: its well-documented capacity to absorb foreign influence into existing institutions. There is no single explanation for this ability, which in fact preceded Western influence in Africa.[17]

Concomitantly, African-Americans have been able to hold on to facets of traditional culture — including ideas about time — as a form of rebellion against oppression.

In addition to different notions of time, enslaved Africans had attitudes toward the past different from their enslavers. For its enfranchised inhabitants "the New World was a place of new fortunes, new hope, new identity, where new ideas could be put into practice with minimal impediment. The past could be scuttled."[18] This sentiment found more contemporary expression in the expansion of laissez-faire capitalism into the hinterland of potential markets. It was in this context that the industrialist Henry Ford once declared that "history is bunk." This new hope and the rejection of the past by a people seeking liberation from the tradition-bound societies of feudal Europe were intricately linked to their squatters' claim to ownership of an untamed and supposedly uninhabited land. In essence, their new hope was tied to their new land. African slaves, on the other hand, had been robbed of both their past and their homeland. In their place was a history of degradation and a land not their own. Thus the content of any meaningful eschatological discourse in the African-American context must take into account the attempts to murder that history and reclaim their land.

The conditions of slavery in the United States made it often impossible or imprudent for African slaves to speak directly of their hopes. They were compelled to find a language that would unmistakably express their hopes for a reversal in their fortunes and at the same time conceal that message from the slaveowners. The apocalyptic language found in the Bible was a ready vehicle. Its striking and colorful images of a radically different future, while rejected by most post-Enlightenment Christian communities, were the cornerstone of African-American public Christian discourse. Talk of rapture, heaven, pearly gates, and winged saints fills African-American folklore and still heavily influences preaching in some African-American churches.

There are at least three reasons that apocalyptic language suited the purposes of newly converted African Christians in slavery. First, this language reflected an ancient cosmology that put God firmly in charge of the universe. Second, it was consistent with the political interests of the oppressed people whom God promised to deliver. Third, this language was the expressive vehicle for the imagination of people convinced of their future liberation. This language did more, however, than simply describe the future; it told a story. The story of God's rectification of the world called its hearers into creative participation in the promised salvation. As slave Christians listened to their preachers describe the vision of John on the island of Patmos, they knew that they were called to *be* among those whom John saw coming up out of the great tribulation. They were not mere observers but participants in God's liberating work. The purpose of this creative, imaginative language was to put the hearer where John was, "In the Spirit on the Lord's Day" (Rev. 1:10), in the right place and the right time. Apocalyptic language contained intimations of a new order and a new reality that spoke to the deepest yearnings of a dislocated and estranged people.

## Eschatology in Black Theology

Eschatology, along with Christology, were the two most controversial themes in early black theology. While Jesus Christ is the primary symbol of the Christian faith, eschatology points to the moving force within the believing community. In nascent black theology three central eschatological motifs were clearly present. The first related eschatology to the existence of evil in the world, reflecting what M. H. Abrams called the "theodicy of the landscape." The second related eschatology to God's benevolence within the created order, reflecting God's terrestrial promise. The third motif related eschatology to the determination of African-American Christians to survive and prosper in difficult circumstances, reflecting the anatomy of hope.

An example of the first motif is found in the writings of James Cone. In his first book, *Black Theology and Black Power*, he rejects the apparent otherworldliness of traditional black religion. Black theology, he argues, cannot accept any perspective that does not compel the oppressed to deal with the evil in this world.

> If eschatology means that one believes that God is totally uninvolved in the suffering of men because he is preparing them for another world, then Black Theology is an earthly theology! It is not concerned with the "last things" but with the "white thing." Black Theology like Black Power believes that the self-determination of black people must be emphasized at all costs, recognizing that there is only one question about reality for blacks: What must we do about white racism? There is no room in

this perspective for an eschatology dealing with a "reward" in heaven. Black Theology has hope for this life. The appeal to the next life is a lack of hope. Such an appeal implies that absurdity has won and that one is left merely with an unrealistic gesture toward the future. Heavenly hope becomes a Platonic grasp for another reality because one cannot live meaningfully amid the suffering of this world.[19]

Cone also argues that there is no place in black theology for the traditional notion of heaven as reward because it would mask the thirst for freedom among the oppressed:

> The idea of heaven is irrelevant for Black Theology. The Christian cannot waste time contemplating the next world (if there is a next). . . . There is no place here for a reward. . . . The free Christian man cannot be concerned about a reward in heaven. Rather, he is a man who, through the freedom granted in Christ, is ready to plunge himself into the evils of the world, revolting against all inhuman powers which enslave men.[20]

Eschatology must rivet the attention of the oppressed on the theodicy of the landscape or the evils of the world. This meant that eschatology had to be related to the historical experience of the oppressed and through them focused on the redemption of the world:

> Black Theology insists that genuine biblical faith relates eschatology to history, that is, to what God has done, is doing, and will do for his people. It is only because of what God has done and is now doing that we can speak meaningfully of the future. With a black perspective, eschatology comes to mean joining the world and making it what it ought to be.[21]

In his next theological text, *A Black Theology of Liberation*, Cone develops and refines his perspective on eschatology. Rather than rejecting the otherworldliness of black Christianity, he critiques the distortions present within much Christian eschatology. Cone points to the escapism of the privileged and their attempts to avoid the question of death and mortality.[22] He affirms that the "eschatological perspective must be grounded in the historical present, thereby forcing the oppressed community to say no to unjust treatment, because its present humiliation is inconsistent with its promised future."[23]

Eschatology must challenge the present order. The power of Christian eschatology is rooted in the resurrection of Jesus Christ, and it is this that introduces the possibility of change within the historical experience of the oppressed.[24] Cone then observes that the function of the concepts of heaven and life after death cannot be adequately assessed on the basis of their misuse by the dominant classes. "Black theology cannot reject the future reality of life after death — grounded in Christ's resurrection — simply because whites have distorted it for their own selfish purposes."[25] While Cone is more sympathetic to the

possible value of traditional notions of eschatology, he resists the use
of these notions to dull the revolutionary fervor of the oppressed. "The
future is still the future. This means that black theology rejects elabo-
rate speculations about the end. It is just this kind of speculation that
led blacks to stake their whole existence on heaven — the scene of the
whole company of the faithful with their long white robes. Too much
of this talk is not good for the revolution."[26]

In his third theological text, *God of the Oppressed*, Cone affirms the
role of eschatological vision in the liberation struggle of the oppressed.
He notes:

> There is included in liberation the "not yet," a vision of a new heaven
> and a new earth. This simply means that the oppressed have a future
> not made with human hands but grounded in the liberating promises
> of God. They have a liberation not bound by their own strivings. In
> Jesus' death and resurrection, God has freed us to fight against social
> and political structures while not being determined by them.[27]

Moreover, Cone argues that while eschatology must be grounded in
history, it is not limited by what is historically possible. Liberation is ·

> ...beyond history and not limited to the realities and limitations of this
> world. God is the sovereign ruler and nothing can thwart his will to
> liberate the oppressed.... Liberation then is not simply what oppressed
> people can accomplish alone; it is basically what God has done and will
> do to accomplish liberation both in and beyond history.[28]

He concludes that traditional notions of eschatology in African-
American Christianity, including its apocalyptic language, have a
constitutive role in the liberation struggle:

> I contend that black people's experience of liberation as hope for a new
> heaven and a new earth represents a new mode of perception, different
> from the experience of white people. When black people sing, "When the
> roll is called up yonder, I'll be there," they are referring to more than a
> metaphysical reality about heaven. For the "roll up yonder" is not about
> an object but about black subjects who have encountered liberation's
> future.[29]

In Cone's theology, one can observe a movement from the rejection of
otherworldliness, to a critique of distorted otherworldliness, to an appreciation of the role of eschatological vision in the liberation struggle
of the oppressed. However, the common element in this perspective
is the relation of eschatology to the evil of the world, or the theodicy
of the landscape.

An example of the second major theme in black eschatology is
found in the writings of J. Deotis Roberts. Whereas Cone relates eschatology primarily to history, Roberts relates it to ethics. In his first book

on black theology, *Liberation and Reconciliation: A Black Theology*, he argues:

> Ethics and eschatology are related in Black Theology. This is the basis of the black hope. This is the bridge between the *now* and the *not yet*, the promised and the fulfilled.... Things hoped for and reached after always elude complete fulfillment, but the promises and ideals of the Christian faith inspire us to keep "reaching." Indeed, a Christian dies reaching.[30]

In this perspective, eschatology is concerned with the intangible dimensions of reality. Thus the symbols of heaven and hell are described in corresponding terms.

> Eternal life is a *quality* of life.... Eternal life is the "abundant" life. The heaven which is the consummation of the Christian experience of forgiveness and sanctification is not a *space* but a state.... Hell is not a place but a state of experience.[31]

Because the symbols of heaven and hell do not refer to physical realities, the telos of human striving, the reign of God, points to the moral and spiritual essence of human existence. Heaven represents the best of human potential and hell is the worst of human possibilities. In this perspective the world is not hostage to evil forces but is moving toward an eventual fulfillment. It embodies the terrestrial promise of God. This promise is the result of God's benevolent outpouring upon all of creation:

> Creation of nature and of human life is good. Whereas the affirmation of creation as good sharpens the question of evil in a world where creation is declared good by a God who is all-goodness and all-power, it also says yes to *this life* and all the material goods and services that make life worth living.[32]

The benevolence of God is the guarantee of the earth's promise to provide what is necessary to make life more human. Eschatology does not refer primarily to the radical transformation of the world but to an anticipatory fulfillment of its potential. In the response to the persistent idea in African-American social and political thought — the acquisition of a separate land where black people could fortify their indigenous customs and values — Roberts claims that since the whole earth is the Lord's, there should therefore be no place on that earth that God's people cannot be at home. The entire earth holds the promise of God. In his second book on black theology, *A Black Political Theology*, Roberts refines the relationship between eschatology and ethics:

> The future of black religion and the black church may well depend upon what black theologians can contribute to a correlation between eschatology and ethics in the black experience.... Eschatology can no longer

be a mere addendum to black theology. It is at the center of any theology which endeavors to bring a meaningful hope to the weak and the powerless. Ethics is also pivotal to a theology that is concerned with the liberation of the oppressed in the here and now. Black theology has a unique promise of ushering eternity into time without surrendering a grasp upon eternal hope.[33]

Roberts makes it clear that eschatology in black theology must take account of the influence of the African past.

> As we look at our African past and our Afro-American past and present, we need to work through all the streams of thought and faith which converge in our understanding of ethics and eschatology. It is important that we take the best from our heritage to enrich our understanding of human destiny here and hereafter, personal and collective. How we handle our personal identity crisis as well as our quest for peoplehood is bound up with the relation between ethics and eschatology. All that we are and all that we hope to be as persons and as a people is at stake.[34]

In essence, the terrestrial promise means that there is no necessary contradiction between one's reach for eternal life and being an agent of liberation and reconciliation in the world.

Gayraud Wilmore's book *Last Things First* is an example of the third motif in African-American eschatology. In light of Mbiti's analysis of time and eschatology in traditional African thought, Wilmore examines the nature of history and hope among Christian slaves in the United States. He argues that "Christian slaves were an eschatological people who believed that Christ was coming again and that there would be a radical transformation of the world and in relationships between people."[35] The anatomy of the hope of African-American Christians must take into account the distinctive problem of the delayed Parousia caused by the conflict between African and European conceptualizations of time and history.

Wilmore suggests three responses of the slaves to this problem. Some slaves turned away from Christianity, never fully embracing the legitimacy of the Gospel preached to them by white Christians. Others adopted an "immediatist" posture and claimed that the pentecostal possession of the spirit was evidence that the reign of God had already come. The third response was to embrace a vision of the reign of God as the model for and judgment upon the present order.[36]

The key to understanding the complexity of eschatology in African-American Christianity is the inseparability of the material and the spiritual dimensions of life. This is reflected in the language that black Christians have used to express their hope for better things to come. Talk about "new shoes" and "white robes" — concrete earthly images — are juxtaposed with talk about "crowns and wings." For Wilmore, this points to "the worldliness and concreteness of the black religious imagination."[37] It draws from ordinary life the tropes of transcendence. It addresses the satisfaction of physical needs *and* the fulfillment of spiritual hunger.

The major signposts in the anatomy of black hope are (1) the variety of influences on the African-American eschatological perspective. Besides the African notion of time, "other influences must be seen in America, including other elements of the African heritage, those coming from Native American religions (with which many slaves had close acquaintance), from white revivalism, and from the slaves' own perception of their situation and what needed to be done to deal with it";[38] (2) the fact that black eschatology is neither "crassly materialistic or hopelessly otherworldly";[39] and (3) that the eschatological vision of God's reign should be understood as "liberation from sin, slavery, and second-class citizenship, but also as freedom from bigotry, hatred, and the alienation of people from one another in the land of their birth and common destiny."[40] The anatomy of black hope is the map of the African-American religious imagination. Indeed, it may be that the hope of American Christianity rests with the people to whom little more than hope has been entrusted.

### History, Hope, and Freedom

Eschatology in black theology is inseparable from the struggle of African-Americans for freedom. As one theologian puts it, "the whole of Black eschatology could be summed up in one word: *liberation*. Black theologians proclaim that God is the Liberator who acts in history to set people free from whatever keeps them in bondage to a life which is less than human."[41] It is impossible to understand fully the significance of eschatology in African-American religious experience without attention to its role in the freedom struggle of black people. Eschatology refers to the consummation and rectification of history and the persistence of hope. The vision of a new order was indispensable to Africans languishing in the foul embrace of slavery because it kept the fires of freedom burning in their hearts. Yet they were not content to claim solely an inner freedom. The idea of the reign of God or the Promised Land compelled them to proclaim and approximate it in their individual and collective existence.

In essence, eschatology plays two roles in the struggle against sin and bondage. First, it makes every historical gain only penultimate. In the struggle for a new social order, there is a great temptation to forget the tragic and ironic dimensions of historical efforts. In the exhilaration of revolutionary zeal, the eschatological vision will not let the Christian settle for anything less than the perfect reign of God. One might say that the difference between the Christian revolutionary and the secular revolutionary is that the Christian asks each day, "How can we make it better?" Eschatology provides the historical model of perfection that prevents us from sacralizing any human social order.

Second, eschatology prevents momentary failures from becoming permanent defeats. Every liberation movement travels an uneven path. Even in the Christian mission to engage the world with the emancipating message of the Gospel, there are always low points when one's efforts meet resistance. But the sight of the Promised Land, though in the distance, continues to revive the weary. The apostle Paul captured this insight when he proclaimed, "We are afflicted in every way, but not crushed; perplexed, but not driven to despair; persecuted, but not forsaken; struck down, but not destroyed" (2 Cor. 4:8–10). Eschatology provides a vision of hope that saves the oppressed from being overwhelmed by historical disillusionment.

Hope in African-American Christianity has more than one dimension. It is multidimensional because the liberation that the Gospel proclaims is multidimensional. Hope has a personal dimension. This aspect of hope is the focus of Christian affirmations regarding the resurrection of the body, immortality, and eternal life. Although this belief suffered greatly under the skeptical gaze of the scientific community, it persists among those who face the specter of death regularly.

Certainly, the doctrine has been problematic in the history of Christian thought. The notion of eternal life has been critiqued as "egoism" among the dominant classes and as an "opiate" among the dispossessed. Despite the abuses, the personal dimension of hope suggests that only those who truly value life and its beauty can fully appreciate the significance of resurrection. This means that pessimism is incompatible with belief in resurrection. Resurrection does not primarily refer to a sensationalist recomposition of decaying flesh, because, as African traditional thought suggests, we are more than flesh. The body is the unity of spirit and flesh. Resurrection, in black religious experience, points to the survival of the personality beyond death, and one's continuing existence in the presence of God and the company of saints. Only those who know what death is can know what the resurrection means. Only those who "die in Christ" can experience the joy of eternal life in Christ. This means that escape into materialism or the cheating of nature and the aging process beyond reasonable measures are incompatible with belief in the resurrection.

Hope also has a collective or interpersonal dimension. This aspect of hope is the content of Christian belief in heaven and hell, damnation and reward. Heaven, in African-American religious thought, usually refers to being in community with others, while hell is often described as a state of alienation, not only from God, but from others. Since in African traditional thought, one's being is intimately related to the community, to be separated from solidarity with others is tantamount to nonexistence. Likewise, one's continued existence is tied to one's ongoing participation in community. This is the reason that, in thought coming out of the African Diaspora, heaven is often referred to as "home," and home often means "Africa." Hell meant the plantations of the American south and the Caribbean, the physical and temporal alienation that characterized slavery and colonization. Heaven meant the return to a state of community, mutuality, and wholeness.

Hope has a cosmic dimension. This aspect of hope is the basis of the Christian affirmation of universal salvation. One of the inherent ironies of the Christian notion of salvation is summed up in the question, "If salvation is not possible for the worst of us, can it be a certainty for any of us?" The idea that salvation is available even to the worst of sinners has stirred its measure of controversy in Christian thought. The primary reason is that the multidimensionality of hope has often been obscured by the all-too-human tendency to claim what can only be God's prerogative. The point of the story of the Prodigal Son (Luke 15:11–32) is that God determines one's fitness for salvation. One must ask, "If the future reality that the gospel proclaims is one in which humanity is divided between the delivered and the damned, to whom is the message of hope directed? Is judgment the opposite of hope? Is is possible that heaven and hell, judgment and redemption are possibilities for all of creation?" The cosmic dimension of hope points to the fact that God creates and redeems all that is. The multidimensionality of Christian hope in African-American religious thought has its roots both in African traditional thought and in the Bible. Both suggest that hope is wholistic, intergenerational, and universal.

History and hope, the origin and telos of faith, are related to freedom in African-American religious expression. The bequest of our African ancestors to their children are roots and wings. This is what Joseph gave to his descendants as they carried his bones into the Promised Land. This is what Jesus gave to his followers in the memory of his resurrection and the anticipation of his return. Our ability to nourish those roots and spread those wings will determine whether African-Americans, as a people, become pallbearers or torchbearers.

# NOTES

## Introduction

1. Gayraud S. Wilmore, *Black Religion and Black Radicalism: An Interpretation of the Religious History of Afro-American People*, 2d ed. (Maryknoll, N.Y.: Orbis Books, 1983), x.

2. Warner R. Traynham, "Theology under Re-Appraisal: Black Theology," in *Today's Church and Today's World*, ed. J. Howe (London: CIO Publishing Co., 1977), 154.

3. See James H. Cone, *Black Theology and Black Power* (New York: Seabury Press, 1969); J. Deotis Roberts, *Liberation and Reconciliation: A Black Theology* (Philadelphia: Westminster Press, 1971).

4. See Gayraud S. Wilmore, "Black Theology: Its Significance for Christian Mission Today," in *International Review of Mission* 63 (April 1974): 211–31.

5. These objections to Christianity were not new, but were, in fact, reformulations of the primary objections to Christianity among black people voiced in the nineteenth century.

6. The historic and even divisive debates around various colonization schemes that would send African slaves back to Africa or to some other tropical destination symbolized the extent to which the African population of the United States had become embroiled in the dilemma of whether or not they were, by now, irrevocably "American." Frederick Douglass, using himself as the prototype, argued that the slaves built the wealth of the United States and therefore were heirs to its anticipated glory. Martin R. Delaney countered that people of African descent would never be "at home" in this land and should find refuge in Africa or Central America. By this time, however, going back to Africa had already ceased to be a realistic historical option for the majority of black people. Thus the debate was, in essence, about "ideology" and not "geography."

## Chapter 1 / Revelation and Liberation

1. I am indebted to my colleague and New Testament scholar Paul Hammer for pointing out to me this important aspect of a pivotal text for black theology.

155

2. Paul Tillich states that "the history of revelation and the history of salvation are the same history" (*Systematic Theology*, *Systematic Theology* [Chicago: University of Chicago Press, 1973], 1:144). In black theology the term "liberation" is used to refer to salvation and more. This "more" is necessary because of the tendency in European-American Christianity to limit the meaning of salvation to some privatistic notion of individual rescue that has no effect on one's social location in relation to God's liberation of the total person.

3. An example of the coincidence of conversion/revelation and liberation is found in the thought of Maria Stewart, an African-American political writer in the nineteenth century. After her conversion to Christianity she immediately relates her personal change to the project of the social transformation of racist American society: "From the moment I experienced the change, I felt a strong desire, with the help and assistance of God to devote the remainder of my days to piety and virtue, and now possess that spirit of independence that, were I called upon, I would willingly sacrifice my life for the cause of God and my brethren. All the nations of the earth are crying for liberty and equality. Away, away with tyranny and oppression! And shall Afric's sons be silent any longer?" (Marilyn Richardson, ed., *Maria W. Stewart, America's First Black Woman Political Writer: Essays and Speeches* [Bloomington: Indiana University Press, 1987], 29).

4. Joseph R. Washington, *Black Religion* (Boston: Beacon Press, 1964).

5. Ibid., 9, 22, 161.

6. Ibid., 33, 161.

7. Ibid., 30, 141, 143.

8. Ibid., 139, 143.

9. Ibid., 41, 103.

10. Ibid., 289. Though this book is dated and Washington appeared to have modified his position on this matter in later works, it is interesting to note that as late as 1981 he continued to argue that the solution to the dysfunctional character of black religion is the total integration of black people into white churches. See Joseph R. Washington, "The Religion of Anti-Blackness," *Theology Today* 38 (July 1981): 146–51.

11. See Albert J. Raboteau, *Slave Religion* (New York: Oxford University Press, 1978), esp. chap. 6.

12. Ibid., 295.

13. Clifford Geertz, *The Interpretation of Cultures* (New York: Basic Books, 1973), 113–14.

14. An excellent analysis of the notion of Afrocentrism is found in Molefi Kete Asante, *The Afrocentric Idea* (Philadelphia: Temple University Press), 1987.

15. Thomas S. Kuhn's classic monograph *The Structure of Scientific Revolutions* (Chicago: University of Chicago Press, 1962) addresses the revolutionary and revelatory consequences of seeing the world in a tradition-shattering manner. He describes these revolutions as "paradigm shifts" in which the data of experience is more adequately explained than in previously held theories.

16. See Victor Turner, *Dramas, Fields, and Metaphors: Symbolic Action in Human Society* (Ithaca: Cornell University Press, 1974), 57.

17. Susan Sontag, *Against Interpretation* (New York: Dell Publishing Co., 1966), 7.

18. Charles H. Long, *Significations: Signs, Symbols, and Images in the Interpretation of Religion* (Philadelphia: Fortress Press, 1986), 46.

19. The parables of Jesus are the most obvious examples of these kinds of transformative stories, but there are others. African-American folktales function in much the same way, revealing the truth to those who are open enough to hear it, and engendering a response in the social existence of the hearers. However, these stories never become philosophical treatises because their aesthetic dimension is indispensable. That is, in them there is no radical separation between their truth and their beauty.

20. Stephen Crites, "The Narrative Quality of Experience," *Journal of the American Academy of Religion* 39 (1971): 291.

21. Ibid., 303, 306.

22. This is one of the central arguments of the Dutch journalist/theologian Theo Witvliet in his insightful analysis of the development of black theology in the United States: *The Way of the Black Messiah* (Oak Park, Ill.: Meyer-Stone Books, 1987).

23. James H. Cone, "The Story Context of Black Theology," *Theology Today* 32 (July 1975): 150.

24. See Stanley Hauerwas, *Truthfulness and Tragedy* (Notre Dame: University of Notre Dame Press, 1977).

25. Cone, "The Story Context of Black Theology."

26. Robert McAfee Brown, "My Story and 'The Story,'" *Theology Today* 32 (1975): 172.

27. Jean-François Lyotard, *The Postmodern Condition: A Report on Knowledge* (Minneapolis: University of Minnesota Press, 1979), 23.

28. For an analysis of the relationship between faith and praxis in liberation theologies, see James H. Evans, Jr., "Faith and Praxis in Contemporary Theology," *Counseling and Values*. For an intriguing discussion of the relationship between doctrine and culture, see George A. Lindbeck, *The Nature of Doctrine: Religion and Theology in a Postliberal Age* (Philadelphia: Westminster Press, 1984).

## Chapter 2 / The Bible: A Text for Outsiders

1. Sacvan Bercovitch, "The Biblical Basis of the American Myth," in *The Bible and American Arts and Letters*, Giles B. Gunn, ed. (Philadelphia: Fortress Press, 1983), 219.

2. Ibid., 223.

3. Ibid.

4. Martin E. Marty, *Religion and Republic: The American Circumstance* (Boston: Beacon Press, 1987), 40.

5. Marty points out that the Hare Krishna youth of the 1960s centered their activities on the distribution and exegesis of their own scriptures, the devotees of Sun Myung Moon had their version of holy writings, and many of the radicals treated the writings of Chairman Mao as a kind of canon (ibid., 40).

6. Ibid., 144. Marty notes that although many Americans hold the Bible to be inerrant, few people are familiar with its contents. Therefore, its icono-graphic function is evident in the tendency to use the Bible as an adjective to legitimate otherwise completely secular activities, e.g., Bible week, Bible camp, etc. (ibid., 153).

7. Ibid., 165.

8. Drew Gilpin Faust, ed., *The Ideology of Slavery* (Baton Rouge: Louisiana State University Press, 1981). See the Introduction, "The Proslavery Argument in History," 1–20. Also see Larry R. Morrison, "The Religious Defense of American Slavery Before 1830," *Journal of Religious Thought* 37 (Fall–Winter 1980–81): 16–29.

9. After 1850 scientific and ethnographical defenses of slavery began to compete with the Bible as the main bulwark of proslavery ideology. Many proslavery voices were uncomfortable with the anti-religious overtones of the emerging scientific and ethnographic disciplines and the fact that many of their findings were contrary to biblical claims. However, as legalized trafficking in African slaves came to an end the emphasis shifted from the biblical sanction of slavery to scientific theories of racial inferiority (see Faust, ibid., 14–15).

10. Some examples of the use of the Bible in the antislavery argument are, William E. Channing, *Slavery* (Boston: James Munroe and Company, 1835); William Hosmer, *Slavery and the Church* (New York: Negro Universities Press, 1853), chaps. 5 and 6; Albert Barnes, *An Inquiry into the Scriptural Views of Slavery* (Philadelphia: Parry & McMillan, 1857).

11. It is important to note here that neither side was significantly in-fluenced by the emergence of "higher criticism" of the Bible. During this period in America, Protestant literalism still prevailed, even in the "moral thrust" argument of the abolitionists, while in Germany biblical scholarship was undergoing a revolution.

12. John Henry Hopkins, *View of Slavery* (New York: W. I. Pooley & Co., 1864), 7.

13. Thornton Stringfellow, "A Brief Examination of Scripture Testimony on the Institution of Slavery," in Faust, ed., *The Ideology of Slavery*, 140.

14. Thomas V. Peterson, *Ham and Japheth: The Mythic World of Whites in the Antebellum South* (Metuchen, N.J.: The Scarecrow Press, 1978), 5, 7. S. A. Cartwright, a proponent of slavery argued in his 1843 essays that the Ham story sealed the destiny of the Southerner as the builder of a great cul-ture, but also compelled Africans to gather on the shores of their continent "drawn thither by an impulse to his nature to fulfill his destiny of becom-ing Japheth's servant" (cited in William M. Swartley, *Slavery, Sabbath, War and Women: Case Issues in Biblical Interpretation* [Scottdale, Pa.: Herald Press, 1983], 33).

15. Cain Hope Felder, *Troubling Biblical Waters: Race, Class, and Family*

(Maryknoll, N.Y.: Orbis Books, 1989), 39. The historian David Brion Davis notes that as a result of the confusion over what the Ham story actually meant "the Babylonian Talmud could point to the Negroes, the supposed children of Ham, as a people cursed with blackness because of their ancestor's disobedience or sexual transgression" (*The Problem of Slavery in the Age of Revolution: 1770– 1823* [Ithaca: Cornell University Press, 1975], 539).

16. Charles B. Copher, "The Black Man in the Biblical World," the *Journal of the Interdenominational Theological Center* 1 (Spring 1974): 7.

17. See George Fitzhugh, *Sociology for the South, or the Failure of Free Society* (Richmond, Va.: A. Morris, 1854). Though the logic of Fitzhugh's argument is perverse, he sets forth a clear statement of the connection many proslavery advocates made between the existence of slavery and the advancement of nineteenth-century capitalist culture.

18. Hopkins, *View of Slavery*, 7–8.

19. Stringfellow, "A Brief Examination of Scripture Testimony on the Institution of Slavery," 140–41.

20. Samuel B. How, *Slaveholding Not Sinful* (Freeport N.Y.: Books for Libraries Press, 1855), 18, 19.

21. Stringfellow, "A Brief Examination of Scripture Testimony on the Institution of Slavery," 155.

22. See Larry R. Morrison, "The Religious Defense of American Slavery before 1830," 19–20.

23. Langston Hughes and Arna Bontemps, eds., *The Book of Negro Folklore* (New York: Dodd, Mead, 1958), 292, 299.

24. Ibid., 286.

25. Albert J. Raboteau, *"Ethiopia Shall Soon Stretch Forth Her Hands": Black Destiny in Nineteenth-Century America*, pamphlet (Tempe: Arizona State University Department of Religious Studies, 1983), 5.

26. Gayraud S. Wilmore, *Black Religion and Black Radicalism*, 2d ed. (Maryknoll, N.Y.: Orbis Books, 1983), 121.

27. Leonard E. Barrett, Sr., *The Rastafarians*, 2d ed. (Boston: Beacon Press, 1988), 103–45. It should be noted that the Rastafarians mingle the Hebrew and the Ethiopic motifs in their worldview. They avoid any apparent contradiction by their assumption that the "Israelite and the Ethiopian are one and the same" (111).

28. Hailu Habtu, *Preliminary Notes on Ancient Ethiopian History*, monograph (New York: City College of the City University of New York, Dept. of History, 1987), 2–3. The author makes an important contribution to understanding the place of the Bible and African-American experience in his discussion of the ancient manuscripts of the Hebrew Scriptures preserved in the Ethiopian language Ge'ez. Evidence suggests that the Ethiopian Bible is older than the version currently in use today (24–25). Barrett notes that the authority of the Ethiopian text is crucial in understanding the role of biblical revelation among the Rastafarians (*The Rastafarians*, 111).

29. Felder, *Troubling Biblical Waters*, 33.

30. Frank M. Snowden, Jr., *Before Color Prejudice: The Ancient View of Blacks* (Cambridge: Harvard University Press, 1983), 101–4.

31. David Walker, *Walker's Appeal in Four Articles* (New York: Arno Press and the New York Times, 1969), 17–18.

32. Ibid., 20.

33. For an example of contemporary biblical interpretation from the Ethiopic perspective see Gene Rice, "Was Amos a Racist?" *Journal of Religious Thought* 35 (Spring–Summer 1978): 35–44.

34. Modupe Oduyoye, *The Sons of the Gods and the Daughters of Men: An Afro-Asiatic Interpretation of Genesis 1–11* (Maryknoll, N.Y.: Orbis Books, 1984), 60.

35. David Damrosch, *The Narrative Covenant* (New York: Harper & Row, 1987), 298.

36. Northrop Frye, *The Great Code: The Bible and Literature* (New York: Harcourt Brace Jovanovich, 1982), xiii.

37. Ibid.

38. J. Severino Croatto, *Biblical Hermeneutics* (Maryknoll, N.Y.: Orbis Books, 1987), 56–57.

39. Katie G. Cannon, "The Bible from the Perspective of the Racially and Economically Oppressed," in *Scripture: The Word beyond the Word* (Women's Division, General Board of Global Ministries, United Methodist Church, 1985), 38.

40. Robert Alter, *The Art of Biblical Narrative* (New York: Basic Books, 1981), 12. Also see Tzvetan Todorov, *Symbolism and Interpretation*, trans. Catherine Porter (Ithaca: Cornell University Press, 1982), 80–91.

41. Ibid., 46.

42. Frank Kermode, *The Genesis of Secrecy: On the Interpretation of Narrative* (Cambridge: Harvard University Press, 1979), xi, 20.

43. Ibid., 47.

44. Elisabeth Schüssler Fiorenza, *In Memory of Her: A Feminist Theological Reconstruction of Christian Origins* (New York: Crossroad, 1984), xx.

45. See Charles W. Chestnutt, *The Conjure Woman* (Ann Arbor: University of Michigan Press, 1972).

46. Kermode, *The Genesis of Secrecy*, 1.

47. Hans W. Frei, *The Eclipse of Biblical Narrative* (New Haven: Yale University Press, 1974), 10.

48. Erich Auerbach, *Mimesis: The Representation of Reality in Western Literature*, trans. Willard R. Trask (Princeton: Princeton University Press, 1953).

49. Ibid., 11.

50. Ibid., 14.

51. Ibid., 10.

52. William A. Graham, *Beyond the Written Word* (Cambridge: Cambridge University Press, 1987), 58.

53. Dolan Hubbard and Bernard H. Sullivan, Jr., " 'Let My People Go': A Spiritually Charged Mascon of Hope and Liberation," in *A.M.E. Zion Quarterly Review* 97 (October 1985): 21

54. Graham, *Beyond the Written Word*, 5. Also see David H. Kelsey, *The Uses of Scripture in Recent Theology* (Philadelphia: Fortress Press, 1975), chaps. 8 and 9.

55. Michael Walzer, *Interpretation and Social Criticism* (Cambridge: Harvard University Press, 1987), chaps. 2 and 3.

56. See Vincent L. Wimbush, "Historical Study as Cultural Critique: A Proposal for the Role of Biblical Scholarship in Theological Education," *Theological Education* 25, no. 2 (Spring 1989): 31; also see Katie G. Cannon, "The Emergence of Black Feminist Consciousness" in *Feminist Interpretation of the Bible*, Letty M. Russell, ed. (Philadelphia: Westminster Press, 1985), 30–40.

57. Robert A. Bennett has argued forcefully for understanding the difference between these tasks as a basis for comprehending their relationship. See his "Biblical Theology and Black Theology," *Journal of the Interdenominational Theological Center* 3 (Spring 1976): 1–16, and "Black Experience and the Bible," *Theology Today* 27 (January 1971): 422–33.

58. See Wimbush, "Historical Study as Cultural Critique," and Renita J. Weems, "The State of Biblical Interpretation: An African-American Womanist Critique," unpublished manuscript, 8–11. Also see her *Just a Sister Away: A Womanist Vision of Women's Relationships in the Bible* (San Diego: LuraMedia, 1988).

59. Vincent L. Wimbush, "Biblical-Historical Study as Liberation: Toward an Afro-Christian Hermeneutic," *Journal of Religious Thought* 42 (Fall–Winter 1985–86): 10.

60. Peter J. Paris, "The Bible and the Black Churches," in *The Bible and Social Reform*, ed. Ernest R. Sandeen (Philadelphia: Fortress Press, 1982), 152; Elisabeth Schüssler-Fiorenza makes a similar observation about feminist hermeneutics: "Rather than seek a 'revealed' Archimedean point in the shifting sand of biblical-historical relativity — be it a liberating tradition, text, or principle in the Bible — a feminist critical hermeneutics has to explore and assess whether and how Scripture can become an enabling, motivating resource and empowering authority in women's struggle for justice, liberation and solidarity" (*Bread Not Stone: The Challenge of Feminist Biblical Interpretation* [Boston: Beacon Press, 1984], xxiii).

## Chapter 3 / The Ungiven God

1. An example of the former is Anselm's *Proslogium*, in which he supposedly proves the existence of God. Examples of the latter are the works of contemporary process theologians, e.g., Schubert Ogden, Delwin Brown, Charles Hartshorne, and Sheila Davaney, who argue that any truly "theological" statement about God must meet certain prescribed "public" criteria.

2. Kamuyu-wa-Kang'ethe, "The Death of God: An African Viewpoint," *Caribbean Journal of Religious Studies* 6, no. 2 (September 1985): 18.

3. Idris Hamid, ed., *Troubling of the Waters* (San Fernando, Trinidad, West Indies: Rahaman Printery Limited, 1973), 7–8.

4. Mokgethi Motlhabi, "Black Theology: A Personal View," in *The Challenge of Black Theology in South Africa*, Basil Moore, ed. (Atlanta: John Knox Press, 1974), 79.

5. Ronald F. Thiemann, *Revelation and Theology: The Gospel as Narrated Promise* (Notre Dame: University of Notre Dame Press, 1985), 5.

6. See Gordon D. Kaufman, *The Theological Imagination: Constructing the Concept of God* (Philadelphia: Westminster Press, 1981), 29–34.

7. Edwin W. Smith, *African Ideas of God* (London: Edinburgh House Press, 1950), 1.

8. See ibid.; also see William A. Brown, "Concepts of God in Africa," *Journal of Religious Thought* 39, no. 2 (Fall–Winter 1982–82): 5–16.

9. It is important here to recognize that any conceptualization of African ideas of God that depends on concepts that themselves are not African in origin creates some dissonance between the concept and the reality. However, an approach that seeks to listen to what Africans have said about God, rather than one that seeks to harmonize African ideas of God with the categories of European theology, is to be preferred. This, I believe, is the one major flaw of John S. Mbiti's classic work, *African Religions and Philosophy* (Garden City, N.Y.: Doubleday, 1969).

10. Smith, *African Ideas of God*, 216, 232–33; Geoffrey Parrinder, *African Traditional Religion* (New York: Harper & Row, 1962), 40–41; Kwesi A. Dickson, *Theology in Africa* (Maryknoll, N.Y.: Orbis Books, 1984), 52.

11. Mircea Eliade described this experience of the absence of God in African religions in his *Deus otiosus* theory. See Justin S. Upkong, "The Problem of God and Sacrifice in African Traditional Religion," *Journal of Religion in Africa* 14, no. 3 (1983): 187–203.

12. Noel L. Erskine, *Decolonizing Theology* (Maryknoll, N.Y.: Orbis Books, 1981), 35; Gwinyai H. Muzorewa, *The Origins and Development of African Theology* (Maryknoll, N.Y.: Orbis Books, 1985), 10.

13. See Melville Herskovits, *The Myth of the Negro Past* (Boston: Beacon Press, 1941), and E. Franklin Frazier, *The Negro Church in America* (New York: Schocken Books, 1964).

14. Albert J. Raboteau, *Slave Religion* (New York: Oxford University Press, 1978), 86–92.

15. Jean Toomer, *Cane* (New York: Liveright, 1951), 26.

16. Raboteau, *Slave Religion*, 92.

17. Theo Witvliet, *The Way of the Black Messiah*, trans. John Bowden (Oak Park, Ill.: Meyer-Stone Books, 1987), 170.

18. Benjamin E. Mays, *The Negro's God: As Reflected in His Literature* (New York: Atheneum, 1969), 14.

19. Ibid., 28.

20. Ibid., 59.

21. Ibid., 61.

22. Ibid., 69.

23. Ibid., 96.

24. Ibid., 97–100.

25. Ibid., 119.

26. Ibid., 127.

27. Ibid., 134.

28. Ibid., 218.

29. William R. Jones, *Is God a White Racist?: A Preamble to Black Theology* (Garden City, N.Y.: Doubleday and Co., 1973), xvii.

30. Ibid., xix.

31. Ibid., xxi.

32. Ibid., 3–5.

33. Ibid., 77, 202.

34. Ibid., 193.

35. Ibid., 194–97.

36. There is a kind of experiential ambiguity about suffering, which is not present in the idea of evil. Suffering may or may not be valued, while evil is, by definition, negative. Clifford Geertz posits a helpful distinction between suffering and evil: "For where the problem of suffering is concerned with threats to our ability to put our 'undisciplined squads of emotion' into some sort of soldierly order, the problem of evil is concerned with threats to our ability to make sound moral judgements. What is involved in the problem of evil is not the adequacy of our symbolic resources to govern our affective life, but the adequacy of those resources to provide a workable set of ethical criteria, normative guides to govern our action" (*The Interpretation of Cultures*, 106).

37. Jones, *Is God a White Racist?*, xiv–xv.

38. See Alice Walker, *The Color Purple* (New York: Washington Square Press, 1982); Toni Cade Bambara, *The Salt Eaters* (New York: Random House, 1981); Toni Morrison, *Beloved* (New York: Knopf, 1987); William L. Andrews, ed., *Sisters of the Spirit* (Bloomington: Indiana University Press, 1986).

39. James H. Cone, *A Black Theology of Liberation*, 2d ed. (Maryknoll, N.Y.: Orbis Books, 1986), 62.

40. Ibid., 65.

41. See Karl Barth, *The Humanity of God* (Atlanta: John Knox Press, 1960), 72.

42. J. Deotis Roberts, *Liberation and Reconciliation: A Black Theology* (Philadelphia: Westminster Press, 1971), 89.

43. J. Deotis Roberts, *A Black Political Theology* (Philadelphia: Westminster Press, 1974), 103.

44. Cone, *Black Theology of Liberation*, 76.

45. See Paul Tillich, *Systematic Theology*, vol. 1 (Chicago: University of Chicago Press, 1973).

46. See Paul Tillich, *Biblical Religion and the Search for Ultimate Reality* (Chicago: University of Chicago Press, 1964).

47. Paul Tillich, *Theology of Culture* (New York: Oxford University Press, 1959), 131.

48. Major J. Jones, *The Color of God: The Concept of God in Afro-American Thought* (Macon, Ga.: Mercer University Press, 1987), 46, 48.

49. Sallie McFague, *Models of God: Theology for an Ecological, Nuclear Age* (Philadelphia: Fortress Press, 1987), 19.

50. Alice Walker, *The Color Purple*, 177.

51. Cone, *A Black Theology of Liberation*, 75.

## Chapter 4 / Jesus Christ: Liberator and Mediator

1. See Joseph H. Washington, *Black Religion: The Negro and Christianity in the United States* (Boston: Beacon Press, 1964), 145–48.

2. Erich Auerbach, "Figura," in *Scenes from the Drama of European Literature* (Gloucester, Mass.: Peter Smith, 1973).

3. Ibid, 12.

4. Ibid., 28.

5. Ibid., 34.

6. Ibid., 53.

7. The following overview is heavily dependent on William Barclay's *Jesus As They Saw Him* (New York: Harper & Row, 1962); see chap. 7.

8. Ibid., 156.

9. David F. Strauss, *The Life of Jesus Critically Examined*, vol. 2 (London: Chapman Brothers, 1846), 2:50.

10. This idea has received its most extensive treatment in W. Wrede's *Das Messiasgeheimnis*, the Messianic Secret. Here the frequent admonitions of Jesus, in the Gospel of Mark, to the disciples to tell no one of what they have seen are argued to be evidence that Jesus not only never claimed the title of Messiah for himself, but that he intentionally distanced himself from the political/messianic hopes of Israel under Roman rule.

11. Gunther Bornkamm, *Jesus of Nazareth* (New York: Harper & Row, 1960).

12. John W. Roberts, *From Trickster to Badman: The Black Folk Hero in Slavery and Freedom* (Philadelphia: University of Pennsylvania Press, 1989).

13. Ibid., 1.

14. Ibid., 5.

15. Wilson J. Moses argues that African-American heroic traditions or "messianic myths" are primarily shaped by "the messianic strains in American culture." See his *Black Messiahs and Uncle Toms* (University Park: Pennsylvania State University Press, 1982).

16. Roberts, *From Trickster to Badman*, 9–10.

17. James H. Cone, *The Spirituals and the Blues* (New York: Seabury Press, 1972). This work offers a theological interpretation of the spirituals and the blues as indigenous African-American musical forms. The author explores the notions of Christ contained in these musical forms. He notes that the uniqueness of the African-American understanding of Jesus, and especially his relationship to God, are evident here. Also see Lewis V. Baldwin, "Deliverance to the Captives: Images of Jesus in the Minds of Afro-American Slaves," *Journal of Religious Studies* 12, no. 2 (1985): 27–45.

18. Roberts, *From Trickster to Badman*, 120.

19. Ibid., 122.

20. Charles Bird, "Heroic Song of the Mande Hunters"; cited in Roberts, *From Trickster to Badman*, 123.

21. Daniel P. Biebuyck, *Hero and Chief* (Berkeley: University of California Press, 1978); *From Trickster to Badman*, 123.

22. Roberts, *From Trickster to Badman*, 125.

23. Howard Thurman, *Jesus and the Disinherited* (Nashville: Abingdon Press, 1949), 7–11.

24. Ibid., 13.

25. Ibid., 16.

26. Ibid., 17.

27. Ibid., 18.

28. Ibid., 29.

29. Ibid., 28.

30. Ibid., 35.

31. Albert B. Cleage, Jr., *The Black Messiah* (New York: Sheed and Ward, 1968), 3; see his *Black Christian Nationalism* (New York: William Morrow, 1972).

32. Ibid., 4.

33. Ibid., 111.

34. Tom Skinner, *How Black Is the Gospel?* (New York: J. B. Lippincott, 1970), 14; for a more contemporary work from this perspective see Carl F. Ellis, Jr., *Beyond Liberation: The Gospel in the Black American Experience* (Downers Grove, Ill.: InterVarsity Press, 1983).

35. This is an instance of the paradigm that H. Richard Niebuhr described as "Christ above culture." See his *Christ and Culture* (New York: Harper & Row, 1959).

36. Ibid., 13.

37. Other contributors to the dialogue on Christology in black theology are Bishop Joseph A. Johnson, Jr., *The Soul of the Black Preacher* (Philadelphia: Pilgrim Press, 1971); Olin P. Moyd, *Redemption in Black Theology* (Valley Forge, Pa.: Judson Press, 1979); and William L. Eichelberger, "A Mytho-Historical Approach to the Black Messiah," *Journal of Religious Thought* 33, no. 1 (Spring–Summer 1976): 63–74.

38. J. Deotis Roberts, *Liberation and Reconciliation: A Black Theology* (Philadelphia: Westminster Press, 1971), 130.

39. Ibid., 139.

40. Ibid., 140.

41. Ibid., 143.

42. Ibid., 140.

43. Ibid., 148ff.

44. J. Deotis Roberts, *A Black Political Theology* (Philadelphia: Westminster Press, 1975), 119.

45. James H. Cone, *A Black Theology of Liberation* (New York: J. B. Lippincott, 1970), 204, 212.

46. Ibid., 217.

47. Ibid., 201.

48. James H. Cone, *God of the Oppressed* (New York: Seabury Press, 1975), 134.

49. Ibid., 136.

50. Cone, *A Black Theology of Liberation*, 209.

51. See David L. Weddle, "The Liberator as Exorcist: James Cone and the Classic Doctrine of Atonement," *Religion in Life* 49 (Winter 1980): 477–87.

52. The most succinct statement on his Christology is Gayraud S. Wilmore, "The Black Messiah: Revising The Color Symbolism of Western Christology," *Journal of the Interdenominational Theological Center* 2 (Fall 1974): 8–18.

53. Ibid., 8, 9.

54. Ibid., 10.

55. Ibid., 12, 13.

56. Ibid., 14.

57. Schubert Ogden, *The Point of Christology* (New York: Harper & Row, 1982).

58. Tom F. Driver, *Christ in a Changing World* (New York: Crossroad, 1981).

59. Dietrich Bonhoeffer, *Christ the Center*, trans. Edwin H. Robertson (New York: Harper & Row, 1978), 28.

60. Ibid., 32, 39.

61. Rita Nakashima Brock, *Journeys by Heart: A Christology of Erotic Power* (New York: Crossroad, 1988), 52.

62. Kortwright Davis, "Jesus Christ and Black Liberation," *Journal of Religious Thought* 42, no. 1 (Spring–Summer 1985): 51–67.

63. Delores S. Williams, "Surrogacy and Atonement in Black Women's Experience" (unpublished paper).

64. Kelly Delaine Brown, "God Is as Christ Does: Toward a Womanist Christology," *Journal of Religious Thought* 46, no. 1 (Summer–Fall 1989): 16.

65. Ibid.

66. Jacquelyn Grant, *White Women's Christ and Black Women's Jesus: Feminist Christology and Womanist Response* (Atlanta: Scholars Press, 1989), 217.

67. Ibid., 218–22.

68. Katie Cannon, *Womanist Ethics* (Atlanta: Scholars Press, 1988).

69. John S. Pobee, *Toward an African Theology* (Nashville: Abingdon Press, 1979).

70. Ibid., 92.

71. Ibid., 98.

72. Elizabeth Amoah and Mercy Amba Oduyoye, "The Christ for African Women," *International Christian Digest* 2, no. 8 (October 1988): 14.

73. Ibid., 15.

74. Ibid., 16.

75. Mercy Amba Oduyoye, *Hearing and Knowing: Theological Reflections on Christianity in Africa* (Maryknoll, N.Y.: Orbis Books, 1986), 98–102.

76. Amoah and Oduyoye "The Christ for African Women," 16.


## Chapter 5 / On Being Black

1. Here the term "black" rather than "African-American," for example, is used intentionally because it embodies the cultural, ethnographic, and *political* dimensions of the experiences of people of African descent in the modern world.

2. John S. Mbiti, *African Religions and Philosophy* (Garden City, N.Y.: Doubleday, 1970), 119.

3. Swailem Sidhom, "The Theological Estimate of Man," in *Biblical Revelation and African Beliefs*, ed. Kwesi A. Dickson and Paul Ellingworth (London: Lutterworth Press, 1969), 100.

4. Ibid., 101.

5. Ibid.

6. Ibid., 103.

7. Mbiti, *African Religions and Philosophy*, 141.

8. See Winthrop D. Jordan's classic work, *The White Man's Burden: Historical Origins of Racism in the United States* (New York: Oxford University Press, 1974), 3–25.

9. Clifton H. Johnson et al., *God Struck Me Dead* (Philadelphia: United Church Press, 1969), 14.

10. See Mechal Sobel, *Trabelin' On: Toward an Afro-Baptist Faith* (Westport, Conn.: Greenwood Press, 1978).

11. W. E. B. Du Bois, "The Conservation of Races," in *The Seventh Son: The Thought and Writings of W. E. B. Du Bois*, ed. Julius Lester (New York: Random House, 1971), 1:176.

12. Ibid., 178.

13. Ibid., 179.

14. W. E. B. Du Bois, *The Dusk of Dawn: An Essay toward an Autobiography of a Race Concept* (New York: Harcourt, Brace & World, 1940), 97–133.

15. George D. Kelsey, *Racism and the Christian Understanding of Man* (New York: Charles Scribner's Sons, 1965), 19.

16. Ibid., 20.

17. Ibid., 24.

18. See the discussion of William R. Jones's *Is God a White Racist?*, in chap. 3.

19. Kelsey, *Racism and the Christian Understanding of Man*, 27.

20. Ibid., 29.

21. Ibid., 32.

22. Ibid., 35.

23. Cornel West, *Prophesy Deliverance! An Afro-American Revolutionary Christianity* (Philadelphia: Westminster Press, 1982), 49.

24. Ibid., 64.

25. See Joseph H. Washington, *Anti-Blackness in English Religion* (Lewiston, N.Y.: Edwin Mellen Press, 1984).

26. Bertrand Russell, "The Superior Virtue of the Oppressed," in *Unpopular Essays* (New York: Simon and Schuster, 1950), 58.

27. Ibid., 61.

28. Ibid., 63.

29. Gustavo Gutiérrez, "Liberation and the Poor: The Puebla Perspective," in *The Power of the Poor in History* (Maryknoll, N.Y.: Orbis Books, 1983), 138.

30. Ibid., 140.

31. Nathan Wright, Jr., "Black Power: A Religious Opportunity," in *Black Theology: A Documentary History, 1966–1979*, ed. Gayraud S. Wilmore and James H. Cone (Maryknoll, N.Y.: Orbis Books, 1979), 48.

32. James H. Cone, *A Black Theology of Liberation*, 2d ed. (Maryknoll, N.Y.: Orbis Books, 1986), 94.

33. Ibid., 101.

34. Ibid., 87.

35. J. Deotis Roberts, *A Black Political Theology* (Philadelphia: Westminster Press, 1974), 84.

36. Ibid., 90.

37. Ibid., 91.

38. J. Deotis Roberts, *Liberation and Reconciliation: A Black Theology* (Philadelphia: Westminster Press, 1971), 110.

39. Ibid., 119.

40. Jürgen Moltmann, *Man: Christian Anthropology in the Conflicts of the Present* (Philadelphia: Fortress Press, 1974), 3.

41. Sallie McFague, *Speaking in Parables: A Study in Metaphor and Theology* (Philadelphia: Fortress Press, 1975), 157.

42. William L. Andrews, ed., *Sisters of the Spirit: Three Black Women's Autobiographies of the Nineteenth Century* (Bloomington: Indiana University Press, 1986), 1.

43. Manas Buthelezi, "The Theological Meaning of True Humanity," in *The Challenge of Black Theology in South Africa*, ed. Basil Moore (Atlanta: John Knox Press, 1974), 93.

44. Cited in Houston Baker, *The Journey Back: Issues in Black Literature and Criticism* (Chicago: University of Chicago Press, 1980), 1.

45. James William McClendon, *Biography as Theology* (Nashville: Abingdon Press, 1974), 30–31.

46. Erich Auerbach, "The Idea of Man in Ancient Literature," in Giles B. Gunn, ed., *Literature and Religion* (New York: Harper & Row, 1971), 118.

47. Mercy Amba Oduyoye, *Hearing and Knowing: Theological Reflections on Christianity in Africa* (Maryknoll, N.Y.: Orbis Books, 1986), 137.

## Chapter 6 / The Community of Faith and the Spirit of Freedom

1. H. Richard Niebuhr, *The Social Sources of Denominationalism* (New York: Henry Holt, 1929), 236.

2. Howard Thurman, *Jesus and the Disinherited* (New York: Abingdon Press, 1949) 43.

3. Charles Johnson and A. P. Watson, *God Struck Me Dead* (Philadelphia: Pilgrim Press, 1969), 1; also see B. A. Botkin, *Lay My Burden Down* (Chicago: University of Chicago Press, 1945).

4. Carter G. Woodson, *The History of the Negro Church* (Washington, D.C.: Associated Publishers, 1929), preface to the 1945 edition.

5. Ibid., 290–92.

6. Ibid., 298–99.

7. E. Franklin Frazier, *The Negro Church in America* (New York: Schocken Books, 1964), 1.

8. Ibid., 4.

9. Ibid., 6.

10. Ibid., 41.

11. Ibid., 45.

12. Ibid., 70.

13. Zora Neale Hurston, *The Sanctified Church* (Berkeley: Turtle Island, 1983), 79.

14. Ibid., 81, 83.

15. Ibid., 80.

16. Ibid.

17. Ibid., 106.

18. Ibid., 91.

19. Ibid.

20. Ibid., 103.

21. Victor Turner, *Dramas, Fields, and Metaphors: Symbolic Action in Human Society* (Ithaca: Cornell University Press, 1974), 202.

22. Ibid., 203.

23. Ibid., 207.

24. Ibid., 208.

25. Ibid., 206.

26. Ibid., 208.

27. Emil Brunner, *Dogmatics*, vol. 3, *The Christian Doctrine of the Church, Faith, and Consummation*, trans. David Cairns (Philadelphia: Westminster Press, 1960), 22.

28. Ibid., 29.

29. Ibid., 30.

30. An interesting connection between the work of Turner and Brunner is that they both drew significantly on the writings of the sociologist Ferdinand Tonnies.

31. The most comprehensive sociological and historical analysis of the African-American church published to date is C. Eric Lincoln and Lawrence Mamiya, eds., *The Black Church in African-American Experience* (Durham, N.C.: Duke University Press, 1990).

32. James H. Cone, *Black Theology and Black Power* (New York: Seabury Press, 1969), 92.

33. Ibid., 105.

34. James H. Cone, *A Black Theology of Liberation*, 2d ed. (Maryknoll, N.Y.: Orbis Books, 1987), 130–32.

35. James H. Cone, *God of the Oppressed* (New York: Seabury Press, 1975), 150.

36. James H. Cone, *Speaking the Truth: Ecumenism, Liberation, and Black Theology* (Grand Rapids, Mich.: William B. Eerdmans Publishing Co., 1986), 124.

37. Colin W. Williams, *The Church* (Philadelphia: Westminster Press, 1978), 154.

38. J. Deotis Roberts, *Liberation and Reconciliation: A Black Theology* (Philadelphia: Westminster Press, 1971), 64.

39. J. Deotis Roberts, *A Black Political Theology* (Philadelphia: Westminster Press, 1974), 177.

40. J. Deotis Roberts, "A Black Ecclesiology of Involvement," *Journal of Religious Thought* 32 (Spring–Summer 1975): 36, 40.

41. J. Deotis Roberts, *Roots of a Black Future: Family and Church* (Philadelphia: Westminster Press, 1980), 94ff.

42. Ibid., 106.

43. Ibid., 92.

44. Frederick Denison Maurice, *The Kingdom of Christ* (London: Macmillan, 1883).

45. Sterling Stuckey, *Slave Culture: Nationalist Theory and the Foundations of Black America* (New York: Oxford University Press, 1987), ix.

46. Albert B. Cleage, Jr., *Black Christian Nationalism: New Directions for the Black Church* (New York: William Morrow, 1972), xvi.

47. Ibid., 249.

48. Ibid., 17.

49. Ibid., 46.

50. Ibid., 32.

51. Ibid., 57–58.

52. Ibid., 34–35.

53. Ibid., 41.

54. Ibid., 60.

55. Ibid., xxxv.

56. Ibid., 42.

57. Ibid.

58. Ibid., 65.

59. This trinitarian schema is also helpful in classifying various "types" of churches. A church of the first person is one that emphasizes rationality and the goodness of creation. It extols native human potential. This type of church is intimated in the works of Walt Whitman, Ralph Waldo Emerson, and Thomas Paine. It was Paine who declared in his *Age of Reason* that "My mind is my own church." One of the few remaining churches of this type is the Unitarian-Universalist church. A church of the second person is one that emphasizes the dialectical relationship between reason and revelation. It recognizes a moral ambiguity in the created order, and the consequent disablement of human potential. Churches of this type are usually centered on the proclamation of the Word that both edifies and convicts. Many churches in the "reformed" tradition fall within this type. A church of the third person is one that emphasizes the priority of extra-rational revelation and the depravity of the created order. It claims that human perfection is possible through the redemption effected by Christ and signalled by the presence of the Holy Spirit. Many "Pentecostal," "Holiness," and "Spiritualist" churches fall into this category. Of course, it is not only possible but even probable that these emphases are present, in differing degrees, in any single congregation.

60. This aspect of its mission has been often neglected in the African-American churches. While there are notable exceptions, most churches put

very little emphasis on their educational ministries. Many churches will spare no expense to insure that they obtain a leader who is skilled in preaching and fund-raising, but readily rely on volunteers who have received very little training to run their Christian education programs. In addition, those programs are most often geared toward young children, because the assumption is that the need to be intellectually formed in the faith ceases with adult conversion.

## Chapter 7 / The Last Shall Be First

1. Max Weber, *The Sociology of Religion*, trans. Ephraim Fischoff (Boston: Beacon Press, 1964), 106.

2. Ibid., 107.

3. Karl Barth, *The Epistle to the Romans*, trans. Edwyn C. Hoskyns, 6th ed. (New York: Oxford University Press, 1968), 46.

4. John S. Mbiti, *African Religions and Philosophy* (Garden City, N.Y.: Doubleday, 1969), 21.

5. Ibid., 25.

6. Ibid., 30.

7. Ibid., 31.

8. Ibid., 34.

9. Ibid., 35.

10. Ibid.

11. Ibid., 36.

12. John S. Mbiti, *New Testament Eschatology in an African Background* (New York: Oxford University Press, 1971).

13. Bonnie J. Barthold, *Black Time: Fiction of Africa, the Caribbean, and the United States* (New Haven, Conn.: Yale University Press, 1981), 7.

14. Ibid., 15.

15. Martin Luther King, Jr., *Why We Can't Wait* (New York: Harper & Row, 1964), 83.

16. Ibid., 89.

17. Barthold, *Black Time*, 20.

18. Ibid., 23.

19. James H. Cone, *Black Theology and Black Power* (New York: Seabury Press, 1969), 123.

20. Ibid., 125.

21. Ibid., 126.

22. James H. Cone, *A Black Theology of Liberation*, 2d ed. (Maryknoll, N.Y.: Orbis Books, 1986).

23. Ibid., 137.

24. Ibid., 140.

25. Ibid., 141.

26. Ibid., 142.

27. James H. Cone, *God of the Oppressed* (New York: Seabury Press, 1975), 158.

28. Ibid., 158, 160.

29. Ibid., 159.

30. J. Deotis Roberts, *Liberation and Reconciliation: A Black Theology* (Philadelphia: Westminster Press, 1971), 168, 169.

31. Ibid., 171, 173.

32. Ibid., 83.

33. J. Deotis Roberts, *A Black Political Theology* (Philadelphia: Westminster Press, 1974), 178, 179.

34. Ibid., 186.

35. Gayraud S. Wilmore, *Last Things First* (Philadelphia: Westminster Press, 1982), 77.

36. Ibid., 79–83.

37. Ibid., 84.

38. Ibid., 87.

39. Ibid.

40. Ibid., 89.

41. J. N. J. Kritzinger, "Black Eschatology and Christian Mission," *Missionalia* 15, no. 1 (April 1987): 15.

# INDEX